Women and British Party Politics

Women and British Party Politics examines the characteristics of women's partic-ipation at the mass and elite level in contemporary British politics; as voters, party members and elected representatives respectively. It explores what this means for ideas about, and the practice of, descriptive, substantive and symbolic representation. The main focus is on the feminization of British party politics – the integration of women into formal political institutions and the integration of women's concerns and perspectives into political debate and policy – in the post-1997 period.

Not only specifically designed to bring together cutting-edge conceptual devel-opments in the sub-discipline of gender and politics, with robust British empiri-cal research, this book also presents reflections on how best to study gender and politics. The empirical findings which are presented through the extensive use of case studies derive from a range of research projects which were undertaken over a period of ten years, and which make use of a variety of research methods and techniques.

This book will appeal to all those with an interest in British Politics, Feminism and European Studies; and will provide the reader with an overview of the complex relationship between sex, gender and politics in a conceptually sophisticated fashion.

Sarah Childs is a Senior Lecturer in the Department of Politics at the University of Bristol, UK.

Routledge Advances in European Politics

Women and British Party Politics

Descriptive, substantive and symbolic representation

Sarah Childs

Routledge
Taylor & Francis Group

LONDON AND NEW YORK

First published 2008 by Routledge
2 Park Square, Milton Park, Abingdon, Oxon, OX14 4RN

Simultaneously published in the USA and Canada
By Routledge
270 Madison Ave, New York NY 10016

Routledge is an imprint of the Taylor & Francis Group, an informa business

Transferred to Digital Printing 2010

Typeset in Times New Roman by Keyword Group Ltd

British Library Cataloguing in Publication Data
A catalogue record for this book is available from the British Library

Library of Congress Cataloging in Publication Data
Childs, Sarah, 1969-
Women and British party politics: descriptive, substantive and symbolic representation / Sarah Childs.
p.cm. – (Routledge advances in European politics; 51)
"Simultaneously published in the USA and Canada by Routledge."
Includes bibliographical references and index.

ISBN 978-0-415-36682-3 (hardback: alk. paper) – ISBN 978-0-203-01944-3 (e-book: alk. paper)
1. Women in politics–Great Britain. 2. Women legislators–Great Britain. 3. Representative government and representation–Great Britain. 4. Women_Great Britain–Social conditions. I. Title.

HQ1391.G7C483 2008

324.2410082–dc22

2007042971

ISBN 10: 0-415-36682-8 (hbk)
ISBN 10: 0-415-59409-X (pbk)
ISBN 10: 0-203-09144-X (ebk)

ISBN 13: 978-0-415-36682-3 (hbk)
ISBN 13: 978-0-415-59409-7 (pbk)
ISBN 13: 978-0-203-01944-3 (ebk)

For Joni Lovenduski
Pioneering Feminist Political Scientist

Contents

Figures

Tables

Acknowledgements

This book draws on more than ten years of research into the relationship between sex, gender and British politics. It draws heavily on a range of research projects, many of which were collaborative projects. My thanks go, first, to those with whom I have worked on particular projects (in alphabetical order): first, Rosie Campbell and Joni Lovenduski, for our work on the 2005 British Representation Study and the 2005 Hansard Society *Women at the Top Report*. Rosie also wrote Chapter 2 of this book and deserves special thanks for having taught me statistical analysis; Karen Celis, Johanna Kantola and Mona Lena Krook, for our ongoing work on the substantive representation of women; Philip Cowley, with whom I worked on women's MPs' loyalty and who also read the whole of this book in draft – and who proffered, as ever, apposite comment. This book is much better for him having read it; David Cutts and Edward Fieldhouse, with whom I worked on the electoral impact of Labour's All Women Shortlists (AWS); Mona Lena Krook for our reflections on 'critical mass theory' which we began when she was a post-doctoral student at the University of Bristol, and with whom I wrote Chapter 5; and Julie Withey for our analysis of sex and the signing of Early Day Motions. I trust they know how important their friendship and collaboration have been to me over the years.

To augment my own empirical and conceptual analysis, and extend *Women and British Party Politics*' coverage beyond Westminster, I have included select Case Studies in most chapters. In this I have benefited from the generosity of friends and colleagues from the wider politics and gender and politics community who have shared their research with me. Chapter 1 includes Case Studies based on research undertaken by Rosie Campbell (2006), Joni Lovenduski and Pippa Norris (Norris *et al.* 2004) and Rosie Campbell and Kristi Winters (2007). Chapter 2 includes a Case Study on the adoption of AWS by the Labour Party, based on research by Joni Lovenduski (2005b). Chapter 3 includes Case Studies based on the Hansard Society *Women at the Top Report* and one based on collaborative research with David Cutts and Edward Fieldhouse, analyzing the impact of AWS at the 2005 General Election (*Party Politics*, forthcoming). In Chapter 5, Case Studies 5.1 and 5.7 present analysis that was co-authored with Julie Withey. Case Study 5.2 draws on Karen Bird's research on parliamentary questions; Case Study 5.3 draws on Paul Chaney's work on the National Assembly for Wales; Case Study

5.4 on research by Joni Lovenduski and Alex Brazier; Case Study 5.6 presents Fiona Mackay and Meryl Kenny's research on Scotland. Chapter 5 also draws on work with Mona Lena Krook, some of which was previously published in 'Should Feminists Give Up on Critical Mass? A Contingent Yes', *Politics and Gender*, Volume 2, Issue 04, December 2006, pp 522–530 and in 'Critical Mass Theory and Women's Political Representation' *Political Studies*, forthcoming 2008.

There are of course other colleagues and friends without whose advice, research, reading of particular chapters, and general support my work would be significantly less insightful. In alphabetical order: Lesley Abdela, James Brazier, Jane Chamberlin, Rob Dover, Clare Ettingshausen, Richard Heffernan, Dan Lyndon, Vicky Randall, Gemma Rosenblatt, Andrew Russell, Meg Russell, David Sanders, Marian Sawer, Judith Squires, Manon Tremblay, Linda Trimble, Wendy Stokes and Lisa Young.

It also goes without saying that had the large number of politicians and party workers not agreed to participate in my research then this book would have been much thinner. They shall remain nameless, as most request, but I thank them for their interest in my work, their time, and the manner in which they have responded to yet further requests for information. Too often our politicians are derided for being only interested in what is in it for them; my experience belies this.

I would also like to publicly thank those individuals who were present at the numerous conferences and seminars where I have presented my work: departmental seminars at the Universities of Alberta, Bristol, Calgary, Essex, Manchester, Surrey and Sussex; the PSA 'Women and Politics' Group Annual Conference and specialist panels at the PSA Annual Conference; the PSA 'Elections, Public Opinion and Parties' (EPOP) Specialist Group Annual Conference; the 'Women in Parliaments' Conference in Ottawa; and the Canadian and American Political Science Association Annual Meeting (CPSA and APSA). At the University of Bristol, my work has benefited from the discussion of the Gender and Governance Research Reading Group, as well as teaching 'the Politics of Gender' unit, over the last four years, to third year undergraduates. The latter is an excellent example of the reciprocity of research-led teaching. Thanks also to three University of Bristol research assistants, all post-graduate students: Christina Rowley for her administration of the 2005 British Representation Study; Hannah Parrott for her bibliographic searches; and Ana Jordan for her copy editing of this manuscript.

The writing up of this book in 2006–7 was made possible through a period of study leave from the University of Bristol, for which I am very grateful. Without this, the book would simply not have been completed. The Hansard Society provided me with a Visiting Fellowship during this time, which enabled me to benefit from their collective insights into British Politics and Parliament as well as the use of their London offices. They also made it a considerably more fun task to undertake. The book also draws on research on political recruitment undertaken at the time of the 2005 General Election with Rosie Campbell and Joni Lovenduski (the British Representation Study funded by a Nuffield Foundation Small Grant (ref: RES-000-23-0841). I thank them for their support.

Completing this research also benefited from the unconditional support of friends and family. They know how much I depend on them – they also know that I do not go in for public displays of affection.

As in the writing of any book, *Women and British Party Politics* is not all that I would have wanted it to be. In part, this reflects gaps in the research: there are so many different ways of exploring the intersection of gender, representation and British Party Politics. However, what I hope I have achieved is to have accurately and engagingly presented the research undertaken thus far and to suggest ways in which future research might proceed. Any mistakes are, of course, my own.

If the research from which this book developed is underpinned by one single premise, it is this: that women's presence in politics matters – even if the precise contours, whether symbolic or substantive, are not always clear. Wanting women to 'do' party politics is about believing that both gender and electoral politics are important; that women's absence from formal politics, whether at the mass or elite level, *should* trouble democrats and *must* trouble feminists. At its most basic, but also perhaps at its strongest and most defensible, this is simply a matter of justice (Phillips 1995). This belief that women's political presence matters is further underpinned by a contention that the integration of women and their concerns into electoral politics is possible – that such politics is not inherently patriarchal but can be transformed (Vickers 1997; L. Young 2000). It might be that, hidden within this assumption, is the hope, at least for feminists, that the transformation that women will effect is a feminist one. But, at the minimum, the intuitive belief remains that the inclusion of women – as gendered beings – will have *some* kind of re-gendering effect.

As part of a wider commitment to the project of feminizing British party politics as well as to feminizing its study, this book was written with Vicky Randall's (1991) comments on feminist research very much in my mind: this should not reproduce the hierarchical relationships between the researcher and researched, and should aim to both 'let women be heard' and to be of use to women. To this end, I hope this book is accessible to and informative for, not only scholars and students but also practitioners, and especially women practitioners, of politics. A final aim for *Women and British Party Politics* is, quoting Joni Lovenduski (2005a, 10), to 'once again ... draw to the attention of political scientists the importance of gender to the study of politics'. In providing, in a single volume, theoretical and empirical research on British party politics, I hope to have made it nigh impossible for mainstream political science, and especially party scholars, to ignore or marginalize feminist political science.

Prologue

A stiletto in the heart

A pair of £120 Russell and Bromley leopard-print kitten heels dominated newspaper coverage of the 2002 Conservative Party Annual Conference. They belonged to Theresa May MP, the Tory Party Chairman. The day after her speech, one third of the *Daily Telegraph's* front page was filled by a photograph of May's shoes. The accompanying headline read: 'A stiletto in the Tories' Heart'. The offending knife in her statement: 'you know what people call us – the nasty party'.

What May had to say in her 2002 Conference speech was prescient: having suffered two election defeats in a row, she was pointedly asking the Conservative party whether it was at ease in Britain of the twenty-first century. May also decried as a 'travesty' the lack of Conservative women MPs. The more perceptive of the media commentators picked up on this and saw in her shoes a metaphor for party change and the feminization of politics. Rachel Sylvester, writing in the *Telegraph* declared: there have been two Conservative Parties on display in Bournemouth this week. The first wears leopard print kitten heels . . . and opens its arms to the voters in a welcoming embrace. The second prefers metaphorical bovver boots . . . proud to be seen as the 'nasty party'. The *Guardian's* Polly Toynbee talked of the 'intellectual transvestitism' of the Conservative party as 'speaker after speaker' climbed onto the stage 'in full drag to reveal their feminine side and recant the erroneous trousers they used to wear'. Another newspaper pondered whether 'the ditching of frumpy loafers in favour of sexy kitten heels' would 'turn out to be the Tories' Clause Four' moment.

Rather than what she said, it was, however, May's kitten heels that 'stole the show'. More than one newspaper revealed that, in addition to their 'spiky heels and silky leopard print', the soles of the shoes were engraved with, 'In love the chase is better than the catch. Too much is not enough'. Other journalists reported that, 'unaware' that leopard print is 'objectionable on every possible count of taste' 'respectable middle-aged women' conference delegates, 'stampeded the Bournemouth branch', throwing off their 'grey courts', and buying up all of Russell and Bromley's stock – along with a good few matching handbags. Fortunately, May had brought more than one pair of shoes with her to the

Party Conference. Later in the week she wore 'multi-coloured velvet' Mary-Janes, and a pair of 'pinstriped black shoes with the red rose of Labour on the instep'. Other commentators contemplated the effect of May's shoes' on the men inside the Conference centre: apparently the sight of her in kitten-heeled 'don't f*** with me' shoes was enough to bring 'tears to the eyes of red-blooded Tories'. Male MPs were in 'a collective lather' experiencing a 'quiver of excitement' – 'not wholly averse to a little public humiliation from a good-looking woman'.

This was not the first time that the media had honed in on, and sexualized, Theresa May's attire. References to her 'trademark', 'exotic', 'attention-seeking' and 'sassy' shoes, together with her penchant for leather jackets and trousers were already peppering media commentary. After her Conference speech, however, such representations became more dominant: between the 1 January and the 6 October 2002 – when May gave her Conference speech – a mere 3 per cent of newspaper articles made reference to her shoes; between the 7 October and the 31 October this jumped to 21 per cent.

Introduction

Women's presence in politics is not only about women participating in party politics or getting women elected to political institutions – if the 'personal is political' then politics is everywhere. Nevertheless, this book focuses on precisely these activities and places. This is both because feminist political science maintains that gender is central to understanding conventional politics – to addressing the question 'who governs' – and because too many questions about women's participation and representation in British party politics are yet to be fully answered (Mackay 2004a). The 'fact', for example, that the 120 women MPs elected to the 1997 Parliament represented a mere 18 per cent of all MPs is often not fully appreciated. Westminster can often look like it is full of women MPs, especially if the TV cameras are focused on the Government's benches, showing Labour's women MPs wearing colourful outfits. Yet, women constitute fewer than 1:5; far from parity. There is, furthermore, little consensus as to whether women's underrepresentation matters and what, if anything, should be done about it. There is a paucity of information about women's political participation and representation in other aspects of British electoral politics too. It is a widely held assumption that women are more conservative than men. However, in 1997 younger women shifted their vote to New Labour, although by 2005 they were said to have 'fallen out of love' with Tony Blair. In respect of party membership it is widely accepted that women constitute the backbone of the Conservative Party. However, the role women play in political parties in terms of policy- and decision-making is rarely systematically considered[1]. Then there is the apparent 'failure' of women representatives, not least Labour's 1997 intake, to *act for* (substantively represent) women. Finally, there are the ways in which the media represent women politicians and the question of whether these representations affect women's participation and substantive representation. Pick up any British newspaper when women politicians are in the news and there is likely to be plenty of gendered copy. Labour's 1997 women MPs are, for example, regularly referred to as 'Blair's Babes'. Or, to provide another striking example: on the appointment of her husband to Cabinet – which she also attends – Yvette Cooper was referred to as 'Mrs Ed Balls'.

Such gender concerns rarely surface in mainstream discussions of British party politics (Ware 2003; Webb 2000). This is a serious lacuna and reflects a failure by party politics' scholars to adopt gendered perspectives. Feminist political science demonstrates, in contrast, that parties' ideologies, structures, processes of candidate selection, and strategies to win women's votes, are saturated with gender (Lovenduski 2005a). Pioneering feminist research has extensively mapped these effects in the Labour Party of the 1980s and 1990s (Perrigo 1996, 1995, 1986; M. Russell 2005) but little has been published in respect of the Liberal Democrats (Evans 2007) or the contemporary Conservative Party (Campbell *et al.* 2006).

Women and British Party Politics aims to fill in some of these gaps. It identifies the characteristics of women's participation at the mass and elite level in contemporary British politics – as voters, party members and elected representatives, respectively. It also explores what this means for ideas about, and the practice of, descriptive, substantive and symbolic representation. The main focus is on the feminization of British party politics in the post-1997 period. Feminization has two dimensions: first, the integration of women into formal political institutions; and second, the integration of women's concerns and perspectives into political debate and policy (Lovenduski 2005a). Whilst it is often assumed that the former engenders the latter, the two dimensions do not necessarily work in tandem (L. Young 2000). Moreover, the feminization of politics is best understood as a process – it is about the *relative* integration of women and their concerns and perspectives.

With increasing party competition over women's concerns, together with women's enhanced participation in electoral politics at the elite level, feminization is likely to become a more significant feature of the British party system. Employing a feminist conceptual lens is, therefore, necessary to understand the story of women and British party politics. At its simplest, feminist analysis looks at how gender relations between women and men are a structuring dynamic of society. In such definitions, gender refers to the socially constructed differences between women and men, rather than any biological differences – the contrast between gender and sex, respectively. Importantly, gender is not a synonym for women (Carver 1996); studying gender in British party politics entails acknowledging and exploring the ways in which both women and men have gendered identities and the gendered nature of institutions. In addition, much, if not all, contemporary feminist theorizing recognizes intersectionality – that gender is cross-cut by other identities. As a consequence, feminist political science must consider the ways in which an appreciation of differences influences our understanding of political participation and representation: for all the celebrations about sex parity secured in the National Assembly for Wales in 2003, both it, and the Scottish Parliament, were wholly white institutions until 2007, when one Black, Asian and Minority Ethnic (BAME) MSP was returned to Holyrood: the House of Commons currently has only 15 BAME MPs, of whom only two are women.

To attain a better understanding of gender and party politics, (and, indeed, British politics per se) scholars need, then, to engage with the more abstract and normative questions found in feminist literature and apply them to empirical study. Feminist political scientists and theorists have been grappling with these for more than two decades (Norris and Lovenduski 1995; Phillips 1995).

Although they do not all necessarily agree, collectively they identify a host of reasons why women's presence in electoral politics matters. Some talk in terms of justice and equity. Others talk in terms of legitimacy, questioning whether legitimacy can be conferred on overwhelmingly male-dominated political institutions, even if they claim to 'stand for' or 'act for' men *and* women. Still others talk about the positive effect women's greater presence in politics would have, arguing that it is naïve to assume that women's concerns and perspectives – whatever they may be – are being fully addressed when those 'doing' politics are all too often male (and middle-class and middle-aged and white, for that matter).

Women and British Party Politics is specifically designed to bring together cutting-edge conceptual developments in the sub-discipline of gender and politics, with robust British empirical research, as well as presenting reflections on how best to study gender and politics in the future. The empirical findings derive from a range of research projects which were undertaken over a period of ten years or so, and which themselves make use of a variety of research methods and techniques. This reflects both a commitment to 'problem-driven' research and recognition of feminist political science's methodological eclecticism (Krook and Squires 2006). Moreover, bringing together research based on different methods in a single volume provides for a much richer account than would be possible if only a single research technique was used. Capturing the contours of women's mass political participation in electoral politics is probably best undertaken by survey research; understanding how women feel about their participation is most likely to be forthcoming in in-depth interviews and in focus groups. Nonetheless, when considering substantive representation, and drawing on recent work undertaken with European and American colleagues (Celis *et al*. 2007), a particular method – process-tracing and comparison – is favoured as the method most likely to best capture women's substantive representation.

Women's early participation in British party politics

The vote

Women's participation in British party politics pre-dated their partial enfranchisement in 1918. The Conservative Primrose League admitted women in 1883. And, before then, women had been active in various social and political movements – including temperance, anti-slavery campaigns and, of course, women's suffrage. In February 1918 the Representation of the People Act enfranchised some 8.5 million women – women over the age of 30 who were householders, the wives of householders, occupiers of property with an annual rent of £5, and graduates of British universities or women who were qualified but not graduates (Atkinson 1988, 39). In 1928 the Representation of the People (Equal Franchise) Act lowered the voting age for women to 21 – the same age as men.

The claim that politics did not concern women, and that women need have no concern for politics, was frequently aired during debates about women's suffrage. It was said that women did not *need* the vote – for they were already represented by their husbands; indeed, women should be *protected from* the vote – for it would threaten their purity and innocence. Instead, women should concern themselves with the domestic, and in their most public roles, the world of the social and of philanthropy (Maguire 1998). In any case, according to anti-suffrage arguments, if women had the vote, they would either: (a) vote in the same way as their husbands or (b) vote as a group. Either way, this would reveal women's lack of agency. In the former case, it would show that women did not need the vote, whilst in the latter instance, that women would vote on what was considered a wholly inappropriate basis.

Participation in political parties

In the first half of the twentieth century, the Conservative Party might rightly be considered the political party most hospitable to women (Maguire 1998; Lovenduski 2005a). By the 1980s and 1990s, this mantle passed to the Labour Party. Feminists who had previously rejected electoral politics joined Labour and, together with existing women members, made substantial demands, not least for parliamentary sex quotas. The re-emergence of a third party in British politics in the 1980s – the Social Democratic Party – was a compounding factor in this trans-formation as it sought to mobilize women as both party members and potential voters.

Women's participation in British political parties has, since the early part of the twentieth century, been marked by two questions. The first is whether women are best served by participating in parties' 'women's organizations' or through their mainstream organizations. This is the 'integration versus separation' dilemma. The second question centres on whether women should opt for an organizational form that seeks to substantively represent women *as women*, most often through parties' 'women's organizations', or one that advances the participation of women *as elected representatives* (Lovenduski 2005b). This is the 'collective versus indi-vidual representation' dilemma. Both dynamics are evident in the history of the two parties that dominated British politics in the twentieth century, the Conservative and Labour Parties.

The Primrose League, one of two Conservative extra-party organizations mobi-lizing women in the late-nineteenth Century, was the first political organization in the UK to give women a major role (Maguire 1998). Following the expansion of the franchise and legislation against electoral corruption, the Conservatives recognized that it would need women volunteers to register and canvass voters. There was no doubt, however, that the women would be 'subsidiary'. The sepa-rate organization of women in the Conservative Party continued for the first half of the twentieth century. There were women's sections at the local and regional levels – by 1924 there were more than 4000 women's branches. After the Second World War, integration was more in vogue and the women's branches were abol-ished. By the 1960s the women's sections had become 'women's constituency advisory committees', infamous for the provision of 'food and drink' and doing 'all the work' at election time (Maguire 1998, 140–1).

In terms of collective representation, the Conservatives' National Union established a women's staff with a Vice Chairman responsible for women. There was also an Annual Women's Conference, Women's Committees at the regional (ultimately called Women's Advisory Councils) and national level. In 1928 the Central Women's Advisory Committee was officially recognized and, later, renamed the Women's National Advisory Committee (WNAC). A parliamentary subcommittee of the WNAC was established in 1946. However, it was not until Edward Heath's modernizing leadership that WNAC-led demands for the integration of women's concerns were accepted. The Party needed to win votes, especially middle-class professional women who were proving resistant to the Party (Maguire 1998, 120–2; Lovenduski 2005a, 60). A new Committee of Women's Rights was established in 1973. From 1975 to 1990, the party was famously led by a woman, Margaret Thatcher – the first British woman Prime Minister (1979 and 1990). Her impact on women's participation and representation in the Conservative Party is, unfortunately, under-researched. But, by the 1990s women members of the Conservative Party were said to be of two distinct types (Maguire 1998): the traditional woman party member, fewer in number than before, as working women found themselves with little time for hosting Conservative tea parties; and the 'career' woman who was seeking political office, but who did not, or rarely publicly at least, see herself as a gendered political actor.

The story in respect of Labour is not so very different. Under the Labour Party's 1918 constitution, and reflecting women's separate involvement in much of the Labour movement pre-1918, Women's League branches became the Labour Party's new Women's Sections. By 1922 some 100,000 women chose to join one of the 650 Women's Sections (Graves 1994). Critics argue that these entrenched 'gender inequality into the very fabric' of the Labour Party (Perrigo 1995, 408); women were neither integrated and equal, nor separate but equal (Graves 1994, 7; M. Russell 2005, 97). With no direct powers of decision-making or direct representation on the party's decision-making bodies, the Women's Sections constituted merely advisory bodies. In the 1930s, and especially post-war, Women's Sections declined in importance – becoming 'little more than a fund-raising supporters club', as women became more active in the mixed constituency parties (Perrigo 1986, 102). The movement towards integration (Graves 1994, 109) meant that some women were able to participate and take office in local constituency parties, but, at the national level, women become less visible in the party and policy-making became the preserve of the male leadership and Trade Unions.

Other aspects of the Labour Party's 1918 constitution denied women's collective representation. One woman sat on each of the party's Executive Committees of the local constituency party; five seats were reserved for women on the National Executive Committee (NEC); there was a Chief Woman Officer, a Woman's Advisory Committee and an annual Women's Conference. Yet, each of these institutional forms was limited (Perrigo 1995; Lovenduski 2005a). The Women's Conference had no real status – Labour's Annual Conference voted down or refused to discuss issues from the Women's Conference almost every year between 1923 and 1930. A 1928 proposal to allow three Women's Conference resolutions a year to go to the Annual Conference was simply ignored by the NEC (Graves 1994). The five reserved seats on the NEC were not chosen by the Women's Sections, or by women party members, but by the Annual Conference (in effect, the Trade Unions). Finally, because women who wanted to be successful within the party were chosen by the wider party and not by women, they were under pressure to conform to masculinized party norms in order to compete against men, and they lacked corporate links with other women in the party.

Descriptive Representation at Westminster

Women's right to stand for election to Westminster was enshrined in the Parliament (Qualification of Women) Act of 1918. Seventeen women stood as candidates at the 1918 general election, including a number of Suffragettes, most famously (and unsuccessfully), Christabel Pankhurst. The first woman to be *elected* to the House of Commons was not, as many people mistakenly assume, the American-born Lady Nancy Astor, but Countess Constance Markievicz, a Sinn Fein MP, who refused to take her seat. Astor was the first woman to *sit* in the House, on winning a by-election in 1919, following the elevation of her husband to the House of Lords (Vallance 1979). By 1929 ten women sat in Parliament. At the outbreak of the Second World War there were 12: six Conservatives, four Labour, one Liberal and one Independent.

In much of the post-war period the percentage of women in the House of Commons averaged around 4 per cent. It was only in 1987 that this rose to 6 per cent, and in 1992 to 9 per cent. The watershed election of 1997 saw both the numbers of women and percentage of women double: to 120 and 18.2 per cent respectively. The General Election of 2001, however, delivered the first decline in a generation: the numbers of women MPs decreased by two to 118, and the percentage fell to 17.9 per cent. The upward trend returned in 2005: 128 women were elected, constituting 19.8 per cent of the House.

In respect of women's participation in Government, there have been both quantitative and qualitative advances since 1997. More women have served in Government under Tony Blair than the total number of women government ministers between 1924 and 1997. The numbers of women in Cabinet have also been unprecedented. Margaret Thatcher was, for the most part, the sole woman in her Cabinet, and none were present in John Major's first Cabinet. Blair had five women in his first Cabinet, and eight in his last. There has also been an improvement in terms of horizontal segregation. Women have been appointed beyond education and health. In any case, the historic characterization of 'soft' and 'hard' departments has become rather suspect in recent times; both education and health are key domestic priorities of the Government and both have significant budgets. Other important 'firsts' since 1997 include: the first female Leader of the House (Ann Taylor); the first female Foreign Secretary (Margaret Beckett); the first female Chief Whip (Hilary Armstrong); and the first black woman in the Cabinet (Baroness Amos). In Gordon Brown's first Cabinet in 2007, Jacqui Smith was appointed the first woman Home Secretary.

What difference the increased presence of women in the UK Parliament since 1997 has made is a question that is levelled collectively at women MPs, irrespective of whether individual MPs accept the assumption that their sex and/or gender plays a role in representation. In the 1997–2005 Parliament senior Labour ministers such as Harriet Harman, Patricia Hewitt, Margaret Hodge and Tessa Jowell were all publicly associated with the government's policies on Childcare, Sure Start, the extension of maternity and paternity rights, rights to flexible working, equal pay and domestic violence (Toynbee and Walker 2005). The basis upon which women representatives seek to act for women, the actions they undertake and the effect they have, has constituted the core research questions for gender and politics scholars.

Structure of the book

Women and British Party Politics is divided into two sections. The first half examines women as voters, party members and elected representatives in British party politics, focusing on women's vote choice in national elections, their participation in the three main UK political parties, and as representatives in the House of Commons. The second half of the book explores what women's participation means for ideas about, and the practice of, representation, in particular symbolic and substantive representation. The book can be read in two main ways. To gain the most from the analysis and the empirical cases, it is probably best to read the main body of each chapter, then the Case Studies. Readers might, though, prefer to 'dip' into particular Case Studies first. The number of Case Studies per chapter varies. This reflects the extent and nature of published research for each topic. By the end of the book readers should be able to consider the relationships between sex, gender and politics in a conceptually sophisticated fashion. They will have a more comprehensive picture of the relationship between women and British party politics, at least at Westminster. They will have a sense of where women are, the kind of political activities they engage in, and what kind of effect they may have.

The first chapter, *Women's Participation and Voting,* is written by Rosie Campbell. It maps the characteristics of women's mass participation in politics, noting that traditional conceptions of political participation often exclude women's activities. Case Study 1.1 questions the assumption that women are less interested in politics than men and argues, instead, that women and men are differently interested in politics. Case Study 1.2 summarizes the findings of the 2004 Electoral Commission Report *Gender and Political Participation* (Norris *et al.* 2004). This breaks down political participation into 'cause', 'civic' and 'campaign' oriented activities and finds that women are more likely to participate in the first two, and less likely to participate in the third. The most substantial part of the chapter turns its attention to gender and voting. Mainstream theories of voting behaviour are outlined, noting the emphasis historically given to class in understanding UK vote choice. Informed by the more extensive US gender and voting behaviour literature, UK research on gender and vote choice is then discussed, with particular focus on the gender generation gap, whereby younger women are found to be more left leaning than older women and younger and older men. In this analysis, acknowledgement is given to intra- as well as inter-sex differences in vote choice (differences between women, and differences between women and men, respectively). Case Study 1.3 examines the role that women's parenthood plays in their vote choice. Whether women and men conceive of, and approach, political choices differently – with women employing a more connected relational frame and men drawing on more abstract disconnected thought – is also examined, together with a discussion of whether women and men evaluate party leaders differently.

Chapter 2, *Feminizing British Political Parties,* explores the role of women, and the particular conceptions of gender and representation, at play in each of the main three British political parties. Each party's women's organizations and formal policy-making structures are described. In each case, relations between gender equality activists and party leadership are explored, together with a discussion of party change. A feminist audit of the three main parties' 2005 General Election manifestos and party leader interviews on BBC Radio 4's Woman's Hour enables consideration of the extent to which gendered analysis was integral to each party's policies at that particular moment in time. The chapter concludes by positing research questions that might contribute to the development of gendered typologies of political parties in future research.

Chapter 3, *Women's Legislative Recruitment,* offers a comprehensive analysis of the political recruitment of women to the contemporary House of Commons. A summary of both supply and demand-side explanations for women's legislative recruitment is followed by detailed analysis of the three main political parties' strategies to increase the number of women MPs at the 2005 and subsequent General Elections. Attention is focused on their formal procedures. The asymmetry in women's descriptive representation by party at Westminster is accounted for by the Labour Party's adoption of All Women Shortlists (AWS). In contrast, the Conservative and Liberal Democrat parties rely on equality rhetoric and promotion. Through a comparison with the Scottish Parliament and National Assembly for Wales, party demand is identified as the key determinant of women's descriptive representation in the UK. Case Studies in this chapter include a discussion of the electoral impact of AWS at the 2005 General Election – which, despite extensive media brouhaha, was not significant, outside of one constituency (Blaenau Gwent) – and analysis of the Conservative Party's 'selection DVD', designed to encourage local parties to select a more diverse group of parliamentary candidates. The chapter closes with a discussion of women's descriptive representation in comparative terms and explores the role that sex quotas play in enhancing women's political presence globally.

Chapter 4, *Representation: Why Women's Presence Matters*, is the introduction to the second half of the book. It outlines and evaluates classic and contemporary feminist theories of political representation. A feminist reading of Pitkin's *The Concept of Representation* is offered. Pitkin's groundbreaking work serves as the context within which more recent feminist engagements with the idea and practice of women's political representation have developed. The examination of feminist debates centres on the claim that women's descriptive and substantive representation is linked, for this is the question that dominates the contemporary academic literature, as well as much of the everyday discussion that surrounds women and politics. Arguments for women's political presence based on substantive representation claim that women are more likely to 'act for' women than men. Especially when crudely portrayed, this claim seems to be both reductive and essentialist; it assumes that the relationship between descriptive and substantive representation is straightforward. In contrast, I contend that the relationship between women's descriptive and substantive representation is complicated; that, in practice, other factors determine whether representatives act for women, a claim that is returned to in the subsequent chapter.

Chapter 5, *The Substantive Representation of Women,* is co-written with Mona Lena Krook. This chapter has two aims and is structured accordingly. First, there is a fulsome and critical engagement with existing feminist conceptions of substantive representation and, in particular, with how gender and politics scholars understand and study the relationship between descriptive and substantive representation. In doing this, it posits an alternative to 'critical mass theory'. After revisiting the landmark contributions of Rosabeth Moss Kanter and Drude Dahlerup, 'critical mass theory' is replaced with the concept of critical actors – understood as those who initiate reforms themselves or play a central role in mobilizing others for policy change. This enables an acknowledgement that women's substantive representation can occur in the absence of large numbers or percentages of women. Hence, rather than looking for 'when women make a difference', or 'whether women act for women', we contend that gender and politics scholars should examine 'how the substantive representation of women occurs'. The development of this approach reflects not only the perception that the link between women's descriptive and substantive representation is more complicated than often acknowledged, but also that existing empirical research itself points to the need for such a shift in research questions and focus. Accordingly we outline a second shift – a move away from analysis of what 'women' do in particular political institutions at the macro level, to an investigation of political actors at the micro level, coupled with an acknowledgement of the multiple sites of women's substantive representation. The second aim of Chapter 5 is to provide, through a substantial number of Case Studies – drawing directly on my own and others' work – a summary of existing empirical work on women's substantive representation at Westminster, in Scotland and in Wales. Together, these empirical studies constitute, in Lovenduski's (2005a, 180) terms, 'a substantial amount of circumstantial evidence' that women representatives 'act for' women.

Chapter 6, *Women Politicians, the Media and Symbolic Representation,* turns its attention to the gendered representations of women MPs in the British print media – one way of studying symbolic representation. It opens with a brief summary of extant literature on the study of gender, politics and the media, noting the three dominant approaches: symbolic annihilation, stereotypical representation and gender frame analysis (where women's sex/gender is the peg upon which the story is hung). This chapter takes a slightly different form than the other chapters, with only a single Case Study. 'Not up to the Job' centres on the media representation of the two women Ministers who resigned from Blair's Cabinet, Estelle Morris and Clare Short. The Case Study draws on national newspaper articles gathered for a one-week period either side of the Ministers' resignations. It is an intra-sex comparison. Using both quantitative and qualitative methods, it analyzes the use of stereotypes, gendered adjectives and traits employed in newspaper headlines and articles, and explores, in-depth, those articles which foreground the resigning Cabinet Ministers' sex and/or gender as either a reason for the resignation or as a basis for the media representation of the resignation. Five gender frames are identified. Three – the 'politics as male', 'not their own woman' (agency) and the 'all women' frames – are employed in respect of both Estelle Morris and Clare Short. The 'women's resignation' frame is applied only to Morris and the 'love' frame only to Clare Short. Such representations point to a distinction between the *male-politician-norm* and the *female-politician-pretender* and a contrast between 'good women' and the 'good representative'.

Women and British Party Politics' concluding chapter summarizes the relationship between sex, gender and British party politics. In so doing, it identifies ongoing conceptual and empirical debates that characterize the study of gender and politics both in the UK and the wider sub-discipline, and raises questions about the direction of future research.

Note

1 One exception is M. Russell (2005).

Section I

Political participation and descriptive representation

1 Women's political participation and voting

Rosie Campbell with Sarah Childs

Introduction

In the past, it was widely held that women were less political than men, if not apolitical. It was assumed that women had lower levels of interest in politics and lower levels of participation in political activities. And when women did vote – the classic, albeit minimal, measure of political participation – it was claimed that they did so on the basis of emotion rather than reason, on the basis of a candidate's personality rather than on policies or in the same way as their husbands. Feminist political science offers a two- pronged critique of such approaches to women's political participation and voting behaviour. First, it challenges the mainstream's conceptualization of politics, with its tendency to exclude or discount forms of participation that fall beyond the boundaries of a narrow definition of what constitutes 'politics'. Adopting a wider conception of political participation, recent studies find that women and men's political activism gap is dramatically reduced, and with women more active than men according to some measures (Norris *et al.* 2004). Feminists also charge the mainstream with failing to fully consider how gendered life experiences might influence and constrain the extent, and nature, of women's political activity. Second, feminist political science asks why the rigorous research designs employed in the academic study of political participation and voting were not applied to the study of sex, gender and political participation. Why, for example, was it acceptable to make statements about women's political interest and motivations in the absence of supporting evidence?

To date, the nature of women's political interest and dimensions of their participation have not received extensive attention by British feminist political scientists. Case Study 1.1 presents new research that explores how interested men and women are in politics, and, in particular, whether women and men are interested in different kinds of political issues. Asking respondents to state how interested they are across five issues (education, the NHS, foreign policy, law, order and crime, and partisan politics), this research establishes that interest in politics is not uni-dimensional. Instead, it has two components: (1) general interest in politics; and (2) domestic politics. Women are less interested in general politics than men but are more interested in domestic politics than men – sex differences that are statistically significant.

It has been as voters that feminist scholars have been most interested in women's political participation. Informed by the more established US literature on the gender gap, they have been keen to investigate whether sex and/or gender influences vote choice in the UK. It has also been observed that women are more likely than previously to turn out to vote, have a greater longevity than men, and a greater propensity to be floating voters. According to the British Election Study (BES), 37 per cent of women, compared with 31 per cent of men, decided how to vote *during* the 2005 election campaign. In such a context, political parties have begun to take an interest in, and increasingly compete for, women's votes. For the media, especially the print media, the possible influence of sex and gender on voting easily generates good copy. In the run up to the 2005 General Election, for example, a *Daily Mirror* front page had Tony Blair, centre-spread, his arms around two of its women columnists, with the headline: 'Can He Turn Women On?'[1]

That there are only a handful of British feminist studies documenting the relationship between sex, gender and voting behaviour, most of which are quite recent, can be explained by the later emergence of feminist political scientists in the UK as compared to the US, especially those trained in quantitative methods of political analysis. Yet, it also reflects the absence of an aggregate gender gap in Britain: overall, men and women in Britain vote roughly in the same way. The British case does, however, provide evidence that sub-groups of men and women differ in their political and voting preferences. Younger women are more left-leaning and feminist than older women and both younger and older men – a gender-generation gap. There is also evidence of motivational gender gaps, whereby men and women may vote for the same parties, but do so for different reasons.

Gender and political participation

Defining and measuring political participation is by no means straightforward. Yet, how one defines political participation has important consequences for the conclusions drawn about the extent and nature of women's participation. Early studies tended to adopt narrow definitions. In some of these, assertions were made about women's behaviour that were not founded upon evidence. To Bourque and Grossholtz (1998) this was simply bad science; Goot and Reid (1975) set out to trace and challenge the myths about women portrayed in this literature, such as the depiction of women voters as 'mindless matrons'. A classic example of the failings of some of the early literature is Gabriel Almond and Sydney Verba's *Civic Culture*. In this, they claimed that 'it would appear that women differ from men in their political behaviour only in being somewhat more frequently apathetic, parochial, conservative and sensitive to personality, emotional and aesthetic aspects of political life and electoral campaigns' (Almond and Verba 1963, 325). No evidence was presented to support their claims.

Other studies exploring women's and men's political participation, employing robust research designs, did find sex differences in participation, with women less active than men.[2] Maurice Duverger's (1955) early study concluded that women were less likely to turn out at election time and less likely to join political parties.

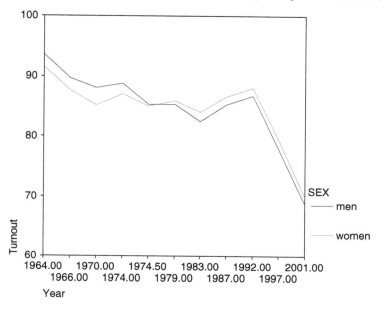

Figure 1.1   Electoral turnout by sex, 1964–2001 (BES).

More recently, Parry *et al.* (1992) found a pro-men 'gender gap' in political participation in Britain. However, this difference was 'distinctly small' – there are 'almost as many (or as few!) politically active women as men': 'men on average undertake 1.6 actions and the women 1.41'. There is also evidence of a closure of the traditional gender gap in voter turnout. Fewer women than men may have voted in General Elections in the first two-thirds of the twentieth century but since 1979 the gap has disappeared, as Figure 1.1 illustrates. In some instances it has reversed, although the difference is not usually statistically significant, and probably reflects women's greater longevity.

Expanding our conception of political participation facilitates a more compre-hensive analysis of political participation and permits conclusions as to whether women are less active than men overall, or whether women and men tend to be involved in different types of activities, as Case Study 1.2 outlines. The 2004 Electoral Commission Report distinguishes between different types of participa-tion: 'cause oriented', 'civic oriented' and 'campaign oriented' activities (Norris *et al.* 2004). Campaign oriented activity equates with the widely accepted tradi-tional conceptions of political participation, which include only those activities that are *directly* related to attempting to influence government. It consists of items such as political party membership, as well as donating to, and campaigning for, political parties. In contrast, both cause oriented and civic oriented activities broaden out the definition of political participation, by including the boycotting of goods and signing of petitions, in the case of the former, and membership of voluntary organizations, in the case of the latter. In this way, political participation encompasses a wider range of activities that may have a more *indirect* effect upon government. The Report concludes that there is only a small activism gap in the UK, and, more strikingly, that men and women tend to undertake different kinds of politics. In turn, this focuses attention onto the question of whether it matters if one sex disproportionately partakes of one form of political activity and, if so, in what ways: if women and men participate differently, but both have equal chances of affecting decision makers, it might not matter for substantive reasons. However, it might matter for symbolic ones if women are the ones signing petitions rather than joining parties or contesting elections.

Alongside the study of political participation, as more traditionally understood, political scientists have, in recent years, become interested in associational membership (individuals' participation in voluntary groups). This renewed interest has largely resulted from the work of Robert Putnam (1995; 2000; Putnam et al., 1993) who has employed the concept of social capital to explain what he considers to be the worrying decline in political participation in contemporary America. This decline mirrors a decline in social capital. Social capital describes the substance gained by individuals in associational life that aids their movement through social networks. There are two types of social capital – bridging and bonding. The former refers to networks of diverse groups of people; the latter, networks of homogenous groups of people. According to Putnam, stable democracies require significant numbers of people to have access to the 'right' kind of social capital; 'bridging social capital' – this brings enormous benefits for society, from community cohesion to the successful implementation of public policy. The link between social capital and electoral political participation lies in the assumption that, whilst developed primarily through membership of non-political organizations, social capital is an important precursor to traditional political activity.

British studies have failed to find a decline of social capital comparable to the US case. More pertinent to issues of gender and political participation, though, is the finding that 'social capital has been sustained in Britain largely by virtue *of increasing participation of women* in the community' (Hall 1999, emphasis added): women's group membership more than doubled between 1959 and 1990. Even so, a feminist reading of the social capital literature contends that the definition of social capital employed is, itself, too narrow, overlooking vast areas of women's participation, from charitable endeavour to informal sociability (Lowndes 2000). Putnam *et al.*'s (1993) original Italian study includes only a fraction of the groups related to health and social services, precisely the kinds of groups that women participate in. Similarly, Hall's (1999) study failed to include childcare activities, which constitute important social networks for women. This omission is not merely definitional: childcare activities constitute an ideal type of activity for the acquisition of the 'right' kind of social capital (Lowndes 2000, 534). Members of childcare groups are likely to be drawn from a variety of backgrounds and their relationships are characterized by 'mutuality' and 'reciprocity'.

If women and men in Britain are roughly equally likely to undertake associational activity (Lowndes 2000), they nevertheless engage in different kinds: men are more likely to participate in sporting and recreational groups, whilst women are more likely to engage in befriending activity and be members of health, educational and social service organizations. The logic of such observations, following Putnam, is clear: if women and men engage in different types of associational life, they will gain different types of social capital. In turn, this might impact on their involvement in more traditional forms of political participation. Indeed, Lowndes (2006, 233–4) concludes that women 'are more likely than men to draw upon social capital as a resource for getting by, for balancing the competing demands of home and work and protecting their own and the families' health and well-being'.

Vote choice in Britain

Mainstream accounts

According to the 'Michigan Model' of voting behaviour most people have little knowledge about politics; voters' beliefs are formed, in the main, by the socialization process (Campbell *et al.* 1960). Applying this model to the British case, the founding fathers of electoral research in Britain, Donald Stokes and David Butler (1969) contended that class was the most important predictor of vote choice. Three-quarters of the respondents to the British Election Study (BES) felt a strong, long-term, and stable affiliation to a political party. This affiliation was closely related to class identification, with most working class voters identifying with the Labour Party and most middle class voters identifying with the Conservative Party.

With their emphasis on class, Butler and Stokes (1969) gave little space to sex and gender. There are no direct references to either term, or to women for that matter, in the index of *Political Change in Britain;* nor does sex or gender feature in any of their tables. In their analysis women were also assigned their husband's occupational class even if they were themselves employed in paid work. There is only one occasion when the impact of sex differences on vote choice is considered, and this is in relation to the effect on the political development of children, rather than an examination of women's vote choice. When analyzing childhood socialization, and 'when the direction of the mother's preference is distinguished from the father's, it is plain that *each parent*, and not only the father, helps to form the nascent partisanship of the child' (Butler and Stokes 1974, 32, emphasis added). Yet it is the father's preference that is considered more significant – as it was more likely to be visible within the family – a claim that is made without further substantiation.

From the late 1970s, the bedrock of accepted accounts of voting behaviour in Britain was shaken by the 'dealignment' debate. This contends that the explanatory power of class and party identification was overstated (Rose and McAllister 1986). A key example of this approach (Franklin 1985) suffers from similar gender shortcomings to Butler and Stokes. There are, again, no references to sex, gender or women in the index to *Decline in Class Voting in Britain*. Moreover, women's class location continues to be determined by their husband's – a move which fails to appreciate that family members may have different social backgrounds. This study also employed head-of-household statistics, by which women are subsumed under the family label. Finally, no distinction is drawn between women and men's influence when the effect of parental party and parental class on vote choice is considered.

The dealignment literature did, however, provide some space for greater consideration of sex and gender, and the development of more sophisticated inter- and intra-sex comparisons (Dunleavy and Husbands 1985). In this, the tradition of assigning all married women their husband's occupational class was, first, criticized. Second, it was claimed that comparisons of women and men's voting patterns should go beyond controlling for class to recognize additional problems associated with comparing vote choice within a particular occupational class. In this respect, it was acknowledged that women are often less successful at attaining career advancement than men, especially if they marry and take time out to care for children. This means that gender must be considered logically prior to occupational class. Third, and consequently, it became necessary to assess the impact of *social* rather than *occupational* class on vote choice. This refers to taking into account differences in men and women's lives and how these might relate to voting behaviour. On this basis, Dunleavy and Husbands (1985, 128) showed that there was considerable variation between the voting behaviour of women in the manual and non-manual class, with 53 per cent of non-manual women voting Conservative compared to 27 per cent of manual women (this difference is larger than the one between manual/non-manual men, with 36 per cent of non-manual men and 29 per cent of manual men voting Conservative).

Gendered voting studies

US literature

The more extensive US literature on gender and voting provides the analytic frameworks within which much of the contemporary British research operates. Much of the US scholarship centres on the modern gender gap: since 1980 there has been an overall difference between the way women and men vote in US elections, with women more likely to vote Democrat than men.[3] The use of the term gender gap in the US is not, however, without controversy. Some have claimed that feminist political scientists (and activists) tend to use the concept to further a political agenda, namely the greater descriptive and substantive representation of women (Greenberg 2001; Steel 2003). Other critics emphasize that the gender gap in the US is not as big as is often assumed, and that other differences are more salient (Seltzer *et al.* 1997, 3): 'in 1994, women voted 7 to 11 percentage points more Democratic than men' but the race gap 'between whites and blacks was a true chasm of 50 points'. At the same time, the gender gap is, at 5–10 per cent, of sufficient size to affect US elections. The US literature also identified other factors which interact with sex to explain vote choice. Analysis of the 1992 US presidential election found that Bill Clinton constantly won a majority of college-educated women's support. However, 'born-again' Southern religious women were found to be mainly responsible for the increase in female George Bush supporters (Bendyna and Lake 1994). Paid employment is another important intra-sex difference: the preference for Clinton over Bush was 10 per cent amongst employed women, whereas homemakers were more likely to vote for Bush – 45 per cent of homemakers voted for Bush, compared to 36 per cent for Clinton.

Attempts to explain the US gender gap draw on a variety of models. These can be roughly divided into two types. The first cites the different material interests of men and women which result from the sexual division of labour. The second set of explanations is based upon psychoanalysis and theories of socialization which place the source of gender difference in early childhood.[4] Box-Steffensmeir *et al.*'s (1997) study compares both approaches. In the second approach, Carol Gilligan's 'ethics of care' – in which women are understood to perceive morality within a connected web of human relationships, in contrast to the rules based approach generally conceived by men – is used to suggest that women might have a compassionate motivation for voting for the Democrat party. Democratic Party voters believe they should support the needs of all society's members. This contrasts with the alternative rational choice hypothesis which depicts the voter as bounded by self-interested behaviour. Here, the gender gap reflects the patterns of women's employment and welfare dependency. Women are more likely than men to work in the public sector, a factor known to be linked to identification with the Democratic Party; women are also more likely than men to be the receivers of state benefits, again, a factor linked to support for the Democrats. The economy is a further important component in this research: women tend to be more pessimistic about the economy than men. However, if the gender gap remains after controlling for personal finances, it can be inferred that the gap does not result purely from women's relatively worse-off position in society. Neither the compassion nor the self-interest arguments are sufficient, alone, to explain the gender gap in US politics (Box-Steffensmeir *et al.* 1997). The reasons that women are more inclined to identify with the Democrats are diverse: women in higher-and middle-income groups are more likely than men, of the same socio-economic status, to be motivated by compassion. A similar, although smaller gap, is present at lower income levels. This probably results from the shared economic vulnerability of lower income men and women; whereas in the higher income groups there may be more scope for a gender gap to emerge.

While the American gender gap literature provides a useful starting point for British research, it is necessary when moving to the British case, to consider how the two countries vary. Most importantly, and as stated above, there has been no comparable 'gender gap' in vote choice at the aggregate level in the UK. This difference in voting patterns might be explained by the 'traditional lack of a strong class cleavage in the electorate, the centrist pattern of two-party competition, or the salience of issues like abortion and affirmative action' (Norris 2001, 302). Other differences between the two countries include alternative health and welfare traditions. Whilst it is the case that in both countries 'women earn less than men and are primary caregivers to their families', in the US 'women live and raise children under limited welfare provisions' (Steel 2003, 3). The unparalleled salience of welfare provision as a political issue in the US, together with the division between the sexes over the issue, means that welfare underpins the US gender gap. Key subgroups of men and women in the UK and US also differ. In particular, religion is a less important indicator of partisanship in Britain and, as a whole, fewer British than American citizens are highly religious.

British research

In the first instance, British gender and vote choice research attempts to explain the absence in the UK of an aggregate level modern gender gap, akin to that observed in the US. It does this by exploring differences between women and men's vote choice (inter-sex differences) and differences between sub groups of women (intra sex differences). Case Study 1.3 examines the interaction of various socio-demographic characteristics on vote choice. It finds, on the basis of an analysis of British Social Attitudes Data from 2001 and 2002, that 'women with children under 11 in the household' are more likely to vote for the Labour Party than the Conservative Party. The same is not true for men: of respondents with a child under 11 in the home, 68 per cent of women, compared to 58 per cent of men, were Labour Party identifiers. Recent studies also explore the ideological and attitudinal differences between women and men that might underpin such gaps, and explores sex differences in the motivations of voters, namely whether women and men or, rather, subgroups of women and men, prioritize different political issues when deciding how to vote. Exploratory focus group research also examines sex differences in leadership evaluations and finds that women respond to politicians in the same way as men, undermining the media portrayal of women as 'wooed' by male leaders.

The modern gender gap and the gender generation gap.

Although the first mass surveys of British public opinion found that women were more likely to say that they voted for the Conservative Party than men (Goot and Reid 1975), the traditional gender gap in Britain was never large (Norris 1999b). At its peak in the 1950s, the gap was about 14 per cent, falling to around 3 per cent post-1979. This has led to suggestions, especially following the 1997 General Election, that a gender dealignment has taken place. The possibility of a modern gender gap – where women are more likely to vote Labour – came very much to the fore in the run up to the 2005 General Election, when Labour's, and especially Blair's, relationship with women voters was widely reported as suffering from a 'seven year itch'. Focus group findings, survey results and private party polling, all found that women were more dissatisfied with the Labour government than men were; support for the Labour Party had fallen six points among married women with children.[5] Yet opinion polls in the year prior to the General Election suggested that women were still more likely to support Labour than men, overall: men 'certain to vote' would distribute their vote 35 per cent Labour, 35 per cent Conservative and

19 per cent Liberal Democrat, while women would vote 36 per cent Labour, 32 per cent Conservative and 24 per cent Liberal Democrat (Mortimore 2005, 80). Analysis of the pre-election British Election Study (BES) data concurred with the direction of these earlier polls, with more women than men reporting that they intended to vote for the Labour Party (Campbell and Winters 2006a). The General Election exit polls,[6] too, found a pro-Labour gap between women and men's votes: 38 per cent of women voted Labour, 32 per cent voted Conservative and 22 per cent voted Liberal Democrat. In contrast, 34 per cent of men voted Labour, 34 per cent voted Conservative and 23 per cent voted Liberal Democrat. However, the post-election data, which measures 'actual turnout', by checking the electoral register to see whether survey respondents did in fact vote, found no such evidence of an aggregate level modern gender gap at the 2005 General Election.

At the same time, the 2005 post-election data did find evidence of a gender generation gap. This refers to younger women's greater propensity to vote for the Labour Party than both younger men and older women and men. Evidence for such a gender generation gap had been forthcoming 'in successive elections from 1964 to 1997', with women in the youngest cohort 'consistently more Labour leaning than men' (Norris 1999b, 156). These differences do not always become evident, however, at the aggregate level because the different voting preferences of older and younger women cancel each other out. At the 1997 General Election it appears that women born after 1945 were more likely to have voted for the Labour Party than men of the same generations (Norris, 1999b); 55 per cent of women under 45 voted Labour, in comparison to only 44 per cent of younger men. In the older age group (over 44) 39 per cent of the women voted Conservative in comparison to 31 per cent of the older men.

Attitudinal gender gaps.

Gender gaps in vote choice are very often underpinned by gender gaps in ideology. Ideology is usually measured using two cross-cutting scales, the left-right or socialist/laissez-faire scale (which asks respondents a number of questions about nationalization, private enterprise and equality), and the liberal-authoritarian scale (which asks respondents about their attitudes to civil liberties). Evidence of an ideological gender generation gap is forthcoming in the 1997 and 2001 BES (Campbell 2004; 2006).[7] Women born post-1945 are significantly to the left of men on the self-placement left–right scale – where respondents are asked to choose how left- or right-leaning they believe themselves to be. This finding is corroborated by the observation that women born after 1957 are also significantly more left-leaning on the socialist/laissez-faire scale than men. Such UK surveys are in line with surveys in other Western industrialized countries (Campbell 2006; Inglehart and Norris 2000). Calculating the sex difference in left/right political positions, Inglehart and Norris (2000) reported ideology gaps for 1981 at –0.03 for the US and –0.06 for Britain. In 1990 the reported gaps were 0.22 for the US and 0.19 for Britain. Thus, the US trend – with women becoming more left-leaning than men – is also evident in Britain.

The impact of *feminist* orientation on women's and men's vote choice has been addressed in two British studies.[8] The first found that feminist attitudes can be used to predict votes for the Labour Party (Hayes 1997).[9] It established that feminist attitudes can be possessed by both men and women, and that feminist attitudes predicted Labour Party votes of men and women equally well. The second study sought to confirm whether feminist orientation is a better predictor of vote choice for younger women, which would provide a possible explanation of the gender generation gap. Women born post-1945 are significantly more feminist than men of the same generation. Moreover, this has a significant effect on vote choice (Campbell 2006). Feminist orientations also prove to be a better predictor of younger women's votes for the Labour Party than younger men's. Suggestive evidence points to the different effects education and occupation might have on the ideological position of men and women. Women who have A-levels or a Degree are significantly more left-leaning than men with the same qualifications. Similarly, women members of the salariat are also more left-leaning than men members (Campbell 2004). These findings might go someway toward explaining the reversal of the traditional gender gap and the emergence of the modern gender gap. Younger women's left-leaning tendencies might reflect the fact that more women are now entering higher education and paid employment.

Motivational gaps.

A motivational gender gap occurs when men and women vote for the same parties, but do so for different reasons (Steel 2003). It usually occurs when men and women have different issue priorities. For example, if women are more concerned about education than men, and men are more concerned about the economy than women, a gender gap in behaviour will occur *if* the parties have significantly different platforms on these issues. Recent British research has identified differences between men and women, and especially different generations of men and women, in issue preference: women are more likely to prioritize education and healthcare issues, and men are more likely to select the economy as their most important election issue. However, the differences between the sexes are most interesting when broken down by age: younger women are more likely to prioritize education whilst older women are more likely to prioritize healthcare (Campbell 2004). In contrast, according to the 2001 BES, men aged between 25 and 34 are the most likely to say that taxation is the most important election issue. It is clear that issue preferences vary by age and sex, but do those differences map on to the party voted for? Logically, the relationship between issue preference and party of vote will vary according to electoral context. If education is more important to women than men, but all the main parties provide similar policy platforms around the issue, then a gender gap in vote choice would not be generated. In the 2001 General Election, the Labour party stressed it's commitment to investing more in health and education. If women's prioritization of these issues transforms into vote choice then it would be expected, in this context, for women to be more likely to vote Labour. Evidence from the 2001 BES suggests that this is what happened. Respondents to the 2001 BES were asked whether they would support increases in taxation if the funds were to be spent on welfare. In all of the generations, the tax/spend on welfare variable had a larger impact on the vote choice of women than men. In the whole sample women who supported increased taxation and spending on welfare were 5.5 times more likely to vote for the Labour Party than those who did not, whilst men who chose increased taxation and spending on welfare were 2.5 times more likely to vote for the Labour Party than those who did not. This data suggests that, although overall women voted for the Labour Party in roughly equal numbers to men, they may have done so for different reasons; women were more likely to be driven by a concern for increased spending on welfare than men.

Leadership evaluations

During the 2005 general election the media took a particular interest in women's ratings of Tony Blair; it is widely assumed that the Labour Party's 1997 landslide election victory and re-election in 2001 owed a great deal to Blair's personal popularity with women. Winters and Campbell's (2007) exploratory focus group study explored whether there was any difference in the way men and women evaluate party leaders. In both the men's and women's groups, Blair received the highest number of positive competence assessments of all three main party leaders and the fewest number of comments which described him as incompetent. There is, though, no evidence, on the basis of these focus groups, to suggest that women and men evaluated Blair using distinct criteria, although men spent more time discussing his leadership qualities than did women. Women's descriptions included: untrustworthy; insincere; convinced of his own rightness; charismatic; ambitious; liar; bully; dictator; knowledgeable; and preachy. Men's comments about Blair included: phoney; a capable and serious leader; liar; strong; reliable; practical; presidential; looks intelligent; tries to please everyone; good politician; and persuasive. In general, then, men and women evaluated Blair according to the same three themes: competence, personality, and integrity, suggesting that the media's interest in Blair's 'love affair with women' was misplaced. These findings are in line with quantitative evidence from the BES which shows that women voters were on average slightly less impressed by Blair than men throughout the whole period of 1997–2005, although the difference is virtually negligible in the 2005 sample (Campbell 2006). This data reveals, further, that Blair was less popular with older women than older men, arguably reflecting the traditional gender gap within the oldest cohorts of the population.

Conclusion

Feminists have long since insisted that political participation is not limited to engagement in electoral politics. This chapter has sought to capture the characteristics of women's mass participation in politics in Britain, through a broader definition of participation than is traditionally assumed, although this is not as broad an exploration as the feminist claim 'the personal is political' demands. It suggests that, when mainstream political scientists fail to look beyond party politics, at social capital and group membership, for example, they miss important dimensions of women's participation. Furthermore, and turning the attention back to more traditional conceptions of politics and political participation, the chapter also set out to highlight how extant claims about participation gaps between women and men are more complex than usually understood. To be sure, women continue to be less involved overall in some aspects of party politics, although this is no longer so in terms of voter turnout. At the same time, however, women are more involved than men in certain, less formal, but nonetheless political activities, such as signing petitions, boycotting goods and belonging to health and education related voluntary groups related to influencing government, as shown in Case Study 1.2. Explaining the dimensions of women and men's mass political participation is not easy: the research points to sociological, psychological and institutional factors. Taking the example of institutional factors – the finding that women's political activity increases in a number of ways in constituencies where there is a woman MP – suggests that the 'apathy' attributed to women in the early political science literature might be a reflection of political disenfranchisement and, importantly, one which may be reversed when women see more 'people like them' involved in politics.

A discussion of sex, gender and vote choice constitutes the core of this chapter. The mainstream literature on voting behaviour is characterized by a gradual shift from sexist and bad political science, to a more nuanced approach, which takes account of differences between women, as well as comparing women and men. As in many other advanced industrialized countries, there is evidence for a gender generation gap in Britain: younger women have moved to the left of men on the ideological spectrum. Whilst robust, ideological differences between men and women do not always clearly map onto vote choice – women are less likely to be strong party supporters than men and their movement to the left does not guarantee votes for the Labour Party. Even so, since 1997 the Labour Party has won more of the votes of young women than young men. The relative success of Labour among women since 1997 is, in all likelihood, attributable to a successful targeting by the party of middle and high-income mothers. Recent research also suggests that men and women prioritize different issues, with younger women most concerned about education and older women prioritizing healthcare, whilst men are more concerned by the economy and taxation (Campbell 2006). It also suggests that the traditional division of labour between women and men socializes women to think about politics in a connected relational way, focused upon the needs of their families. In contrast, men are more likely to engage in more abstract disconnected thought. In short, women might 'do' voting differently from men.

Despite the advances made over the last decade or so in British gender, political participation and voting research, there are still many unanswered questions. The relationship between gender and vote choice is complicated: inter- and intra-sex differences mean that, to take gender seriously, political science must be careful not to discuss women and men voters as though they are members of a homogenous group. Any differences between women and men should also be considered gender, and not sex, differences. The impact of gender on voting behaviour, importantly, also depends upon electoral context and, in particular, issue salience.

Case Study 1.1

Not interested or differently interested?

That women generally have lower levels of interest in politics than men is a well rehearsed political 'fact'. But is it that women are less interested in politics than men, or, rather, that women and men are differently interested? Extant studies have established that men's and women's political knowledge differs by issue area (Norris *et al.* 2004), and that men and women prioritize different issues (Campbell 2004): women are more interested in health and education, whilst men are more interested in the economy and taxation. Given these observations, a simple uni-dimensional measure of whether an individual is interested in politics – on a scale from 'not at all interested in politics' to 'very interested in politics' – is unlikely to capture the full range of women's political interests.

In addition to the standard 'interest in politics' question (Thinking about politics in general, how much interest do you generally have in what is going on in politics?) respondents in an ESRC[10] funded YouGov electronic survey ($n = 2890$) were asked to rate how interested they would be in news items covering five areas:

- Thse state of education in Britain
- The state of the National Health Service
- British foreign policy (the conflict in Iraq, Israel-Palestine, EU)
- Law and order and crime (including domestic security)
- British partisan politics (Blair and Brown, party conferences, party campaigning)

The results show that there are two dimensions to interest in politics: (1) general interest in politics, and (2) interest in domestic politics. The questions relating to partisan politics, foreign policy and general interest in politics fit together well, as do the questions relating to health, education and law and order. Differences in men's and women's interest in the two dimensions, by age-groups, are portrayed in Figures 1.1.i and 1.1.i.i.

The results show that women are, indeed, less interested in general politics than men, but they are more interested in domestic politics than men; these differences are statistically significant. In both cases the gender differences are largest among the under 45s.

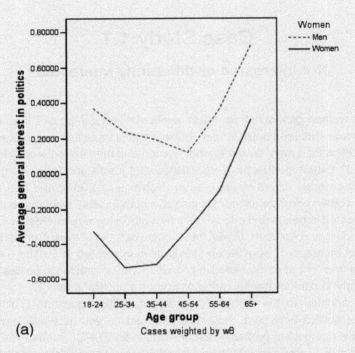

(a)   Cases weighted by w8

Figure 1.1.i Average general interest in politics by sex and age group

Having established that a gender gap exists, it is important to ask why women have lower levels of interest in general politics and higher levels of interest in domestic politics than men. There are a number of possible explanations. First, there may be barriers to women's interest and participation in party politics, produced by the time constraints imposed by the care of young children. At the same time, and intuitively, it seems likely that, because the gaps are largest among the under 45s, the responsibilities of motherhood may provide a possible explanation: women's continuing disproportionate share of childcare responsibilities may lead them to be more interested in issues relating to education and social services. Hence, it can be hypothesized that the inclusion of a measure of parenthood should reduce the gender gaps in both interest

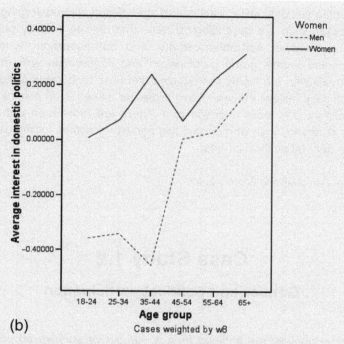

(b)

Figure 1.1.ii Average interest in domestic politics, by sex and age group

in general and domestic politics. Second, there is evidence that the modern gender gap is strongest among high income parents (Campbell 2006). Here it can be suggested that high status men become more interested in partisan and international politics because they see themselves as protected, or remote from, the need for state welfare. On the other hand, low-income individuals (men and women) and high-income mothers may continue to be more focused upon domestic issues and welfare provision, both in terms of their own interests and those of their children. Thus, the hypothesis is that high income men will be the least interested in domestic politics. The results of the analysis suggest that the second explanation has more power than the first. All women, and not simply women who are mothers, are less interested in general politics and more interested in domestic politics than men. However, high-income men are the least interested in domestic politics and the most interested in general politics. The gap between men and women remains, even after the dummies for parenthood and high income men are included. The only measures which have any real impact upon the size of the sex difference are those of agency and communion. Agency and communion are psychological traits that tend to vary by gender. Agency involves self-enhancement and self-assertion, whereas communion entails group participation and cooperation with others. Individuals who are highly self-directed and have high levels of agency and efficacy believe they can have a greater influence on politics and, accordingly, pay more attention to it. There are more men with high levels of agency than women and this partially accounts for the gender gap in general political interest.

Source: Campbell and Winters 2007.

Case Study 1.2

Gender and political participation

Bringing together the findings from a number of surveys on political participation and undertaking systematic secondary data analysis of academic studies, the Electoral Commission's 2004 Report 'Gender and Political Participation' provides analysis of the ways in which gender determines the nature of women's and men's political participation in the UK. On the basis of their findings, the Report refutes widely-held assumptions about women's apolitical nature. Rather, the level of men's and women's activism in the UK differs according to the type of political activity.

Key findings:

- There is no gender gap in voter turnout at national, regional, or local elections; at the 2001 General Election 66.8 and 67.7 per cent of men and women voted.
- Women are more likely than men to be involved in 'cause oriented' activities – activities such as signing petitions or boycotting products. For example, women were found to be 6 per cent more likely than men to have signed a petition in the last year; 7 per cent more likely to have bought a product for political reasons; and 1 per cent more likely to have boycotted a product for political reasons.

- Women are significantly less likely to participate in campaign-oriented activities – activities such as contacting politicians, and donating money to, working for, or being a member of, a political party. Men were found to be 3 per cent more likely than women to have contacted a politician in the last year; 3 per cent more likely to have contributed money to a political campaign; and 2 per cent more likely to have worked for a party.

- Overall, women are less likely than men to join voluntary organizations. However, this observation masks significant differences in the type of organizations men and women join. Men were 13 per cent more likely than women to be a member of a sports club and 7 per cent more likely to be a member of a professional organization; women were 7 per cent more likely to belong to a church group and 1 per cent more likely to belong to an environmental group.

- In parliamentary constituencies with women MPs, women are more politically active. In a constituency where the MP is a woman, women constituents were found to be 4 per cent more likely to have voted than men; and in constituencies with a woman MP, 3 per cent more women than men reported being 'very interested' in the election.

These sex differences in political participation beg questions about the causes and effects of the gender gap. In respect of the former, the Report asks whether women do not participate in campaign politics because they can't (they lack the resources), won't (because they are not interested), are not asked to (because they lack networks), or are put off from participating (by the rules of the game)? Similar questions might, of course, be posed as to why men engage more in some, and not other, forms of political participation.

The report also asks whether women's preference for boycotting or buying particular products, signing petitions and demonstrating is problematic if it means women are not, at the same time, engaging in campaign politics. As some feminists suggest, this lower participation in campaign politics may not only reduce the legitimacy of our elected political institutions but might also mean that women's concerns are absent from the political agenda of party politics.

In accounting for the gender gap in political participation, the Report finds that it is at its widest among the least educated, narrows in households with above average income and educational attainment, and is larger among respondents who have children living at home. Britain's ethnic minority women are also found to be less politically active than other women, with Black women 8 per cent less likely to vote than

Black men, and Asian women 2 per cent less likely to vote than Asian men. One explanation found for women's lower participation is their weaker sense of political efficacy – the belief that their activities will make a difference – women's average level of political efficacy was 0.81 (of a point on a five point scale) lower than men's.

As well as finding a number of sociological and psychological explanations for the gender gaps, the Report establishes that they may have potential institutional causes. It finds, as stated above, that in parliamentary constituencies where there is a sitting woman MP, according to several measures, the gender gap in political participation reverses: in seats where a woman MP was elected in 2001 women's turnout was 4 per cent higher than men' at that General Election; women represented by a woman MP are far more likely to agree that 'government benefits people like me' – 49 per cent compared to 38 per cent. Where a man represented the seat, this gap reversed; in seats with male MPs, women are less interested in the election campaign, and less likely to say they would volunteer to work for a candidate or party. Crucially, if there are institutional causes of the gender participation gap, then institutional changes may positively affect women's participation in those areas where they currently under-participate. For example, an increase in the number of women MPs returned to Parliament might reduce the gender gap in campaign orientated political participation.

Source: Norris *et al.* (2004).

Case Study 1.3

Intra-sex differences and vote choice: Mother's parenthood

Previous British research has revealed that understanding the interaction between sex and other background characteristics is key to explaining how gender impacts upon vote choice. Most notably, the lack of an aggregate level sex difference in vote choice in Britain has been shown to mask the fact that older women tend to be more likely to vote Conservative than older men, and that younger women tend to be more likely to vote Labour than younger men. In sum, crude operationalizations of gender, which use sex as a proxy, miss important intra-sex differences; capturing the influence of gender on vote choice requires us to consider how women differ from each other, as well as how they might differ from men. Moreover, most of the background characteristics, such as class, income and education, that are included in models of voting behaviour, have a gender dimension: for example, men and women are segregated in the workplace both horizontally and vertically. For these reasons, it is essential to explore how the interaction between different identities, stages in the life cycle, and life experiences might produce gendered attitudes and behaviours.

To date, little attention has been paid to the impact of parenthood on vote choice. There are several competing approaches to explaining gender differences in attitudes and behaviour that might be tested using a measure of parenthood. These can be roughly divided into 'ethics of care' and 'rational choice' approaches. Eleven ethics of care explanations are based upon a simplification of Carol Gilligan's (1982) work and suggest that the moral development of women leads them to an altruistic concern for others, whereas men's moral development is more abstract, individualistic and rules based. In line with this, women should be more likely than men to prioritize spending on welfare, irrespective of whether it benefits them directly or not. Alternatively, a rational choice explanation would contend that, because women still undertake the majority of childcare, they will focus their attention upon issues such as education and health when they are mothers. Testing whether the modern gender gap in vote choice is only evident among women who are mothers provides a crude comparison of these two approaches. The analysis is conducted upon a combined dataset, comprising of the 2001 and 2002 British Social Attitudes surveys (BSA). This dataset yields a large sample size, of over 6000, which facilitates the analysis of subgroups of the population, although it suffers from not being conducted at election times. Partisan identification is used as a proxy for vote choice.

Overall, there is more similarity than difference in men's and women's partisanship. In common with BES data, the BSA data shows that women's historic tendency to vote for the Conservative Party in greater numbers than men is not evident among respondents born since 1945. Furthermore, age has a more profound effect on the Labour/Conservative support of women than men. The most interesting finding in the study is that 'women with children under 11 in the household' were more likely to vote for the Labour Party than the Conservative Party. The same was not true of men. Of respondents with a child under 11 in the home, 68 per cent of women, compared to 58 per cent of men, were Labour party identifiers. This ten point gap is not a chasm, but is large enough to have an impact upon election results. In regression analysis, parenthood had a significant effect on the Labour vote, but this effect disappears when a dummy variable for motherhood is included. Thus, the pro-Labour leanings of parenthood are accounted for entirely by mothers. Further examination suggests that the parenthood gender gap is only statistically significant within middle and high-income earners; the gap appears to be stronger among higher status individuals. Thus, there is some weak evidence that rational choice or materialist accounts provide better explanations of the gender gap than 'ethics of care' approaches.

Source: Campbell 2006.

Notes

1 *Mirror*, 15 April 2005.
2 See also Barnes and Kaase 1978; Merriam 1924; Tingsten 1937; Verba *et al.* 1978.
3 The gender gap is calculated as follows: (the percentage of women voting Democrat minus the percentage of men voting Democrat) minus (the percentage of women voting Republican minus the percentage of men voting Republican).
4 Though, even here, the sexual division of labour plays an influencing role as daughters are thought to maintain a stronger sense of connection with their mother.
5 *New Statesman*, 21 February 2005; *Observer*, 27 February 2005.
6 MORI Final aggregate analysis pooled campaign surveys, 16 May 2005. Total n. 17,595. www.mori.com; *Observer*, 8 May 2005.
7 No study has been undertaken, as yet, on the 2005 data.
8 International studies include: Inglehart and Norris 2003; Tolleson Rinehart 1992.
9 Hayes conducted her analysis on the 1992 BES, using three variables to measure feminist orientations. The first asks whether women are given too few opportunities within political parties, the second whether women should have an equal role with men in running business industry or government, and the third whether equal opportunities for women in Britain have gone too far.
10 ESRC Grant number RES-000-22-1857.
11 In practice the division is often tenuous: for example men's interest in the economy and taxation is usually interpreted as self-interested, but could equally be conceived as altruistic, relating to a male-provider model of the family.

2 Feminizing British political parties

Introduction

In the run up to the 2005 general election, the *Guardian* columnist Polly Toynbee reflected on the Conservative party's policy proposal to give those eligible, but not already drawing, childcare tax credits, £50 a week for each child to spend how they saw fit.[1] In her opinion, this was a better deal than what Labour had to offer. But more than that, this was proof that the 'ideological tectonic plates' of British party politics had shifted – of how the political terrain over which British political parties compete had become more feminized: 'childcare and nursery education are here to stay, *whoever is in power*' (emphasis added). Such changes are likely to go unnoticed by mainstream party scholars. Their attention is usually focused on typologizing parties in terms of membership, organization and electoral strategy, as if gender did not matter (A. Russell 2005; Heffernan 2003).

Lisa Young (2000, 204) outlines a framework for evaluating political parties according to criteria of feminist transformation. In a *feminist* party there will be: first, sex parity amongst elected representatives, or, at least in the interim, sex parity among newly elected candidates (these outcomes will be secured either because women no longer face barriers to their participation or through the use of specific mechanisms to guarantee sex parity). Second, in a feminist party the position of Party leader is in reach of women and a woman leader's failures would not be attributed to her sex. Finally, feminist concerns and perspectives are integral to the development of party policy, figure prominently in the party's manifesto, and are enacted with the same commitment as other policy commitments.

The possibility of 'co-option', where parties are feminist in respect of the integration of women but unresponsive in terms of women's concerns, is included in Young's framework. However, greater analytic space should be given to the possibility of parties making positive, neutral and negative responses – or rather, feminist, neutral, and anti-feminist responses – along both dimensions of feminization. As Table 2.1 shows, this framework allows for an anti-feminist party which is, nonetheless, a feminized political party. Such a party integrates women as elected representatives and party members. It also integrates women's concerns into their policy agenda, but it does so in an anti-feminist fashion. In order to illuminate the extent and direction of the integration of women into

Table 2.1 Feminization and party types

		Responsive Party I (feminist both dimensions)	Party II	Anti-feminist Responsive (feminist on 1st dimension, feminist 2nd Dimension)	Co-optive Party (feminist on 1st dimension, neutral on 2nd)	Co-optive Party (feminist on 1st dimension, anti-feminist on 2nd)	Non-responsive	Anti-feminist Party
1st Dimension	**Integration of women parliamentary elites**	High/moderate representation; Well designed and fully implemented quotas; or absence of obstacles to women's representation	Low representation; absent or poorly designed/implemented quotas	High/moderate representation; may have quotas	High/moderate representation; may have quotas	High/moderate representation; may have quotas	Low representation; absent quotas	Low representation; rejects principle and practice of quotas
	Integration of women party members	Parity of members; Quasi Women's Policy Agencies (QWPA) fully integrated into party policy making	Fewer women members; integrated QWPA	Parity of members; auxillary women's organizations	Parity of members; auxillary women's organizations	Parity of members; either anti-feminist QWPA fully integrated into party policy making or organizations 'auxillaries'	Indifferent to representation of women; auxillary women's organizations rather than integrated QWPA	Indifferent to representation of women; either anti-feminist QWPA fully integrated into party policy making or auxillary women's organization
2nd Dimension	**Integration of women's concerns**	Positive and in feminist direction	Positive and feminist	Neutral or where positive, in a neutral direction	Positive but in anti feminist direction	Positive but in anti feminist direction	Negative	Positive in an anti-feminist direction

Source: Amended from L. Young 2000.
NOTE: These are ideal types. Empirical enquiry would need to establish whether they exist in particular political systems. Thanks to Adrian Flint for this insight.

political parties, it is necessary to document women's participation as ordinary party members, party elites and elected representatives, and to analyze parties' women's organizations; whether they are 'ladies auxillaries' engaged in 'political housekeeping' (L.Young 2000) or quasi-women's policy agencies (QWPA) seeking to act for women as a group (Lovenduski 2005a). To reveal the extent and direction of the second dimension of feminization – the integration of women's concerns – requires examining the extent to which gendered and feminist analysis is present in parties' policy making processes and policies.

The Labour Party: From 'manly' old Labour to a feminized and feminist New Labour?

The Labour party has undergone widely acknowledged ideological and organizational change over the last two decades (Heffernan 2001; Fielding 2002). Much of the debate that surrounds the organizational reforms – changes to the composition and role of party conference, the selection of the leader and parliamentary candidates, and the powers of local parties – focuses on claims that, collectively, they constitute a centralizing tendency, empowering the leadership and reducing intra-party democracy. Yet, Labour's new organizational structures also invite evaluation in respect of their gender effects. As Meg Russell (2005, 265–6) observes, the equal participation of women within the Labour party became established as central to the ethos of 'new' Labour within the space of two decades. Questions remain as to whether, and to what extent, the second dimension of feminization, the integration of women's concerns, operates within the party (Perrigo 1999); whether there are sufficient spaces for women party members to engage in 'real debate and dialogue' and effect a feminization of policy.

Windows of opportunity for women to feminize the Labour party opened up in the 1970s and 1980s. As Box 2.1 outlines, party change occurred over distinct time periods characterized by different relationships between women and the party leadership and the different dimensions of feminization. Changes in the wider political context included the rise of Thatcherism and Labour's successive electoral defeats. The decline of manufacturing industry and rise of service industries, together with women's increased participation in the paid workforce, transformed the economic and social characteristics of British society (M. Russell 2005). More specifically, in the 1980s Labour witnessed a shift away from demands for women's collective representation to individual representation (Perrigo 1995, 1996). In making this new – or 'pragmatic', as the party Leadership perceived it – claim, Labour women first sought internal party quotas. This enhanced their presence within party structures. Then they compromised in their demand for parliamentary sex quotas, down from all, to half of all, vacant-held and winnable parliamentary seats. To bolster their claim, the pro-Conservative gender gap, and the electoral challenge from the 'woman friendly' Liberal Democrats was emphasized. Post-1987 the desire for electoral victory on behalf of the Leadership was key. Neil Kinnock came to recognize that electoral

success was compatible with, if not partially dependent upon, a greater feminization of the party: Labour had a problem with its 'male dominated' image. After
Labour's defeat in 1992 the new Party Leader, John Smith, who was personally
committed to sex quotas, astutely played his hand at the 1993 Party Conference.
The issue of All Women Shortlists (AWS) for selecting parliamentary candidates
was conjoined with the issue of 'One Member One Vote' (OMOV) into a single
Conference resolution.[2] As Case Study 2.1 outlines, the inclusion of the AWS
clause was dependent upon the actions of Labour's women's organizations, not
least the NEC Women's Committee. Three factors are critical to understanding its
successful passage (M. Russell 2005, 56; Lovenduski 2005b): the abstention of
the MSF (Manufacturing Science and Finance) union, despite its opposition to
OMOV; an internal party quota that guaranteed women's presence at Labour's
Conference – as both constituency and trade union delegates; and Smith's threat
to resign.

Box 2.1   Feminizing the Labour Party 1980s–1995

Pre-1979: A Gendered Organization?	The party privileges the male actor (male trade unionist with a wife) and has a traditional, familial and paternalistic gender order with women and men occupying different spheres; the separate women's organization lacks access to the main decision-making bodies of the party; the party functions according to rule-bound, bureaucratic modes requiring a long apprenticeship which fosters fraternal feelings; leadership pays very little attention to individual members as the party is dominated by trade unions; there is no inter-party incentive for Labour to take gender issues seriously; feminists are largely indifferent to formal electoral politics.
1979–83 Gender Struggles and New Opportunities	The party experiences organizational instability and bitter inter-factional disputes; leadership loses control of party as TU no longer constitute moderating allies; the left of the party seeks greater accountability from the parliamentary party; a wider hostile political and economic climate, coupled with the feminist 'turn' towardsthe state and a left wing shift leads to a collaboration between feminist women outside and women inside theparty, although older women are suspicious; there is a revival of the Women's Sections – by 1981 there are 1200; the Labour Women's Action Committee (WAC) demands changes to increase the collective representation of women by enhancing the constitutional status of women's organizations; 1982 sees the publication of the NEC's 'Charter for Women's Equality in the Party' and Jo Richardson is appointed spokesperson on women's rights.

1983-7 Leadership Containment: regard women activists as hard left but under pressure to respond positively	The new Leader Neil Kinnock re-establishes leadership authority, shifts control of policy making back to PLP, marginalizes the left and seeks to transform the party's image – including its male-dominated image; the establishment of Social Democratic Party (SDP) with a sex quota at parliamentary candidate short-listing stage, creates inter- party competition over women's votes; the WAC mounts highly effective campaign around its demands for collective representation, forces debate at national conference and works through the NEC's Women's Committee to press claims on the party leadership; the 1986 Annual Conference accepts the principle, and in 1987, the constitutional requirement that at least one woman should be included on any shortlist of any constituency in which a woman is nominated; support increases for women's issues amongst women in the party including the new intake of women MPs and from the TU; the Party proposes a Women's Ministry but the National Labour Women's Committee are refused participation in the Policy Review.
1987–1995 From Rhetoric to Action: leadership modernization and the demands of women increasingly congruent	Modernization accelerates; links are made between modernization and the representation of women; women drop their demand for collective representation in favour of individual representation as MPs; the National Labour Women's Committee are excluded from the Policy Review on the grounds that it is dominated by 'left-wing' women; subsequent establishment of Monitoring Committee chaired by Jo Richardson; Plans for a Ministry for Women; there is a strategic alliance between Deborah Lincoln (Labour women's officer) Clare Short MP (member of NEC Women's Committee) and male allies including: Larry Whitty (General Secretary), Gordon Brown and John Prescott MP; the party's new National Policy Forums have to consider implications for policy on women; Women's Conference reforms enhance TU women vis a vis left wing constituency activists; 1988 Labour's Women's Network established; Emily's List established; 1989, Composite 54 accepts the principle of quotas and in 1990 the introduction of quotas for candidate selections; quotas for women are set across the party at 40%, including, in 1992, 40% of policy forums; in 1992 a number of feminist women are elected to House of Commons; in 1993, with the support of the then party leader John Smith, All Women Shortlists (AWS) are agreed at national conference. There would be AWS in 50% of all key seats and 50% all vacant Labour-held seats

Source: Perrigo 1999, 1996, 1995, 1986; Short 1996; Stokes 2005; Lovenduski 2005a,b; Kittlison 2006.

The emphasis on women's participation as parliamentary representatives carried with it the significant risk of weakening women's organization within the party and limiting the collective representation of their concerns – something acknowledged by some women activists at that time (M. Russell 2005): by 1997 there were fewer than 200 Women's Sections, down from 650 in 1992 and 970 in 1979. The Party Leadership was less worried by such an outcome. Although interpretations are contested (M. Russell 2005, 96), women's parliamentary representation was considered less disruptive of existing intra-party and gendered power relations.

The focus on ensuring women's individual representation continued under Tony Blair's Leadership. Following the legal ruling against AWS in 1996, party and extra-party gender equality activists campaigned for new legislation. The Sex Discrimination (Selection Candidates) Act, was passed in 2002 (as discussed in Case Study 5.5). By the time of the 2001 general election, Blair had been persuaded of the necessity of returning to AWS. His intervention in Cabinet was 'itself required to guarantee' the inclusion of the Bill in the first Queen's speech of the 2001 Parliament (Lovenduski 2001, 192).

Box 2.2   Time line of Labour Party gender reforms

Year   Major gender reforms

1986   New structure of voting at Women's Conference: TU 50%, constituencies 45% and other affiliates 5%; this has a two-fold effect on gender relations within the party (1) it moderated the women's conference and brought together TU and feminist women and (2) it enhanced the legitimacy of the conference

1989   Quota of three votes in Shadow Cabinet elections which must be cast for women

1990   Annual conference agrees women's quota across the party: 40% nationally, 50% in local parties – two out of four elected officers in each branch, three out of seven constituency officers, 50% delegations to general committees. Local parties sending one delegate to Annual Conference are required to send one woman at least every other year, whilst those sending more than one to apply 50% quotas – importantly, where such quotas could not be met the position would be left vacant; 50% of women in the PLP over ten years or three general elections; phased programme for increasing women on NEC to reach four of twelve TU members and three of seven constituency members by 1995; TU delegations to annual conference should be representative in terms of sex make-up of their union.

1993   Establishment of National Policy Forums – 40% women's quota; Conference agrees AWS: 50% women in vacant held and winnable seats; this is a compromise from earlier demand for AWS in *all* vacant held seats

1994   Women's Conference: resolution-based conference replaced with 'political education' model involving policy seminars and skills workshops; this experimental format subsequently will alternate with traditional conference;

the last resolution based conference is held in 1995

1995 Tony Blair announces that AWS will be employed for only one general election

1996 Industrial Tribunal (Jepson and Dyas-Elliot v Labour Party) rules against party and finds AWS in breach of Section 13 of Part II of Sex Discrimination Act

1997 Introduction of Partnership in Power (PIP). NPF operates with women's quota roughly 40%; abolition of women's reserved seats on NEC.

1998 NEC's Women's Committee and National Women's Officer-led consultation on future of women's organizations; Annual Conference abolishes women's councils, women's sections at branch level; creates constituency-wide Women's Forums; restructuring of regional women's committees and conferences; NEC Women's Committee reduced in size and drawn from women on NEC

2002 Sex Discrimination (Selection Candidates) Act

2003 NEC Women's Committee becomes Women, Race and Equalities Committee

Women's organizations in the Labour Party

Quasi Women's Policy Agencies (QWPA) in the Labour Party refer to a wide range of institutions, organizations, campaigns and networks (Lovenduski 2005a, 108). At the national level there is the Women Race and Equalities Committee (WREC), the National Women's Forum (NWF) and the Women's Conference; at the local level there are Constituency Women's Forums (CWF) and local women's policy forums organized by CWFs; at the parliamentary level is the Parliamentary Labour Party's (PLP) Women's Committee, and at the governmental level the Women's Minister and associated gender machinery; and at the unofficial but associated level, there are Labour Women, Labour Women's Network (LWN) and Emily's List. The Party also employs a National Woman's Officer. She services the WREC, liaises between them and the PLP Women's Committee and is involved in campaigning and outreach work.

Emily's list and LWN

Both Emily's List and LWN are concerned primarily with the political recruitment of women. Neither has formal party status nor receives party funding. Emily's List, which was an important organization in the 1990s, contributing funds to pro-choice women candidates, has, in the words of its founder, probably 'had its day'. LWN, meanwhile, has an extensive network of women within the party and continues to deliver substantial amounts of party training for aspirant parliamentary candidates.

Local constituency women's forums

Despite the abolition of Women's Sections in 1998, the tradition of women's separate organizations within the Labour Party continues with Women's Forums (WF) (Stokes 2005, 102): when a woman joins the Labour Party she is designated a member of the local constituency WF. Each WF has a dedicated Woman's Officer, who is responsible for drawing up an annual plan, a programme of activities and coordinating the forum. According to the 'Rules for Women's Forums', WF activities are focused around three strands: (1) supporting women members to 'play an active part in all the party's activities'; (2) building links with women in the community; and (3) ensuring that women's voices are properly heard in the party'. In respect of the latter, this means 'feeding' their views to local and national policy forums, and to their local constituency General Council, as well as 'encouraging women to play an active role in these and other bodies', and holding local policy forums for women. Information about the number, membership and activities of WF is not, however, centrally held by the Party.

On paper, WF encourage women to participate in the party – through networking, mentoring, and supporting women to stand for elected office. Moreover, the formal 'Rules' emphasize the importance of women's participation in the integrated parts of the Labour Party, and for standing for elected office, both inside and outside of the party. WF can also nominate candidates for parliamentary and European candidates. Lovenduski (2005a, 89) notes, however, that the shift from Women's Sections at branch level to WF at constituency level has reduced the potential for nominations simply as the byproduct of the reduction in numbers of WF relative to Women's Sections.

In respect of the second dimension of feminization, WF constitutes a collective site for women's substantive representation in the local constituency. Formally recognized, and with the agreement of the constituency Labour party, WF are a party-funded, woman-only space. They act as a body in respect of the GC of the local constituency party. Equivalent to branches in the LP, WF can elect two delegates to the GC and to the local government committee, and, as stated above, nominate candidates for parliamentary and European candidates, members of the party's NEC and National Policy Forum (NPF). At formal meetings of the WF (where, amongst other qualifications, there must be at least ten eligible women members present) the forum may agree motions to be sent to their local GC. WF can also make submissions directly to policy commissions. The autonomy of WF is not absolute: their annual plans are, like branch activities, subject to the agreement of their local constituency GC/EC.

Women's conferences and national women's forums

Distinguishing between the annual Women's Conference and the twice yearly National Women's Forum (NWF) is, in respect of their remit, largely redundant. One remaining difference relates to size. All women members are entitled to attend both, and current figures suggest that the annual Women's Conference attracts some 1,200 women, whereas the NWF is likely to attract no more than 150 women. There is overlap in attendees. Both the NWF and the Conference are sites for the discussion of policy and campaigning, the provision of selection training and networking – the last resolution-based Labour Women's Conference was in 1995. The agenda of the Conference and NWF is decided by the NEC, WREC and the Women's Officer.

Policy discussions at both the Conference and NWF influence policy through the presence of a designated policy officer or member of the NPF attending the NWF and annual Women's Conference. They take notes on discussions and later 'feed' these into policy commissions and related documents, in the same way that local and regional submissions are made to the NPF. The influence that women party members have on policy is, consequently, informal rather than formal, as the term 'feed in' suggests; it is a potential power rather than one guaranteed by particular mechanisms. It is for this reason that Meg Russell (2005, 203) considers Labour's Women's Conference one which follows a 'top-down education' model, rather than a 'bottom' up institution, for 'democratic control'. Many participants, however, report their satisfaction with the new form the conference takes, even if participation remains on an individual rather than collective or corporate basis.

Women, Race and Equality Committee

The WREC is a sub committee of the National Executive Committee (NEC). It is accountable to them and is serviced by the National Woman's Officer. The Committee is comprised of 14 members of the NEC and non-voting co-opted members, to 'represent' the views of disabled, BME, lesbian and gay members, TU equality officers or any other group as decided by members. It meets no less than four times a year. The WREC's remit includes both women's participation in the party and influencing party and government policy, as Box 2.3 details. At its meetings it receives reports from the Ministers for Women and other Equalities ministers and from the National Women's Officer.

Box 2.3   WREC roles and responsibilities

1. Women's recruitment, retention and participation in the Party in elected office and the development of women's forums at local level;
2. Black, Asian and ethnic minority recruitment, retention and participation in the Party;
3. Lesbian, gay and bisexual representation and participation within the Party;
4. Disability access and increased representation and participation of members with disabilities;
5. Considering effective Party responses to Employment Framework Directive based on Article 13 (Treaty on European Union) and the European Union Action Programme to Combat Discrimination;
6. Responsibility for driving the Party's equality agenda and the development of an inclusive organization at all levels;
7. Link with Organization Committee and Young Labour Co-ordinating Committee on issues of age discrimination;
8. Biannual women's forum;
9. Biannual ethnic minorities' forum.

The women's minister, the women's unit, the women and equality unit

The feminist credentials of most of Labour's Women's Ministers since 1997 are unquestionable: to Lovenduski's (2005a, 163) list of Harman, Hewitt, Morgan and Ruddock, can be added Jacqui Smith and Meg Munn. Only two – Jay and Roche – sought to publicly distance themselves from feminism (*Vogue*, March 1999; March) (Londer Conde Nest Squires and Wickham-Jones 2002) while Ruth Kelly's position was less straightforward as she seeks to combine her Catholicism with feminism (Dod's 2005, 351). Even so, it would not be unfair to say that Labour's Women Ministers have had something of a chequered history (Bashevkin 2000). Harriet Harman, the first Women's Minister, was only belatedly appointed, having already been made Secretary of State for Social Security. Then Joan Ruddock MP was appointed her Junior Women's Minister, but without remuneration – a situation which was repeated in 2005 with Meg Munn. The Harman-Ruddock tenure was short-lived; both were sacked in Blair's first reshuffle. Their replacements' priorities were elsewhere: Jay was Leader of the House of Lords, and at the time was more concerned with the time-consuming issue of Lords reform (regarded as proof that New Labour wanted to minimize its commitment to the posts (Bashevkin 2000, 418)); Jowell was concurrently Minister for Education and Employment and admitted to spending only 20 per cent of her time on the women's brief (Squires and Wickham-Jones 2002, 67). Even when she did act, Jowell was roundly ridiculed in the media for hosting a summit on young women's 'body image'.[3]

Despite having Cabinet status, Labour's Women's Minister is a watered down commitment from the Party's plans for a Women's Ministry in the mid-1980s. Early assessments of the Women's Unit – the institutional support for the Women's Minister – emphasized its marginal location, lack of resources and agenda setting role (Squires and Wickham-Jones 2002, 2). The reconfigured Women and Equality Units of Labour's second term – with its new priorities of the gender pay gap, work/life balance, women in public life, domestic violence and public services – brought it more into line with government priorities, thereby increasing its impact (Squires and Wickham-Jones 2004). Yet, it remains reliant upon making an economic efficiency argument (NAO cited in Squires and Wickham-Jones 2004, 93) and good personal relations (Veitch 2005, 603), especially with other women MPs, women ministers and ministers with a 'keen interest' in gender equality.

Feminizing policy

Policy in the Labour Party is 'made through a process called Partnership in Power which is designed to involve all party stakeholders, members, local parties, trade unions, socialist societies and Labour representatives, as well as the wider community in shaping party policy' (Labour Party 2005; M. Russell 2005). In essence, Labour in 1997 established a two-year rolling programme of policy formation. In the first year, membership submissions and input from external organizations and individuals are considered by policy commissions. In the second year, these are fed into the NPF, which meets two or three weekends per year and which is comprised of 183 representatives, 40 per cent of whom are women. The next stage is consideration by the Joint Policy Committee (which is chaired by the Prime Minister, alongside other members of government, NEC and NPF), before moving on to the NEC and, finally, the Annual Conference, which remains the sovereign policy-making body of the Party. Three types of documents are submitted to the Conference: consultative, final policy documents and annual reports of the policy commissions: 'alternative positions' in NPF policy documents are put to a vote at Conference.

Currently, the policy development cycle starts with policy commissions bringing forward annual work programmes. These consider issues arising from the implementation of the party's manifesto as well as identifying specific topical issues for wider consultation (Labour Party 2005, 6). There were, as of summer 2006, six policy commissions: (1) Britain in the World; (2) Creating Sustainable Communities; (3) Crime, Justice, Citizenship and Equalities; (4) Education and Skills; (5) Health; (6) Prosperity and Work. The policy commissions have between 16 and 20 representatives from government, the NPF and the NEC. They are responsible for accepting submissions from branches, CLPs, policy forums and affiliates and preparing policy papers.

Medium term policy development has three stages: (1) 2006: a 'Big Conversation' style single document considers the big challenges that face the party as it develops policy[4]; (2) 2007: Documents outlining policy choices. This will take the form of either specific policy areas or cross-cutting themes; and (3) 2008: Policy documents to be considered at a 'Warwick type' NPF. 'Final' draft documents will be circulated widely and, working through their NPF representatives, party units will be entitled to submit amendments and have them considered at the NPF (Amended from Labour Party 2005, 6).

Mainstream critics of Partnership in Power contend that it has reduced intra-party democracy (Seyd 1999) and empowered frontbench parliamentary elites (Webb 2000), although defenders counter that it has created new sites of dialogue between leaders and members (M. Russell 2005). Some groups, such as Labour students and Black socialist societies, have guaranteed group representation on the NPF – one and four representatives out of 183, respectively. There is no provision for representatives of women *as women*. Neither is there a designated women's policy commission, although equality is part of the third commission. At the same time, the party's sex quotas means that 40 per cent of the NPF are women, leading to suggestions (M. Russell 2005, 138) that it is a more women-friendly arena, with a more consensual and deliberative style. Moreover, WF are able to directly submit amendments to the NPF on the basis that party units are entitled at stage three of the policy development cycle to submit amendments.

The Conservative Party: Tory ladies, making tea or making policy?

Over the last few years, but reflecting considerably longer and less public efforts, there has been a mobilization of gender equality activists within the Conservative Party demanding feminization, in both its dimensions. Women in the party who had, in the past, held differing views about the role of women in politics and different conceptions of gender equality, acquired a new sense of confidence and purpose by 2005. They denounced the failure to integrate women's concerns and perspectives into Conservative Party policy at the 2005 General Election and challenged the meritocratic basis of Conservative Party selection procedures. The most public manifestation of this was the establishment of women2win. As Case Study 2.2 outlines, women2win, is a Conservative ginger group committed to women's parliamentary representation. Its founders recognized the opportunity for feminization which was opened up by the Party Leadership election in 2005. The new Conservative Leader, David Cameron, similarly recognized the opportunities that feminization offered him: feminization, or at least, the *rhetoric* of feminization, symbolizes that his is a new and not a 'nasty' Conservative party.

Women's organizations in the contemporary Conservative Party

Conservative Women's Organization (CWO)

The CWO was first established in 1928. It exists to assist Conservative Party electoral success by:

> Providing a focus for women of all ages, all backgrounds and from all parts of the country within the Conservative Party; encouraging and enabling women to participate and stand for office at all levels of the Conservative Party, Government and public appointments [through training]; ensuring that Party policy takes women's views into account; helping the Conservative Party regain the women's vote; making the Conservative Women's Organization relevant and valued in today's political climate.[5]

The reputation of the CWO often comes before it: it is widely regarded in the popular imagination, and reportedly amongst some parliamentary colleagues, as an effective mobilizer of women in the constituencies – the famed backbone of the party prepared to undertake the 'nuts and bolts of fundraising' and 'envelope stuffing'. At the same time, the CWO often feels not terribly well regarded. The party's ambivalence towards the organization came to a head in the late 1990s and early 2000s as its very existence was questioned and the relationship between it and the wider party deteriorated. The Hague reforms (Party leader between 1997–2001) downgraded its role and provided an opportunity to exclude CWO representatives, and in some cases put pressure on Conservative Women Constituency Committees to close down – the CWO 'may', but did not have to, be included on all of the mainstream voluntary committees at regional and constituency levels. Some women MPs also stood accused of having distanced themselves from the organization. The establishment of women2win might further be regarded as an implicit, if not explicit, criticism of the CWO's ability to deliver women's greater parliamentary representation.

Despite these criticisms, the case for a separate women's organization for women in the Conservative Party is no longer disputed by activist women, or publicly by the Party more widely. Indeed, the current CWO leadership envisages a renewed organization, and one more centrally concerned with policy. All the

Regional Chairmen have been instructed to include the CWO on their committees and, within their Regions, to ask the Area and constituency committees to do likewise. A Convention Strategy Committee has been formed which includes the Regional Chairmen, the Convention Officers, and the Chairmen of the CWO and Conservative Future. The CWO leadership is also taking steps to ensure that the CWO functions more effectively alongside the party's mainstream bodies, although it is expected to take time to ensure that Constituency Chairmen include CWO representatives and their views. An annual newsletter is produced to improve links with the parliamentary party and the CWO has created CWO 'champions'. In 2006 these included: the Rt Hon William Hague MP, Don Porter (Chairman of the Conservative Convention and Deputy Chairman of the Conservative Party) and Cllr Shireen Ritchie (Chairman of the Candidates Committee). Evidence of greater goodwill amongst women across the party is forthcoming; the significant cross-membership between CWO and women2win suggests support for, rather than hostility towards, the new organization.

Membership of the CWO is automatic for women, and men are welcome at CWO events. Organizationally, Conservative Women Constituency Committees (CWCC) operate at the constituency level, although there are no central figures on the total number of CWCCs across the country. CWCCs are connected upwards into Areas and then the 12 party Regions. The CWO is supported by a website, email and an online forum. The Executive Committee of the CWO is made up of its Regional Chairman, Officers of the CWO and Co-opted members. It meets three times per year and holds an AGM. There are also usually three annual Officers and Co-option meetings. EC meetings mostly discuss organizational matters although issues of women's selection to parliament and policy are also addressed. The CWO seeks information from its membership through feedback from the Regions and more directly through member questionnaires. Sometimes Parliamentary spokespeople ask the CWO to garner their members' views on a particular topic.

The CWO Annual Conference is currently experiencing an upsurge of interest following a period of decline: 2005 saw 250 attend, whilst 2006 was a sell-out, with 300 individuals in attendance, and more turned away – a larger hall was booked for 2007. Similar to Labour's Women's Conference, the CWO Conference, conforms to a 'top-down education' model. Whilst there is some opportunity for 'Q&A' sessions, the overarching structure is one of information-giving rather than information-gathering. The programme is devised by the CWO Chairman and Officers. In 2006 this reflected women's 'particular' interest in food; a session on farming followed up on a CWO mini-conference on 'Women Go Green'; and the panel on international women's human rights reflected a CWO leadership visit to the US. In the absence of formal resolutions or mechanisms of accountability from the CWO Conference to the party proper, the CWO's influence is limited to a looser notion of diffusion. Reports from the Conference are placed on the CWO website and parliamentary spokespeople associated with conference themes attend.

The CWO has recently established the 'Conservative Women's Forum' (CWF). This is, in part, recognition of the ageing membership of the CWO and the changing work/life patterns of younger women – women in their late 20s and 30s are perceived to be less likely to be involved full time in the Party because of childcare responsibilities. It is also an acknowledgement of the need to engage with women and women's organizations beyond the Party – taking forward David Cameron's agenda of reaching out to new women. CWF usually open with a short presentation by a Shadow Minister and a spokesperson from a relevant pressure group or interested party, before questions are taken from the floor. By Spring 2007, eight had been held in London, with the intention to roll them out. Attendees number 30–40, mostly white women in their late 30s and 40s; the meetings last approximately two hours. Topics so far include childcare, 'attachment theory', charities and stalking. The CWO have also set up a series of Summits to engage with outside organizations and established a Conservative Women's Muslim Group to engender dialogue and understanding between Muslim and non-Muslim women.

Formally, the CWO links with the mainstream party through the National Convention, which is composed of Constituency Chairman, Regional Chairman, Chairman of Conservative Future and Chairman of the CWO, and other representatives (see Appendix C). Currently the CWO has 42 places out of over 800. These are filled by both CWO Officers and Co-optees. Critics contend that the Convention is too large to constitute a robust discussion body. Transmission of CWO opinion to other parts of the Party – 'ensuring that Party policy takes women's views into account' – occurs through informal means. This leaves the CWO dependent upon good personal relations with others inhabiting key party posts. In the recent past, the CWO had regular links with the Party Chairman via the Vice-Chairman for Women: under Joan Seccombe there was a routinized reporting system between the CWO and the Vice-Chairman for Women. Today, the CWO Chairman adopts greater individual responsibility. Direct contact with Ministers is one way of her doing this. Once again, this relies upon the efforts of an under-resourced CWO Chairman and good personal relations with Ministers. The most extensive – in the sense of day to day – links the CWO has is with the Shadow Minister for Women (in Spring 2007, Eleanor Laing MP), Theresa May MP (then Shadow Leader of the House) who has responsibility for candidates, and with Vice-Chairman for Women (Margot James). Links with women2win are formalized as Fiona Hodgson, Chairman of the CWO, is a member of the Advisory Board. In terms of the Party's responsiveness to the CWO, this continues to mostly rely upon good personal relations. Only very recently have 'abrasive relationships' begun to be emolliated and tensions remain regarding the role of the CWO in a modernized Conservative Party. Nevertheless, the CWO regards itself as a supportive organization – '100 per cent' behind the Party Leader. Nor is now the time for demanding specific policies; it is the CWO's belief that a troublesome organization will not be listened to.

VC for women

The position of Vice-Chairman for Women, accountable to the Party Chairman, was revived in December 2005 following its abandonment at the time of the Hague reforms. Supported by the Women's Officer, the VC for Women is a voluntary job that takes up two and a half days a week. The post-holder has two responsibilities: to support the process of getting more women selected for parliament and to ensure that Conservative policies have 'women's interests and concerns uppermost'. Historically, it seems that the VC for Women was more involved in the political recruitment side than she is today – the post is currently two-thirds policy, one-third recruitment. Not only are there other party bodies engaged in recruitment, the current incumbent, Margot James, is herself a prospective parliamentary candidate, which – at least in the eyes of some of her colleagues in the party – makes it harder for her to be central to this task. When Parliament is sitting all Vice- and Deputy Chairman meet weekly for an hour with the Party Chairman and the VC for Women has an individual monthly meeting with, and files a monthly report to, him.

In the past, the VC for Women saw herself as a 'standard bearer' for women in the party and worked very closely with the CWO. Currently, the VC for Women is also responsible for building up relations with women's organizations and women *beyond* party members. Acknowledging that the Conservative Party needs to win back women's votes, their brief is therefore wider than 'acting for' members of the CWO. Although the CWO are themselves more engaged in reaching out to women outside of the party, meetings between the VC for Women and the Chairman of the CWO have the potential, at least, to bring together viewpoints that are distinct: one set drawing predominantly from the views of women outside of the party and the other from viewpoints predominantly from within the party.

As VC for Women, Margot James has formed two groups: (1) the Women's Overview Group and (2) the Women's Policy Review Group. The former consists of all those in the party who focus on women. It is chaired by Theresa May MP.[6] The group meets 'reasonably regularly' to update each other 'with what is going on' in the party to do with women. The Women's Policy Group (WPG) is chaired by Eleanor Laing.[7]

Shadow Minister for Women

The post of Shadow Minister for Women sits rather uncomfortably in the Conservative Party: fewer Conservative women MPs have considered themselves feminists or been gender-conscious and concerns about being sidelined, pigeon-holing and the concept of merit remain. However, with the post now carrying additional responsibility for equality this has lessened, although there is still a perception that it is not considered to be very important by older men in the parliamentary party.

Feminizing policy

To modernize Conservative Party policy Cameron set up six policy reviews. These would consider a series of 'challenges': (1) the competitive challenge; (2) quality of life; (3) public services; (4) security; (5) social justice; and (6) globalization and the global challenge. The Review Groups would report in 2007, at which point the leadership would decide which recommendations to accept as party policy for the next General Election. There was no corporate representation for women on the Review Groups. Rather, the self-appointed responsibility for gendering the reviews rested with Eleanor Laing MP, as Shadow Minister for Women, and the WPG. But with no formal requirements for the Policy Review Groups to contact, listen, or respond to, the Shadow Minister, WPG or the VC for Women, the Review Chairmen could decide to ignore their submissions. In such a context it seems inappropriate to talk of accountability between the Policy Review and women in the party. Issues of resources are also relevant. The Shadow Minister for Women and the WPG receive little administrative or research support, and yet they were seeking to influence six Review Groups.

The Shadow Minister for Women met with all the chairs of the Policy Review Groups in 2006 to ask them to consider women's perspectives from *the very beginning* of the review process; it was made clear that this was not about how many women members a particular review group had, but was about taking into account women's different perspectives. A second round of meetings, between Eleanor Laing and Margot James and the Chairmen took place in Spring 2007. What impact these meetings had on the final policies remains to be seen. However, Laing's reception in the initial meetings was said to have been favourable.

The WPG's strategy to feminize policy was to make submissions to the Policy Review Groups and to produce an agenda-setting policy document in 2007 that would be directly reported to the Party Leader and Party Chairman. The agenda-setting document would also be presented to each of the Policy Review Groups, and would incorporate any 'sensible' responses from them. Its focus was on topics 'of concern' to women: security, domestic violence, welfare and family policy, equal opportunities, education and employment, health, and women prisoners. The document would be informed by existing research, 'robust' statistics, interest group briefings and focus group discussion with women councillors, organizations, party members, and women outside the party, from across the country.

It is too early to draw conclusions about the extent of the feminization of Conservative Party policy under David Cameron. The centering of women's concerns and perspectives – and importantly the direction of those policies – will become clear only when policy is fully formulated and the party's manifesto for the next General Election written. The Party Leader might hold the Policy Review Groups to account if they deliver reports that are gender-blind – Cameron is widely considered by leading gender equality activists in the party to be 'onside' and personally committed to 'gender equality'. In contrast, Cameron's role in the feminization efforts to-date can be considered. Crucially, these transformations should not be understood as simply top-down. To be sure, Cameron opened the door, when other potential leaders might not have, as Case Study 2.3 suggests. But, as discussed above, gender equality activists played a strategic role in gendering the very Leadership election of which he was the beneficiary. They had also been pushing at the door for at least a decade, even if in the past they were less public and less single-minded. The watershed was the 2005 General Election – the Conservative Party's third successive defeat. The CWO fringe meeting at the Party Conference that year heard calls for positive discrimination to increase the number of Conservative women selected for Parliament and the then chairman of the CWO, Pamela Parker, produced a highly critical report of the Party's general election manifesto. This, she strongly believed, had lost the Party the women's vote. The Report's conclusions were carried in the mainstream media, namely, that the party had failed to communicate with women voters and had ignored the CWO submissions in the drawing up of the party's manifesto. In addition, parliamentarians like Theresa May, who had spoken out previously, became more publicly vocal. Finally, the establishment of women2win created a new group around which women from across the party could coalesce in order to push for party change.

The Liberal Democrat Party: Are women individuals or women?

The Liberal Democrat Party's response to feminization of British party politics is paradoxical: at the 2005 General Election the party arguably offered the most feminist manifesto of the three main parties, as Case Study 2.4 demonstrates. At the same time, there is a reluctance to acknowledge that low numbers of women Liberal Democrat MPs might warrant measures that will guarantee a greater presence in the House of Commons.

Women's organizations in the contemporary Liberal Democrat Party

Women Liberal Democrats (WLD) is a Specified Associated Organization (SAO) of the Federal Party. SAOs must have at least 250 members (who must also be members of the party); present a constitution and annual accounts; and be compliant with the Political Parties Elections and Referendums Act (PPERA) (Evans 2007). SAOs may use the Liberal Democrat logo and are resourced officially through the party, although they also engage in their own fundraising (Russell and Fieldhouse 2005). In terms of policy-making, they are entitled to submit policy motions to the party's bi-annual conferences.

WLD operates at the Federal, state, regional and local level, although, apart from the Scottish WLD there are only a 'few local branches'. Unlike the Conservative Women's Organization, membership of WLD is not automatic, although many women members of the party mistakenly assume this is the case. Membership currently costs a minimum of £7 per annum and is open to all men and women. Membership currently stands at approximately 530, a tiny fraction of the party's total membership of circa 75,000. These members come from across the UK, although there is a trend for younger women to be predominantly London-based. WLD are supported by a website and members receive a quarterly magazine. Resource-wise the WLD are limited in absolute terms and relative to the Liberal Democrats' Youth and Students SAO (LYDS): since 2001, WLD have received £16k to help with the cost of employing a part-time administrator for 16 hours per week, but its other workers are volunteers or interns.

Sharing the same 'aims and objects of the Party', the WLD Preamble declares, inter alia: 'We are pledged to eliminate all inequality based upon gender ... we endorse the feminist principles of encouraging, supporting, preparing and promoting

---

Box 2.4   WLD aims and objects, WLD Constitution Sept 2004

2.1   [WLD] ... shall campaign for full participation of women at all levels and in all activities of the Party.

2.2   ... shall seek to achieve the objects set forth in the Preamble to this Constitution. In order to achieve such objects WLD shall:

2.2.1   Campaign, publish and in every way publicize its objectives and activities;

2.2.2   Formulate, advocate and advise on matters of policy;

2.2.3   Actively participate in education, organization and promotion of its members and of women in general;

2.2.4   Seek to secure the election of Members of Parliament, UK members of the European Parliament, MSPs and AMs, members of local government and other elected public authorities; nominate candidates to appointed bodies; and especially seek the election and appointment of women;

2.2.5   Undertake all such activities and do all such things as the Executive deems necessary in pursuit of these Aims and Objects.

---

women to realize their full potential in shaping society'. WLDs 'work to widen the opportunities open to women in professional and public life', while recognizing and appreciating the traditionally female roles of 'mother, carer and homemaker'.

The work of the WLD is three-fold – in order of importance: (1) acting as a networking hub for women in the party; (2) constituting a site for gendered policy discussions; and (3) supporting, albeit predominantly in an informal way, aspirant women candidates. The organization is headed up by an Executive consisting of WLD officers – twelve elected members, up to four Vice-Presidents, up to three co-opted members and one member elected by the Scottish WLD members. Officially, its work includes: conducting the business of WLD subject to the approval of the Annual General Meeting; governing the organization and finances of, and fundraising for, WLD; determining WLD priorities and approving its expenditure; electing or appointing ad hoc Sub-committees; appointing any paid staff; acting as an equal opportunities employer; establishing ad hoc working groups for specific purposes; formulating, advocating and advising on matters of policy and contributing to the policymaking process of the Party; organizing and promoting campaigns within and outside the Party; and organizing and promoting such meetings, conferences and activities (including participation in conferences of the Party) as the Executive shall think fit. The Executive meets at least six times a year. Non-Executive members may attend Executive meetings, although in a non-voting capacity. In practice, the EC spends its time evenly split between policy discussions and organizational matters in Executive meetings. The Executive is directly accountable to its membership at its AGM – reports are presented on the organization's finances, the activities of officers. The AGM is where WLD campaigns are discussed.

The policy side of the WLD is mostly undertaken by its EC. This is driven largely by expediency, with the Executive believing that they are better able to meet the deadlines for submission to the party's conferences. Importantly, conference motions submitted to the Federal Party's biannual conferences are the central medium through which the WLD seeks to influence policy making. WLD aim to submit one motion per Conference.

Beyond conferences, WLD benefit, alongside the LDYS and relative to other SAOs, by their presence, albeit part-time, in Cowley Street, the Liberal Democrats HQ. This enables them to 'raise the profile of the organization', which in turn, 'increases their chances of being able to influence the political agenda' (Evans 2007, 6). They also strive to get members on policy working groups and meet on an informal basis with the party's MPs and Peers, and the Women and Equality Spokesperson MP: WLD let the latter 'know' what they are 'working on', not least in respect of Conference motions, via phone, email and having lunch with them, 'as and when'. The Executive itself acknowledges that it has not as yet 'gender mainstreamed' all policy areas. Just as in the Conservative party, there is a sense that WLD are not wholly embraced by the wider party: WLD face a 'slight rolling of the eyes', and questions about the continued necessity of a women's group within the party.

The Campaign for Gender Balance

The Campaign for Gender Balance (CGB) was formerly known as the Gender Balance Task Force (GBTF). It was set up by the Federal Executive Committee to achieve the targets for women's parliamentary representation agreed in September 2001. The targets include: 40 per cent of held-parliamentary seats and those requiring a swing to win of less than 7.5 per cent to be contested by women and an additional 500 women on the approved list (the latter target was reduced to 150 in 2005, see Box 2.5 below). The full group meets once every three months and it reports to every meeting of the FE as well as to every Federal Conference. Since 2001, £95K has been given to the organization by the Federal party.

Box 2.5 2005 Conference Motion: Conference calls for:

I   The Party to work towards a long term goal of gender balance at all levels of representative government in the UK.

II   The Party to set a target of at least 40 per cent of its new MPs and at least 25 per cent of its total MPs to be women after the next General Election.

III   The Party to set a target of at least 150 additional approved women candidates by the next General Election.

IV   The Federal Executive to ensure that the Campaign for Gender Balance is adequately funded in order to carry out its function in finding, training and developing female candidates.

V   The Campaign for Gender Balance to continue to report back to every Federal Conference and every meeting of the Federal Executive on progress until this goal has been reached.

According to its website the CGB has:

> ... set up, and are always seeking to expand, a network of volunteers to help and support women through all stages of the approval and selection process. From filling in the form to becoming an Approved Candidate, to planning where and when to go for selection, to designing your campaign literature once you have been short-listed, we will put you in touch with someone who will lend you their experience and support.
>
> We also co-ordinate training events, including at Federal and regional conferences, for the many women who feel more confident in a women-only environment. We also work closely with party officials, MPs and the press to ensure that the need to enable and encourage women candidates continues to be taken seriously across the whole party.

The existence of two different women's organizations (WLD and CGB) within the Liberal Democrats, with overlapping aims of encouraging women's selection as parliamentary candidates, creates the possibility of tensions between them. Indeed, rumours of such tension are longstanding, even if rarely publicly acknowledged by key actors in these organizations (Harrison 2006a, 10). The establishment of the GBTF was perceived by some members of WLD as a slight – they considered WLD as *the* women's organization. It is not the case, however, that the WLD or CGB map onto the division in the party over positive discrimination. The distinction reflects their different status and remits: WLD is a membership body, accountable to its members, with SAO status, and focused on representation, policy and networking; the CGB constitute a leadership strategy, funded with the specific aim of encouraging women to stand for elected office and to support them through the provision of training, mentoring and networking. In any case, more recently, WLD and CGB are claimed to have worked together on various projects, with WLD supporting the CGB bid for more funding from the party.

Since 2006 the Party has had a third body whose aim is to increase the numbers of women in Parliament. The Diversity and Equality Group seeks the better representation of women, people with disabilities, Black and minority ethnic populations and lesbian and gay people in public life. Established by the Federal Executive, the group has acquired funds from the Joseph Rowntree Foundation to support women and ethnic minority candidates. Although WLD and CGB can make recommendations on how the candidates fund is spent, neither have a formal monitoring role, suggesting that, despite the CGB constituting a leadership-led organization, it, along with the WLD, plays only an informal role in the Diversity and Equality Group. Accountability to the WLD and CGB relies, therefore, upon good interpersonal relationships and day-to-day workings with individuals in the Leader's Office who monitor the Diversity and Equality Group.

Parliamentary spokespersons

The Liberal Democrats have two parliamentary spokespersons on women and equality: in the Spring of 2007, Lorely Burt MP in the Commons and Lord Lester of Herne Hill in the Lords. The Women and Equality position shadows the Women and Equality Minister (in Spring 2007 in the Department for Communities and Local Government (DCLG)) and reports directly to the Liberal Democrat DCLG shadow spokesperson. Their remit is wide-ranging and cross-cuts through all departments; in short, it is as 'wide' as the post-holder's imagination. Relatively autonomous, the spokesperson acts independently on uncontroversial issues or those in line with party policy. Relations with other parts of the party are less regular: the Liberal Democrat frontbench do not frequently consult the Women and Equality spokesperson, whose influence is dependent upon proactively poking their nose into issues which they consider to be part of their brief. Moreover, the post has no budget, other than the MP's own parliamentary budget.

The second dimension to the Women and Equality post concerns the political recruitment of women MPs and women in 'all aspects of party life'. In this respect, when she was the spokesperson, Burt was 'always on the look out for talent' and took part in the 'shadowing' scheme whereby MPs have responsibility for a particular group of prospective candidates. Burt was also involved with the CGB and the Diversity and Equality Group, and there were plans for more formal networking and work with Operation Black Vote, an organization which seeks to increase the number of BAME MPs. With regard to women members – as a corporate body – Burt was Vice-President of the WLD and took an active role in their activities, for example writing articles for their newsletter and speaking at their conferences. Importantly, though, this relationship, as practiced by Burt when she was the spokesperson, was not mandated by the position of Women and Equality brief and there is no formal accountability to the WLD.

Policy making in the Liberal Democrat Party

Organizationally, the Liberal Democrats is a 'self-avowed' federal party, although there are academic debates regarding the location of power within the party in the face of the apparent dominance by the parliamentary party and party HQ (Russell and Fieldhouse 2005, 64–5). Responsible for UK-wide policy preparation, parliamentary elections and fund-raising, the Federal Party has four central committees: the Federal Executive; the Federal Policy Committee (FPC); Federal Conference Committee (FCC); and the Federal Finance and Administration Committee. A 30 per cent quota guarantees women's presence on all party bodies (Russell *et al.* 2002).

The bi-annual Federal Party Conferences are the sovereign policy-making body of the Liberal Democrats, although this is 'co-ordinated and refined' by the Federal Policy Committee (Russell and Fieldhouse 2005, 58). Each local party, the parliamentary parties, officers of the party and adopted candidates, send delegates with voting rights. A local party is entitled to at least three representatives, and subject to their being sufficient nominations, at least one shall be a man and one a woman. For SAOs there is no sex requirement. Conference motions come from the FPC, state parties, SAOs, local parties and groups of ten conference representatives. If these motions are passed they become party policy.

The impact of Liberal Democrat women's organizations on party policy has been little studied.[8] Motions submitted to the Federal Party's biannual conferences are the central medium through which the WLD seeks to influence policy making. Over the last five years three out of twelve WLD motions have been accepted at conference: Rape convictions at Brighton in 2006; Equal Pay Audits at Blackpool in 2005; and Improving Gender Balance in Politics at Bournemouth in September 2001.

Inter-party competition at the 2005 General Election: The integration of women's concerns[9]

The claim that the political terrain over which British political parties compete has become feminized suggests that women's concerns are increasingly part of political party programmes and a site of inter-party competition. An audit of the three main political parties' policies at the 2005 General Election reveals the relative coverage they give to women's concerns at one particular moment in time. However, as the analytical framework described in Table 2.1 outlines, a party can, if it chooses to, integrate women's concerns into its policy programme, in a feminist, neutral, or anti-feminist fashion. Only a *feminist* audit therefore reveals the extent, and ways in which, feminism is present in, or underpins parties' policies. To counter criticism that such an approach relies upon a universal definition of feminism, a list of questions produced in advance of the election by the Fawcett Society was applied. As Box 2.6 outlines, Fawcett – the UK's leading women's rights civil society group – considered the following the key questions for British women in 2005:

BBC Radio 4's 'Woman's Hour' undertook three special pre-election Party Leader interviews in February 2005. Case Study 2.4 documents, in full, the different conceptions of gender equality voiced publicly by Tony Blair, Michael Howard and Charles Kennedy. Although the precise questions put to each differed slightly, Blair and Kennedy generally held more egalitarian views on gender roles whereas Howard held more traditional ones. At the same time, Blair and Howard acknowledged a tension between women's employment rights and the interests of business. In respect of women's presence in Parliament, Kennedy belatededly accepts the need for specific measures to increase the numbers of women MPs, whereas Howard advances a meritocratic critique of such measures. In sum, the Conservative Party Leader is adrift from the other two party Leaders.

If analyzing Party Leader interviews are likely to reveal the personal views of the different leaders, analyses of party manifestos reveal those statements, policies and images that the party wishes to be put in front of the electorate at a particular General Election; the manifestos are likely to reflect both internal party debates as well the wider political context, not least the state of inter-party competition.

> **Box 2.6 Fawcett Society make your mark. Use your vote!**
>
> - What will you do to close the pay gap between women and men?
> - How will you provide affordable childcare for all? How will you support mothers and fathers who want to stay at home with children?
> - How will you make employment more flexible so that women and men can be equal partners at work and at home?
> - Will you introduce state pensions that recognize the value of caring for family?
> - How will you reward unpaid carers for the important work they do?
> - How will you tackle violence against women and ensure victims get justice and support? How will you ensure that women offenders are given sentences that fit their crimes and help the wider community?
> - How will you reform our education system to ensure that girls and women fulfill their true academic and professional potential?
> - What will you do to help the poorest women in our society escape poverty?
> - How will you provide effective health services for women's specific needs?
> - How will you ensure women feel safe on public transport? How will you tackle bogus minicab drivers who target women?
> - How is your party ensuring women reach the top in business and public life?
> - How will your policies help women in other countries who are suffering because of war, disaster and violence?

The 2005 manifestos took widely differing formats. Labour's was a 112 page paperback book; the Conservatives a 28-page A4 brochure-style manifesto; and the Liberal Democrats a tabloid-sized newspaper. The time taken to read each was more than an hour, 20 minutes and 40 minutes, respectively. The varied formats undoubtedly influenced each manifesto's content: in its book, Labour presented detailed accounts of its second term and outlined proposals for a third term; the Tories devoted eight whole pages to large print, handwritten, single statements, while on other pages there were numerous colour photographs; and the Liberal Democrats presented detailed policy statements accompanied by photos, profiles and views of the respective party spokespeople. Two of the parties, Labour and the Liberal Democrats also produced special women's manifestos, downloadable from their websites.

The parties' coverage of 'women's concerns' in the 2005 manifestos was asymmetric, with Labour's coverage the broadest. However, many of Fawcett's questions are not addressed in the manifestos, as Table 2.2 shows. A simple ranking on a feminist scale positions the Liberal Democrats slightly ahead of Labour, with the Conservative Party bringing up the rear.

With the least comprehensive of the three manifestos, the Conservative Party trail in third place. In his foreword to the manifesto, Howard states that 'to be treated equally is a birthright', and that discrimination is 'wrong'. And he goes on to state that a Conservative government will govern in the interests of everyone in our society – 'black or white, young or old, straight or gay, rural or urban, rich

Table 2.2 Analysis of manifesto policy commitments

	Labour	Conservative	Liberal Democrats
Maternity leave/pay	Nine months maternity leave by 2007 (worth extra £1,400); one year maternity leave by end of 2005 Parliament; consultation on option of shared parental leave	Flexible maternity pay – either nine or six months	Raise maternity pay from £102 to £170 for first six months
Equal pay	Take further action to narrow the pay and promotion gap; The Women and Work Commission will report to the PM 'later this year'		
Equal opportunities	Introduce duty on public bodies to promote equality of opportunity between women and men; establish Commission on Equality and Human Rights; Single Equality Act		Single Equality Act
Domestic violence	Expand specialist courts and specialist advocates		
Health	Faster test results for cervical smears; choice over where/how women have their babies and pain relief; every woman to be supported by a personal midwife		End age discrimination that prevents older women from receiving routine breast cancer screening
Pensions	2nd Pensions Commission Report due Autumn 2005 – 'must address the disadvantages faced by women'		Citizen's pension (for over 75s) based on residency rather than national insurance contributions
Childcare	By 2010, 3,500 Sure Start Centres; increased rights to free part-time nursery provision (rising to 20 hours in longer term); tax credit for nannies/au pairs; consultation on extending rights to flexible working for older parents	Families receiving working tax credit will receive up to £50 per week for under 5s childcare, including familial childcare	
Politics	All-women shortlists		Proportional representation to better reflect 'diversity'
Sexuality	Committed to improving the rights/opportunities of gays and lesbians		Equality Act will ensure fairness for same sex couples in pension arrangements

or poor'. Women are not included. And when women are addressed in the manifesto, it is in terms of the party's maternity and childcare provision – with women having a choice of receiving maternity leave over six or nine months and receiving financial support for familial as well as formal childcare, although there is little specific detail. Women are also depicted as victims of crime – a series of photographs show a woman having her handbag snatched – and as matrons being brought back to 'deliver clean and infection-free wards'. Beyond this, though, there is very little on women. Indeed, the party's discussion of education policy includes a commitment to 'root out political correctness', a form of words that suggests hostility towards feminist analysis of educational provision.

Labour's general appeal to women in the 2005 election was unquestionably on the basis of its package of policies related to 'hard working families'. These included: family tax credits, Sure Start, Child Trust Funds, the expansion of child care provision, and the reduction of child poverty. Looking more closely at the party's record for women (something which their choice of manifesto format permitted) the manifesto: emphasized the extension of maternity leave from 14 to 26 weeks and the 'doubling' of maternity pay; stressed how its Pension Credit had particularly benefited women; highlighted parents' right to request flexible working arrangements; pointed to the 'tailored help' for lone parents; and emphasized the various childcare policies that they claim have improved the work/life balance. They also – and in bold print – state that the Conservatives opposed their improvements in maternity and paternity pay and the introduction of flexible working rights. The manifesto also stresses legislative changes that have advanced lesbian women's opportunities and rights, namely, civil partnerships, the repeal of Section 28, and reform of sexual offences legislation.

Labour's discussion of maternity, paternity and parental leave, while quite detailed, is not accompanied by specific and guaranteed commitments: there is much talk of consultation and aims. Furthermore, the party acknowledges that there is a 'need to balance the needs of parents and carers, with those of employers, especially small businesses' – suggesting, as Blair's interview on Woman's Hour also had – that the party's intentions may be constrained by their perception of the business interest, for example by limiting regulations to only certain kinds of employers. The right to request flexible working is, in the same vein, not the same as a right to flexible working; a goal or target is no guarantee.

The party's 'What is Labour Doing for ... Women?' web page repeats many of the same points made in the main manifesto. There is a little more detail on the impact of the minimum wage on women and in respect of the "most radical overhaul" of domestic violence legislation. But the material is not a detailed supplement. It also makes reference to women's multiple roles – as mothers, pensioners, students, workers, taxpayers, patients, victims of crime, mortgage payers and the majority of those working in and using our public services. Nonetheless, the Labour Party's literature, overall, has a tendency to equate women with motherhood.

Women, and particularly older women, are more central to the Liberal Democrat's manifesto. Charles Kennedy's foreword addresses women's pensions explicitly: 'it's time we redressed the scandalous discrimination against women in the state pension system'. The Liberal Democrat citizen's pension would, they declare, 'provide women who have spent their time caring for children and elderly parents a pension in their own right'. The party's mini-manifesto for women presents a list of the 'top five' Liberal Democrat policies for women. These are: (1) Maternity income guarantee; (2) Citizen's pension; (3) Abolition of tuition fees; (4) Free personal care for the elderly; (5) Childcare. In this document the gendered impact of policies, using a distinctly feminist language of discrimination and equality, is more explicitly stated. For example, a link is made between women's unequal pay and the cost of University tuition and top-up fees – 'unequal pay makes student debt harder on women, with female graduates earning on average 15 per cent less than their male counterparts at the age of 24'. The discussion of pensions emphasizes that two-thirds of the 2.2 million poor pensioners in the UK are women. It also emphasizes that those who would benefit most from free personal care would be women, and claims that the party would 'take immediate steps to alert women' who paid the reduced 'married women's national insurance rate' and allow women to pay back National Insurance contributions. Similarly, there is recognition of the gendered patterns of poverty and employment – with many women working part-time, for low wages, and as home-workers. These insights provide the basis upon which the party intends to tackle discrimination in the workplace, through providing: a maternity income guarantee; a comprehensive Equality Act; a requirement of certain (although unspecified) employers to address EO/equal pay issues; an extension of 'appropriate' (again, unspecified) workplace protection to home-workers; the establishment of an annual review of the minimum wage; a voluntary code against inadvertent discrimination drawn up by CBI, FSB and the TUC (Confederation of British Industry, Federation of Small Businesses and the Trade Union Congress, respectively); and the encouragement of good practice through the publication of employers' diversity strategies and measures. In respect of women's reproductive health, the Liberal Democrats committed themselves to ensuring that all contraceptive options are available in all GP surgeries; providing free condoms in GPs surgeries and other sexual health services; and improving access to emergency contraception. Regarding crime, the party recognizes its gendered nature – by noting women's greater fear of crime – and suggests that their policy of more police will reduce this fear. There is notably though, no specific discussion of domestic violence or rape.

The Liberal Democrat's manifesto feminist rating relative to the other main parties is impressive. But, another reading of the Liberal Democrat main manifesto reveals the party's lack of women MPs. In contrast to the prominence of the party's shadow spokesmen (with photographs and accompanying statements mostly in the same place on each page) there are only two photographs of its current women MPs. And both (Sandra Gidley and Sue Doughty) are given smaller space and less formally presented. They are also, along with Baroness Shirley Williams, on the same double-page spread.

Conclusion

This chapter has sought to provide a preliminary, and largely descriptive, account of the location, roles and potential influence of women in the three main British political parties, together with a consideration of the relative integration of women's concerns in the party's policies at the time of the 2005 General Election. Information on the number of women members of the parties is only known for one party, the Labour Party, with a 60:40 men:women ratio. Thus, despite claims that at least some women in all three of the parties are becoming more established in senior positions (Kittilson 2006, 134–5), it is not clear that they are equally present throughout all the different parts of the political parties. Nor is it the case that women's organizations are fully integrated into policy development or that women's concerns are central to party policy. The analysis of the parties' policy programmes at the 2005 General Election reveals limited coverage of women's concerns and an asymmetry between the parties in respect of the integration of feminist perspectives. What is, however, apparent is that the choice between integration or separation, and between individual or collective representation is an unnecessary one. Today, women in British political parties are demanding individual and collective representation – as individual representatives for elected office *as well as* collectively, through gendered policy. Party leadership responses to these demands, at least in the Conservative and Labour parties, have been similar, albeit separated by time: a reforming leadership recognizes that feminization is electorally useful. Feminization signals party 'modernization' to an electorate that has turned way from the party.

Continuing gaps in research mean that it is not yet possible to draw strong conclusions about the extent of the feminization of the political parties or to map the parties onto the models outlined in Table 2.1 at the beginning of the chapter. To enable such analysis future research should investigate: (1) the level of women's participation in party structures, including, but importantly not limited to, the parliamentary party. Such enquiries should explore whether the party employs specific mechanisms in both party structures and the parliamentary party to guarantee women's participation; (2) whether women's participation in the parties is substantive across the party's various structures and activities or symbolic and limited to certain forms or places; (3) the nature of the role, remit and ideology of QWPAs and, in particular, whether such QWPAs are integrated formally into the wider party structure and policy making bodies, and to whom they are accountable, both upwards and downwards; (4) whether a party regards women as a corporate entity capable of being represented (both descriptively and substantively) and if so, whether the party is susceptible to feminist arguments for this. This might include whether the party makes gender based and/or feminist claims rather than non-gendered, neutral or anti-feminist claims; and finally (5) the extent to which party policies are gendered and feminist – in recognition of the possibility that parties may be feminized but not feminist.

Case Study 2.1

Gendering the 'OMOV' debate

The resolution advocating All Women Shortlists (AWS) at the 1993 Labour Party Annual Conference coupled it with the 'One Member One Vote' (OMOV) reforms to the procedures for selecting parliamentary candidates. The OMOV reforms would permit only full party members to vote in the selection of parliamentary candidates, although Trade Unions would maintain their role in nominating and short-listing prospective parliamentary candidates. The AWS clause stipulated that AWS would be held in half of the party's winnable and safe seats at the next General Election. Unsurprisingly, many unions, including the Transport and General Workers Union (TGWU) and the General Municipal and Boilermakers' Union (GMB), were opposed to OMOV. Notwithstanding such opposition, the resolution was passed by 45.7 per cent to 44.4 per cent. The success was due to one union – the MSF union – abstaining. It did so on the basis that, whilst it was opposed to OMOV, it would break its mandate for the good of women's representation.[10]

The framework of the Research Network on Gender Politics and the State (RNGS) – a cross-national research project – seeks to establish whether or not policy debates are framed both in gendered and feminist terms. The former refers to an acknowledgment that the nature of political problems, as well as possible solutions, will differentially affect women and men. The latter looks to the inclusion of women's movement frames. To this end, RNGS asks the following questions: (1) are (Q)WPAs active participants or symbolic bystanders in policy debates; (2) do they advocate women's movement goals? and (3) do they contribute to successful outcomes for women? In the case of OMOV/AWS the research questions were: what was the dominant frame of the debate, and to what extent was the debate gendered and feminist? What are the characteristics and activities of WPAs, QWPAs and the women's movement? And, how open was the policy environment?

In the language of RNGS the policy environment in which the issue of AWS was debated was 'moderately closed'. There was a complex configuration of procedures, officials and factions within the party. Internal party sex-quotas ensured that feminist actors were included. Even so, this was accessible only to well-established, politically skilful Labour movement activists, as the traditionally masculinist culture of the Party continued to be a barrier to women.

The dominant framing of the OMOV/AWS debate at the Labour Party Conference centred on the relationship between the party and the Trade Unions. Party modernizers embraced OMOV. Traditionalists favoured the retention of some form of electoral college, a state of affairs that privileges the Trade Unions. The dominant public discourse centred on arguments about fairness, equity, representation and policy improvement – concerns that mapped onto demands by women for greater descriptive representation in the parliamentary Labour party.

The gendering of the OMOV debate was made explicit in the clause of the resolution that established AWS. Contributors to the debate made reference to the rights of women voters to be represented by women and the rights of women party members to be nominated. Within the party, discussion of AWS ranged across substantive policy issues, the necessity for the party to present a women-friendly image, and the necessity for women to be represented by women. Opponents of AWS were not much heard in the Conference, as critics focused instead on OMOV.

Women's Policy Agencies were not active in the OMOV/AWS debate. Neither the Equal Opportunities Commission (EOC) nor the Women's National Commission were empowered to intervene. In contrast, the Labour Party's QWPAs were extremely active in ensuring that AWS was put before the Conference, in gendering the debate and ensuring a feminist outcome. These included: the NEC Women's Committee, the Shadow Minister for Women (Clare Short) and the Party's Women's Officer (Deborah Lincoln). Other senior women in the Party, Labour's Women's Network, and Women's Sections at branch, constituency, regional and national level were also vocal in their support. AWS further benefited from the support of key male allies in the party, including the Labour leader, John Smith. Beyond the party proper, Trade Union equality officers, not least the MSF's Anne Gibson, were favourably disposed towards AWS.

Source: Lovenduski (2005b).

Case Study 2.2

women2win

WE DECLARE our determination to increase the number of Conservative women MPs, by campaigning for more women to win nominations for winnable and Tory held seats, by pressing for any positive and radical reforms of the selection procedures for Conservative Parliamentary candidates short of compulsory all-women shortlists, and by providing support and advice to Conservative women who wish to enter Parliament;

and we hold it as self-evident that for the Conservative Party to represent the United Kingdom population successfully, it must itself become more representative of society as a whole, especially of women, and that this will also increase the quality of Conservative representation in Parliament, just as the promotion of able women has improved the quality of management and decision-making in other professions, in commerce and industry, and elsewhere in public life.

Women2win was established in response to the Conservative party's failure to elect greater numbers of women MPs at the 2005 General Election and the de-selection of a number of women candidates in the run up to that election. Anne Jenkin – herself a defeated Conservative parliamentary candidate in 1987 and grand-daughter of Joan Davidson, the only Conservative woman MP returned at the 1945 General Election, and great-grand-daughter of Sir Willoughby Dickinson MP, a leading campaigner for women's suffrage – realized that she was the 'someone' who should be 'doing something about women' and was persuaded that the Conservative Leadership campaign offered the perfect 'opportunity' to put the issue onto the new Leader's agenda. With a meeting instigated by Theresa May MP – who had already spoken at the launch of the Hansard Society Report 'Women at the Top' the previous week – Jenkin, alongside May, Eleanor Laing MP, Laura Sandys, Shireen Ritchie and Anne's husband, Bernard Jenkin MP, met to discuss establishing a new organization. A joint Conservative Women's Organization, Fawcett Society and EOC Party Conference event constituted another important trigger; as did the publication of a letter written by six Tory MPs in support of women's representation, published in the Daily Telegraph, and orchestrated by Bernard Jenkin. With no budget or structure, women2win was launched, paid for by a fee Anne Jenkin had received for a *Sunday Express* article published the previous weekend.

Women2win was launched on 23rd November 2005 at Millbank Tower, a building forever associated with 'new' Labour's 1997 election victory. More than 200 women, along with a handful of men, shared a continental breakfast before listening to a series of presentations and participating in a 'Q & A' session. Women from all parts of the Conservative Party were represented. There were women MPs – newly elected ones, such as Maria Miller, MP for Basingstoke, and more senior ones, such as Theresa May, Eleanor Laing and Caroline Spelman. Women from the professional and voluntary party included Fiona Hodgson, Chairman of the Conservative Women's Organization, Shireen Ritchie, Chairman of Kensington and Chelsea Conservative Association and Lady Trish Morris, previously Vice-Chairman for Candidates. Sandra Howard, wife of the then Party Leader, also dropped by. Supportive male MPs present included Bernard Jenkin and Peter Viggers. Chairing the event was the *Guardian* journalist Jackie Ashley. Also represented were WPAs, women's civil society groups and academics: Jenny Watson, Chair of the EOC, the Fawcett Society's Director, Dr Katherine Rake, and Dr Sarah Childs (as one of the authors of the 2005 Hansard Society 'Women at the Top' Report).

If the women present at the launch of women2win were symbolic of the new face of women in the Conservative Party, then it was smart, stylish, and resolute that the party had to elect more women to Parliament at the next General Election. Interestingly, many of those present were the same women who had been active in the Conservative Party for many years before – what women2win constituted was a new women's militancy; better organized, more vocal, and more politically and media savvy. Not only were the women speaking with one voice, they were also strategic in getting support from women's advocacy groups outside of the Party and bringing men onside – Bernard Jenkin had convinced them that 'you will never make progress until you get the men involved'. The presence at the launch of sympathetic journalists from the *Guardian,* and BBC Radio 4's *Woman's Hour* similarly increased the chances that women2win would be covered in both the mainstream and women's media. Finally, because women2win's launch purposively coincided with the Party Leadership contest, the group was able to lobby both Leadership contenders, David Cameron and David Davis, before the new Leader was elected.

Case Study 2.3

The Conservative Leadership Election

Apparently asked for 'a dare', the 'boxer/briefs?' question put by Martha Kearney to David Davis and David Cameron catapulted BBC Radio 4's

Woman's Hour interview with the two Conservative Leadership contenders in November 2005 into the national consciousness. For the record, Cameron claimed to be a boxers man and Davis a briefs man.[11]

Opening the interviews, each David was given one minute to make a direct appeal to women. Both rejected 'positive discrimination' in the selection of parliamentary candidates. Davis, who spoke first, stated that he would 'invest the whole authority' of his leadership 'in persuasion not imposition'; he would 'head hunt women, train women and promote women'; and it would be his job 'to persuade local parties [that] it's in their best interest to select more women candidates'. David Cameron similarly stated: 'I agree with David, no positive discrimination, no AWS, but everything short of that'. Cameron, however, offered the possibility of more radical change: he included a commitment to 'changing the selection procedures'. When directly asked about an 'A list' of top candidates, Cameron thought it a 'good idea worth looking at' and, prompted by Kearney, commented that a sex ratio of '50:50 would be good', although he stressed the importance of local constituencies having the ultimate decision and acknowledged that local candidates might be preferred. Davis, in contrast, rejected the 'A list' – 'I don't agree with that idea either'. His reasoning was (quite rightly) that the 'A list' failed to guarantee local constituencies' demand for women candidates. Yet he offered nothing other than persuasion in its place. At this point, Cameron interrupted Davis and questioned the set of attributes and skills currently seen as desirable in parliamentary candidates, not least the 'ability to make one big speech'. In contrast, he claimed that 'if you emphasize those parts of the job [listening, empathizing, advising in surgeries] we'd end up with more women'. The interview continued with Kearney explicitly identifying selectorate discrimination against women: Davis rejects evidence of this and reiterates the importance of persuading local constituencies, whereas Cameron talks of needing to 'break down the barriers to make the Conservative Party more attractive to women' and make it 'easier' for women to get onto the list of candidates.

In terms of policy, Davis explained the Tory party's loss of the women's vote with reference to sleaze and the party's over-focus on Europe. His solution was to be 'strong on principles' and he emphasized education, childcare, health, pensions, crime and drugs. Cameron's pitch was more explicitly gendered: 'there are some issues that particularly affect women, the scandal of unequal pay, the issue of childcare and flexible working, the importance of making sure women have access to good pensions which they don't at the moment'. He also stressed the importance of style in politics – rejecting 'Punch and Judy politics'.

Turning to the issue of marriage and families, both men consider marriage a 'good institution' (Cameron) and the 'best odds' for families (Davis). Both agreed that transferring income tax allowance when one parent stays at home is a 'good idea' (Cameron) and 'worth looking at' (Davis); there is also agreement about informal care by grandparents and that perhaps this should be paid for by the state – something Kearney suggested is not 'really' Conservative. On the question of paternity leave, the Leadership rivals are less sure. Cameron thought 26 weeks too long as he worried about the negative impact on small business. Signalling the impending birth of his third child he added – 'I'm not sure what my constituents would say if I buzzed off for 26 weeks from February'. Later he explicitly stated that he would not take this amount. Davis is unsure about 12 weeks. Again, the concern is with small business, but he also considered whether extensive maternity rights would engender discrimination against women, as employers might opt not to employ women. Regarding the issue of the gender pay gap, there is greater distance between the two men, with Cameron keen on pay transparency and Davis fearful that the 'burden of proof' would fall back on the small business.

Both men were also on the receiving end of individual critical questions: Davis was asked about the infamous 'Double DD' t-shirts worn by his supporters at the Conservative Conference the previous autumn, to which he responds that there has been a 'humour failure all around'. Neither does he 'regret it' as Kearney suggests he might. Indeed, he adds that the 'idea actually came from a girl' – he might better have said young woman. Cameron is asked directly about his membership of a men-only London Club. His response is that this was somewhere he met his 'dad' for lunch and, in any case, 'I don't think we have to be politically correct in every aspect of our lives'.

Case Study 2.4

The Party Leaders on *'Woman's Hour'*

With fatherhood impending, Charles Kennedy was provided with the opportunity to declare that he would be a 'hands on' father: 'everything about our marriage is very much a union of equals and I don't doubt ... that bringing up junior is going to be any different'. In a similar fashion,

Tony Blair celebrated young men's involvement in childcare: it is 'extremely healthy' that it 'wouldn't occur' to young men that they would 'have any more right to opt out of the responsibility for children'; he also wants to extend the welfare state 'to catch up with' such changes. Hence Blair's advocacy of the 'basic principle' of extending maternity leave and, in particular, providing transferability of the leave between parents.

In contrast, and on being asked to reflect upon changes in gender roles, Michael Howard chose not to comment on whether he thought they were for the better or the worse. Later, when he was asked when had he last cooked supper he reveals that this had not been 'for a very long time'; he 'wasn't a good cook' whereas his wife was, and that the traditional division of labour between them 'works for us'. Howard's support for marriage as an institution was made explicit when he talked about how evidence showed that it was better for children to be brought up by married parents. Moreover, and despite saying three times that governments should not be 'prescriptive' nor tell people 'how to live their lives', he added, 'where there are things which government can do to achieve that [strengthen marriage] then I think its sensible for government to think about them'. A preference for traditional gender roles is also apparent in discussions about paying women to stay at home to look after children and in discussions of allowing child care by grandparents to be covered by child care tax credit. Without drawing a distinction between grandmothers and grandfathers, he states: 'grandparents know pretty much all there is to know about childminding so we would fast track grandparents'.

In respect of maternity rights, Howard favours an increase in pay rather than longer leave, together with a rejection of extending rights to request flexible working: 'we live in a fiercely competitive world … it's no use giving people rights at work if there's no job to go to'. His discussion of paid statutory leave for those who care for elderly relatives reveals the same prioritization. The question is '"whose going to pay?", if it's the tax payer … there's a limit to what you can ask the tax payer to do'. Here, in a nutshell, is Howard's philosophy: a low tax economy enables individuals to purchase what they need based on the choices they, and not the state, has made. Hidden in this is a very particular conception of gender and the family – a male breadwinner and female carer. The presumption of individual responsibility (and the traditional family) is also present in Howard's rejection of citizen pensions precisely because it breaks the link between contributions, although he did state that he wanted to scrap 'some of the rules', for example the ten year contribution rule that 'works particularly harshly on women'.

Blair lists what he considers to be Labour's transformation in the kind of support provided for parents and emphasizes the importance of helping 'mothers who want to return to work with skills'. There are, though, many occasions in his discussion of maternity pay/leave, pensions and equal pay statements where he fails to make detailed commitments and, like Howard, perceives a tension between women's rights and the wider economic and business interest: it is important to 'work with' and persuade business so that what they once thought 'completely unacceptable' becomes part of the 'accepted way of working'. On equal pay, he talks of the 'delicate balance ... with people often struggling to run small businesses'. Indeed, his rejection of state support for grandparents' care for children, a non-means tested carer's allowance, and payments for stay-at-home mothers, together with a rather equivocal statement on citizen's pensions' are made on the grounds of economic cost, his commitment to a low tax economy, and, regarding the former, concerns about fraudulent claims. Pressed on equal pay, Blair throws the question back to the interviewer: 'how do you make sure you enforce equal pay without getting into bureaucracy and unnecessarily intrusive measures for employers?' to which Jenni Murray retorts: 'demand they publish it'. This, in turn, is answered by Blair with: 'how much, you know, hassle do you end up giving them in order to try and make sure the rules are obeyed'?[12]

Notes

1 *Guardian*, 30 March 2005.
2 OMOV refers to the role of members in the selection of party leaders and parliamentary candidates (M. Russell 2005).
3 In the autumn/winter 2006/7 Jowell's concern seemed apposite as 'too skinny' models were 'banned' from certain continental European catwalks (*Guardian*, 16 September 2006).
4 Labour's 'Big Conversation' was a consultation process launched in the autumn of 2003; it involved the publication of a 77 page document, an interactive website and text messaging service, along with a series of ministerial visits around the country (http://news.bbc.co.uk/1/hi/uk_politics/3245620.stm).
5 http://www.conservatives.com/tile.do?def=party.useful.link.page&ref=cwnc
6 Other members include: Shireen Ritchie (Chairman of the Candidates Committee), Eleanor Laing MP, Liz St. Clair in her capacity as Women's Officer at CCHQ, Baroness Trish Morris, Anne Jenkin and, latterly, Lorraine Fulbrook who is now the Director of women2win.
7 Other members are Margot James, Liz St. Clair, Mary Macleod (Chairman of the Candidates Association), Shireen Ritchie, Alexandra Robson, Laura Sandys, and Fiona Hodgson (Chairman of the CWO). Neither Robson nor Sandys has a formal role in the party. Both are on the approved list for candidates.
8 Russell and Fieldhouse (2005, 60) state that of the Party's SAOs it is the Councillors' and Youth and Students SAOs that are particularly 'worthy of further investigation'.

9 This section draws on research that was previously published in A. Geddes and J. Tonge (Eds) *Britain Decides* (Basingstoke: Palgrave).
10 This point is made by Meg Russell (2005, 56).
11 There was much discussion of the appropriateness of this question: did this mean that women politicians could be asked about their choice of underwear, asked Philip Cowley of the University of Nottingham, as did Melanie Phillips writing in the *Daily Mail*. India Knight, in the *Sunday Times*, retorted: 'you can tell a lot about a man by his underwear'; men who wear boxers 'are by and large jolly, not aggressively macho, open to suggestion, familiar with the odd beauty product, keen on children and dogs, well mannered'.
12 Only Kennedy and Howard faced questions about women's descriptive representation. Kennedy accepted the case for equality guarantees; Howard rehearsed the classic meritocratic critique and emphasized the autonomy of local constituency parties in Conservative Party selection.

3   Women's legislative
recruitment

Introduction

The 2005 General Election saw a record number of women MPs elected to the House of Commons – a welcome increase of ten from the 2001 Parliament. This remains, however, far from parity – women constitute fewer than one in five Members of the House of Commons. Westminster also compares unfavourably to the devolved institutions in Scotland and Wales where, in 2007, women constitute 33 per cent and 47 per cent, respectively. Women's descriptive representation in the UK Parliament is also asymmetric by party: Labour has the highest number of women, 98, and the highest percentage, at 27.5 per cent. At the last three General Elections it returned 101, 95 and 98 women MPs. In comparison, the Conservative Party returned 13, 14 and 17 women MPs, flat-lining at 9 per cent, while the figures for the Liberal Democrats are three, six and ten, in 1997, 2001 and 2005 respectively, constituting, in 2005, 16 per cent. In the 2005 Parliament there were only two Black, Asian and Minority Ethnic (BAME) women MPs, both Labour representatives.

Supply and demand theories

The increases in the number of women MPs since the 1990s, as well as the inter-party differences, beg important questions about the legislative recruitment of women. In their ground breaking study, Pippa Norris and Joni Lovenduski (1995) separate out four levels of analysis. At the first level are the *systemic* factors that set the broad context: the legal, electoral, party systems and the structure of party competition, the strength of parties, and the position of the parties across the ideological divide. The second level looks towards the *context* within parties – their organization, rules and ideology. At the third level are the *individual* factors such as the resources and motivations of aspirant candidates, as well as the attitudes of the party selectorates. Finally, there are the individual elections that determine the outcome of the process for the composition of parliaments.

In Britain systemic factors are not significant inhibitors of women's descriptive representation. Women do not face legal barriers to their election, although the 'First Past the Post' (single member simple plurality, SMSP), majoritarian

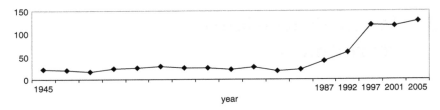

Figure 3.1 Numbers of women MPs elected to the British House of Commons 1945–2005

electoral system used for Westminster is widely considered to be less favourable for women candidates than proportional representation systems. Nonetheless, the recent increases in the numbers of women MPs have occurred during a period in which the electoral system has stayed constant. More important than the electoral system per se is, then, the acknowledgement that the overwhelming majority of MPs elected to the UK Parliament are representatives of political parties. In such contexts, the question of 'who our representatives are' is one of whom our political parties select as their candidates.

The outcome of particular political parties' selection processes is often understood in terms of the interaction between the *supply* of applicants wishing to pursue a political career and the *demands* of selectors who choose candidates on the basis of their preferences and perceptions of abilities, qualifications and perceived electability (Norris and Lovenduski 1995). Supply-side factors likely to limit the overall level of women seeking selection include gendered socialization

Table 3.1 MPs elected to the House of Commons, 1983–2005, by sex and party

Party	1983	1987	1992	1997	2001	2005
Labour	209	229	271	418	412	354
Women	10	21	37	101	95	98[1]
% of total	**4.8**	**9.2**	**13.7**	**24.2**	**23**	**27.7**
Conservative	397	376	336	165	166	198
Women	13	17	20	13	14	17
% of total	**3.3**	**4.5**	**6**	**7.9**	**8**	**8.6**
Liberal Democrat	23	22	20	46	53	62
Women	0	1	2	3	6[2]	10[3]
% of total	**0**	**4.5**	**10**	**6.5**	**11**	**16**
Other	21	23	24	30	25	31
Women	0	2	3	3	4	3
% of total	**0**	**8.7**	**12.5**	**10**	**12.5**	**9.7**
All MPs	650	650	651	659	659	645
Women	23	41	60	120	118	128
% of total	**3.5**	**6.3**	**9.2**	**18.2**	**17.9**	**19.8[4]**

Source: Childs *et al.* 2005.

and the sexual division of labour. Women are, on average, likely to have fewer resources than men, whether that is the necessary free time to engage in politics, money to fund selection and election campaigns, and/or lower levels of political ambition, confidence and experience. On the demand side, women have been found to suffer from selectorate discrimination, that is a lack of party demand for women candidates (Shepherd-Robinson and Lovenduski 2002). This can take different forms. Direct discrimination refers to the positive or negative judgment of people on the basis of characteristics seen as common to their group, rather than as individuals; it reflects the attitudes of the selectors, and can be seen where gender discriminatory questions are posed during the selection process (Norris and Lovenduski 1995). Indirect discrimination refers to instances where the idea of what constitutes a 'good MP' count against women – where, for example, party selectorates prefer candidates with resources primarily associated with men and masculinity. Imputed discrimination is where party members may be unwilling to choose a woman candidate because they are concerned that by so doing they would lose votes. Here, the discrimination reflects what the selectors perceive to be the attitudes of the electorate.

The relative importance of supply- and demand-side explanations for women's legislative recruitment at Westminster has varied over time and between the political parties. Historically, it was said simply that there were insufficient qualified women in the supply pool: as soon as greater numbers of women participated in the public sphere, and especially in those professions such as law that constitute the recruiting grounds for politicians, then more women would seek political candidature. These women would, in turn, be selected by parties and, ultimately, elected as MPs. When women's participation in the public sphere increased in the absence of a corresponding rise in the number of women MPs, the argument was transformed. The problem was now portrayed as a failure on behalf of qualified women to seek selection. This was said to be particularly true for some parties, namely the Conservative Party (Kittilson 2006, 2; Norris and Lovenduski 1995). Today, there is a consensus, at least amongst feminist political scientists, if not amongst all political actors, that the problem is less of supply and more one of demand. Admittedly, the total number of women seeking selection as parliamentary candidates for each of the main parties is fewer than the number of men. And it might be that this sex difference will remain in societies where women and men have different responsibilities for the home and child-caring. But this acknowledgement does not undermine the claim that there are sufficient women candidates for all of the three main political parties, if they so wish, to select women for half their vacant and target seats at each General Election. If parties chose to adopt such a strategy this would deliver parity of representation amongst newly elected MPs and, would, over a short period of time, significantly alter the representative balance between women and men MPs.

There are three main strategies available to political parties to enhance the descriptive representation of women: equality *rhetoric*, equality *promotion* and equality *guarantees* (Lovenduski 2005a). Equality rhetoric and promotion are widespread and largely uncontested in all of the main UK political parties, whereas the adoption of equality guarantees is both more limited and contested. Equality rhetoric consists of party statements, oral and written, that publicly acknowledge the claim for women's descriptive representation. It aims to exhort women to participate in party politics and to seek political candidature. Equality rhetoric can also help persuade party selectorates to choose women as candidates. Accordingly, equality rhetoric has the potential to impact on both the supply and demand sides of legislative recruitment, although it is more likely to impact on the former (Lovenduski 2005a, 92). It also constitutes an opportunity around which gender equality advocates, inside and outside of parties, can mobilize.

Equality promotion measures attempt to bring those who are currently under-represented into political competition. It refers to a range of activities and measures that provide women with the necessary resources to successfully compete in the political recruitment process. As such, this approach is largely underpinned by supply-side arguments: women are regarded as deficient in the resources desired by party selectorates. The most widespread example of equality promotion is candidate training, something all the main UK political parties provide. Often this is women-only. The provision of training for women is, however, subject to three main criticisms. First, aspirant women candidates are known to declare that they 'don't need any more training'; second, training women to compete according to the current rules of the recruitment game does little to unpack parties' assumptions about what makes a good candidate (Harrison 2006b); finally, training candidates may be insufficient to negate selectorate discrimination against women. Other equality promotion measures, such as the provision of financial assistance, take on greater significance where the cost of fighting party selections is high.

Equality promotion can also take the form of 'soft targets' – for example, Labour's intention to achieve a Parliamentary Labour Party with 35 per cent women following the 2005 General Election. It can also refer to measures that, on first glance, look like equality guarantees, but whose finer details and/or implementation reveal that they fall short (Dahlerup and Freidenvall 2003). Measures that merely 'facilitate' or 'encourage' or 'expect' the greater *selection* of women remain examples of equality promotion, albeit strong forms. Party rules that set a minimum quota at the nominating or short-listing stages of candidate selection have the potential to increase the numbers of women selected but this does not guarantee that they will. Nor do they guarantee that any selected women candidates will be subsequently *elected*. Qualitatively distinct, equality guarantees *require* an increase in the number or proportion of particular parliamentarians and/or makes a particular social characteristic *a necessary qualification* for office (following Lovenduski 2005a, with emphasis added). Importantly, equality guarantees create an artificial demand, although they may also indirectly encourage an increase in the supply of women, as women perceive a new demand on behalf of a particular political party.

Equalities guarantees can take different forms, as Table 3.2 outlines. The distinction between equality promotion and equality guarantees can be clarified through considering the implementation of Labour's AWS. In both 1997 and

Table 3.2 Equality guarantees used in British Politics

	Definition	Illustrative Examples
All Women Shortlists (AWS)	A certain percentage of local constituency parties must select their candidate from a list made up only of women aspirant candidates	Labour for the1997 and 2005 General Elections. Labour for devolved elections in Wales 2003
Twinning	Constituencies are 'paired'; one male and one female candidate is selected for the twinned constituencies	Labour for the Scottish and Welsh in 1999 elections
Zipping	Men and women are placed alternately on the list of candidates	Liberal Democrats for the 1999 European elections

Source: Lovenduski (2005).

2005, Labour employed AWS in a proportion of its vacant-held seats and, in 1997, also in a proportion of its winnable seats. This strategy meant, first, that all candidates seeking selection in these particular constituencies were women. Second, because the selected candidate was contesting a Labour-held or winnable seat, she would, ceteris paribus, be *elected* as an MP. The same distinction between equality promotion and equality guarantees applies to twinning and zipping. If the twinned seat contested by women candidates is always 'unwinnable' and the one contested by the men always 'winnable', then twinning cannot be considered an equality guarantee. Zipping in list systems and multi-member seats is likely to constitute an equality guarantee, unless a party is only likely to win one seat and men head up each list.

The decision by a political party to adopt particular equality strategies is influenced by the wider political context within which parties operate, together with the demands and actions of gender equality advocates and party leaders. As Table 3.3 illustrates exogenous factors provide the incentive for parties to increase the number of women; the timing of the adoption reflects the strategies of gender equality advocates (Kittilson 2006). Gender equality advocates' demands are most likely to be effective when they are 'framed' in terms of a party's electoral strategy.

Party strategies at the 2005 General Election

At the 2005 General Election, all political parties could have made use of the opportunities provided by the Sex Discrimination (Election Candidates) Act 2002 to employ equality guarantees.[6] Labour's decision to return to AWS distinguishes them from their two main rivals, who both relied upon equality rhetoric and equality promotion.

Labour

The form of equality guarantee adopted by Labour for 2005 was once again AWS. The party recognized that, seeking an unprecedented third term, it was unlikely to win any new seats. Thus, to be effective, AWS would be needed in those seats Labour already held. Sitting MPs in England and Wales (Scotland was excluded because of the reduction in its parliamentary seats) were, therefore, instructed to inform the party of their intention to stand down prior to December 2002. If too few of these constituencies subsequently volunteered to be AWS, then the party's National Executive Committee (NEC) would impose them in 50 per cent of cases. All post-December 2002 retirements would be classified as 'late retirements' and automatically declared an AWS, although the NEC could authorize exceptions.

It was always likely that AWS would, in reality, constitute fewer than 50 per cent of vacant held seats, as the party also sought to increase the numbers of BAME

Table 3.3 Ideal opportunity structure for increasing women's representation in Parliament

	Exogeneous to the party	*Endogeneous to the Party*
Political opportunity structure	Electoral instability • declining strength of traditional class based groups • existence of gender gap	Reorganization of power within the party • party elite turnover or conversion transform calculus electoral support • enhanced women's presence in party leadership demanding women's numerical representation
	New issues • diffusion of feminist attitudes and mobilization of women around women's issues • emergence of post-materialist values/issues • women's under-representation recognized by international bodies, e.g. UN Party system Competition • proactive or entrepreneurial party targets women's votes • reactive parties create contagion effect	Changing perceptions of party leadership • party leaders see their interests in a new light

Table 3.3 Ideal opportunity structure for increasing women's representation in Parliament—cont'd

	Exogeneous to the party	*Endogeneous to the Party*
Institutional opportunity structure	Electoral System Rules • party competition • high turnover	Internal party structure • de-centralized parties accommodate bottom up demands by women; centralized parties permit leaders to act[5] • highly instituitonalized parties (i.e. with standardized and bureaucratic rules) impedes party change; weakly institutionalized parties tend to bias candidate nomination to those with 'personal' political capital • pragmatic parties are less constrained than ideological parties in their response to new demands; • leftist parties better able to respond to new issue that is consistent with party's present values

Source: Amended from Kittilson 2006.

candidates, and to avoid a perception that 'no men need apply'. Even so, in terms of numbers it is clear that, once again, AWS delivered. Yet, two other stories surround their use in 2005. The first, and more widely covered in the media, was the failure of the AWS Labour candidate Maggie Jones to win the very safe Labour seat of Blaenau Gwent. Together with the loss of seven other AWS, this was interpreted as proof that AWS was a 'bad' policy.[7] However, as Case Study 3.2 outlines, Blaenau Gwent was very much the exception. It was not so much that AWS women lost because they had been selected on AWS but because they were new candidates (Cutts *et al*. forthcoming). The second 2005 AWS story was the failure of any BAME women to be selected via AWS (Criddle 2005). In part, this reflects the party's informal decision to locate AWS predominantly in constituencies without significant BAME populations, suggesting a lack of local supply. But, it also appears to be a question of party demand, with BAME women likely to face selectorate discrimination. Although Dawn Butler was selected for West Ham on a (by default) all Black shortlist, Black and Asian male councillors stand accused of trying to sabotage her selection campaign.[8]

Labour did not just rely on equality guarantees for the 2005 General Election. Equality rhetoric was voiced by Labour Party Leaders, published in party literature and articulated via party women's organizations, for example, Labour Women's Network. Specific equality promotion measures were aimed at increasing the selection of women as candidates: at the Nomination Stage, party Units were asked to submit nominations for a man and a woman while affiliated organizations were 'entitled' 'to nominate both a man and a woman'. At the Short-listing stage, there was a sex balancing rule: 'if four or more are nominated there shall be a minimum of FOUR in any shortlist (i.e. at least TWO men and TWO women)'. Furthermore, the party's literature on candidate selection (Labour's Future and the NPP Application Pack) stressed the importance of candidate diversity – candidates should be 'drawn from the widest possible pool of talent'. Party members were instructed to avoid 'making assumptions based on physical characteristics, dress, body language or voice'. Guidelines emphasized that candidates with caring responsibilities 'may not have work-related or trade union experience, but may be active in the community'. Candidates should also be judged in respect of their commitment to equal opportunities: 'work which candidates have been involved in could focus on race, gender, disability, sexuality, economic equality, or any work which increases the opportunity or influence of under-represented or disadvantaged groups in society'. At hustings meetings sexist questions and those that enquired into a candidate's marital state or domestic circumstances were proscribed. Finally, and privileging sex, party members voting in the selection had to sign the following: I am aware that in casting my vote in this selection procedure I must vote for a candidate purely on the basis of merit. I will not allow the gender of a candidate or any consideration that might favour one gender over another to affect my judgment (Labour's Future, 60).

Liberal Democrats

Divided over the issue of equality guarantees, the Liberal Democrat party relied in 2005 on equality rhetoric and promotion. The party's 'guidance notes for candidates', for example, is explicitly sensitive to gender difference – 'domestic' is included as an occupational category and in the section on 'motivations, qualities and goals', and it suggests that 'planning a big wedding' might constitute an example of strategic planning. The party's Assessment Day's exercises were also devised to be 'seen to be fair'. In terms of constituency selection, the party's Returning Officers have to have undergone training, whilst Selection Committees must ensure the 'fair and equal treatment of all candidates' and should themselves be representative, inter alia, in terms of sex. In target and party-held seats all members of the Selection Committee (and in other seats at least two) 'must' have received the Party's training, 'especially as regards conducting interviews and ensuring equal treatment of applicants'. Two equal opportunity forms 'monitor whether particular groups of candidates are finding it more difficult to get through the selection procedures successfully'.

At the Short-listing stage the Liberal Democrats operated a sex quota: subject to there being a sufficient number of applicants of each sex, shortlists of three or four must include at least one member of each sex, and shortlists of five or six must include at least two members of each sex.[9] Whether or not a particular candidate had a 'husband or a wife, supportive or not, or several children or not' could not be taken into consideration. And whilst not at that time 'illegal', it would not be 'in the spirit of the party' to discriminate on the grounds of 'age or sexual orientation'. Appreciation that fairness does not necessarily mean sameness is also evident in the party literature: 'a softer line may be more appropriate for a "fragile flower" type of candidate'. At hustings, candidates cannot be asked about financial contributions nor can questions be asked 'which discriminate against groups such as women or candidates with disabilities'.

The Conservative Party

In 2005 the Conservatives were opposed to equality guarantees on the basis that they offended principles of meritocracy, preferring instead equality rhetoric and promotion. Having reformed its selection procedures the Party was, however, confident that it had levelled the playing field. At the approval stage, and informed by equal opportunities good practice, the Parliamentary Assessment Boards evaluated six core competencies: (1) Communication skills – listening and speech making (2) Intellectual skills – taking on board and distilling complex information (3) Relating to different kinds of people (4) Leadership and motivation – enthusing, supporting, enabling (5) Resilience and drive, whilst avoiding arrogance (6) Conviction – to Conservative ideas and commitment to public service. Approved women would receive candidate training, some of which would be 'women only'. At the Selection stage, there were various equality promotion measures. These included: the removal of education from CVs, to avoid decisions based on attendance at the 'right school or university'; the encouragement of the 'sift' of applications to be undertaken in London so that this could be overseen – to ensure there was 'nobody languishing' in the 'no' pile who 'shouldn't be there'; and an invitation to non-party members in local constituencies to participate, although not vote, in the selection process.

More dramatically, although ultimately to little effect in 2005, the party introduced American-style primaries and the 'City Seats Initiative' (CSI). In respect of the former, the selectorate was effectively extended beyond members of the local Association. Open primaries were open to anyone who was registered to be involved and who was on the electoral register for that particular constituency; closed primaries were limited to registered Conservatives in the constituency. In both cases, however, members of the local Association continued to determine the shortlist from which the final selection was made, and endorsed, through a special general meeting, the chosen candidate. The City Seats Initiative was part of a wider strategy to revive the party's fortunes in the inner cities: teams of would-be MPs were brought together to campaign city-wide. Only close to the election were individual candidates 'slotted' into particular seats; to counteract any resistance, local parties were given the opportunity to reject individual candidates as members of their city team.

Women MPs at the 2005 general election

The strongest explanation for the relative success of each of the three main parties' in 2005 lies in the type of seat their women candidates was selected for. Table 3.4 shows the distribution of women candidates by seat marginality. Seats are deemed winnable if the party won the seat in 2001 or came second within a margin of less than 10 per cent. In 2005, Labour's women candidates were more likely than women in the other two parties to be selected in seats the party already held. Thirty new women were selected for vacant-held Labour seats via AWS and 23 of these were successfully returned to Westminster. The 2005 Parliament may not have topped Labour's 1997 high-water mark of 101 women MPs, but it reversed the party's 2001 decline and was impressive given that the party lost nine sitting women MPs. In contrast, the majority of Conservative women candidates were placed, not in Conservative held seats but in the party's unwinnable seats. The same is true for the Liberal Democrats. Labour's success in 2005, relative to the other parties, illustrates the potential for measures such as AWS to 'trump' other strategies designed to enhance women's descriptive representation: there is a positive relationship between the Labour party's use of AWS and increases in the number of its women MPs – in 1997 the party jumped from 37 to 101 Labour women MPs; in 2001, when it did not employ AWS, it only returned 95; in 2005 it returned 98 women.

Legislative recruitment post 2005

With the higher levels of women in the UK parliament intimately tied up with the overall electoral success of Labour (because of their use of AWS), a swing away from that party at the next General Election has the potential to reduce women's descriptive representation: women Labour MPs sit in 12 of the 43 hyper-marginal Labour seats. In the absence of new proscriptive legislation requiring that all parties adopt equality guarantees, only Labour chose to continue with its equality guarantee measures.

The Labour Party

Labour's equality rhetoric includes a commitment to 40 per cent women's presence in the next PLP – 5 per cent higher than the 2005 target. This is stated in a number of NEC Organization Committee Documents – the documents that set out the selection procedures. Specific women- and BAME-only training constitutes one aspect of their equality promotion strategy. Others take the form of particular requirements to promote women and BAME aspirant candidates at the Nomination and Short-listing stages of the selection process:

> 10.D. Where party branches nominate, with the exception set out in 10(e) below [AWS seats], they shall be obliged to submit the names of up to

Table 3.4 Women candidates and MPs by type of seat 2005

	Seats won 2001		Winnable 5 %		Winnable 10%		Unwinnable		Total	
	candidates	MPs	candidates	MPs	Candidates	MPs	Candidates	MPs	Candidates	MPs
Labour	115	98	2	0	2	0	47	0	166	98
Consv	14	14	4	1	7	1	93	1	118	17
Libdem	4	4	2	1	5	1	114	4	125	10

Note: the type of seat calculated using the 2001 election results. Seats are deemed winnable if the party won the seat in 2001 or came second within a margin of less than 5% or less than 10%, all other seats are classified as unwinnable.

three candidates with at least one being a woman and at least one being a BAME candidate in the event that at least one BAME candidate has expressed an interest in the seat at the deadline for expressions of interest. Other party units and affiliated branches need only make one nomination but may nominate up to three candidates if they so wish.

10.E. Where there is an AWS in operation, party branches choosing to nominate shall be obliged to submit the names of up to two women with at least one being a BAME candidate in the event that at least one candidate has expressed an interest in the seat ... other party units and affiliated branches need only make one nomination, but may nominate up to two women, with at least one being a BAME candidate in the event that at least one candidate has expressed an interest in the seat ...

11.E. Where no sitting Labour MP is contesting the seat, and other than where an AWS has been designated by the NEC, there shall be at least 50 per cent women on the shortlist. If six or more [aspirant candidates] are nominated there shall be a minimum of six on any shortlist. This is subject to a sufficient number of both men and women being nominated (i.e. should five men and two women be nominated, the shortlist will be three men and two women). Where an AWS is in place, there shall be a minimum of six on the shortlist, provided six women have been nominated.

Notwithstanding these efforts, the key to Labour's strategy is, once again, AWS. The party took four new and additional factors into consideration in reviewing its selection procedures post-2005: first, English and Welsh boundary reviews meant that, in some instances, more than one sitting MP would compete for a single seat and new seats would need to be reclassified as safe, marginal or unwinnable; second, there was an expectation that higher numbers of Labour MPs would retire; third, that there was an expectation that the party's new Leader, would 'have their own views' as to how to implement AWS; and finally, and for the first since 1997, Labour would be contesting winnable seats, not least those they lost due to anti-Iraq and anti-tuition fee sentiment in 2005, such as Cambridge, Bristol West and Manchester Withington. The role of 'politics' in the process of selecting candidates – whether that was local party hostility to AWS or a preference for 'well-funded TU backed' candidates – was more explicitly appreciated by party HQ this time around, and they saw it as their job to manage these issues.

In March 2006 the NEC Organization Committee outlined the criteria for determining which constituencies would be designated AWS. The preferred outcome, as in 1997 and 2005, was the voluntary adoption of AWS. However, where such agreement was not possible, the Organization Committee would determine which seats would be so designated. In the post-Blaenau context, the local political situation would be considered by the Regional Directors. Anti-AWS activity in constituencies would not, though, be tolerated: 'Where deliberate attempts are being made to frustrate the process, this should be reported to the Organization Committee'. Constituency parties are reminded that the 'final decision' lies with the

Organization Committee and that whilst they would have 'fully taken into account' local members' views, this should not be interpreted as meaning that the 'Organization Committee and the constituency will be in agreement'. This is, in black and white, Labour's response to Labour party critics of AWS. It is a statement that acknowledges persuasion may not always be sufficient to ensure local parties volunteer for AWS. It is such provisions, if fully implemented, which would make Labour's AWS for the next General Election equality guarantees, rather than equality promotion.[10]

Liberal democrats

The problem of women's recruitment, according to the Liberal Democrat Leadership is one of supply – only 25 per cent of the party's current Approved List is female. The party strongly disputes that it has a problem of demand. Tables that show the distribution of women Liberal Democrat candidates by type of seat, such as Table 3.2, create, in their view, a misleading impression. In particular, they reject the distinction drawn between winnable and unwinnable seats on the basis that it relies upon an outdated notion of a uniform national swing. Instead, the Party maintains that it does select women candidates for seats that it deems winnable. Accordingly, the 'surprise' victories of women candidates in, for example, Hornsey and Wood Green at the 2005 General Election were not *unexpected* to the party Leadership or Party HQ.

Given their perception of the problem, Liberal Democrat efforts for the next General Election are mostly focused on encouraging more women to seek selection. Examples of equality rhetoric and equality promotion are evident in much of the paperwork that supports the Liberal Democrat selection processes.[11] For example, in the 'Becoming a PPC' document, the Gender Balance Task Force and Women Liberal Democrats are listed under 'Mentoring and Support' (as are the Liberal Democrat Disability Association, Ethnic Minority Liberal Democrats and Liberal Democrats for Lesbian, Gay, Bisexual and Transgender Equality); the 'flyer' for the rolling 'training programmes' includes images of women and BAME individuals; and the application form itself recognizes 'domestic' work as an occupation. The accompanying guidance notes spell this out more clearly: 'Think laterally about your achievements and the skills you use in your everyday life, especially if you have spent time at home with a family or have not followed a standard career pattern'. Training sessions are run at the Party's Annual and Spring conferences and a system of mentoring is in place. Assistance for the production of professional manifestos, a resource in which women are regarded as showing a deficit, advice on the hustings speech and tips on time management and meeting local members, is also provided. Selection Committees, once again, should be representative of sex and there are training requirements for Selection Committee members – in target seats all must be trained. A particular constituency must use 'the guidance and training provided by the party to ensure fair, equal and non-discriminatory treatment of applicants for the seat'.

The procedural cornerstone of Liberal Democrat efforts to increase the number of women selected lie in their Short-listing rules, which are 'sex neutral' in that they specify the minimum presence of aspirant candidates of both sexes: short-lists of three or four must have at least one applicant of each sex; shortlists of five must have at least two applicants of each sex. Where there are insufficient applicants to meet these rules, the Returning Officer 'allows the *direct* canvassing of approved candidates in a given area to alert them to the selection in question and invite their applications' (Clause 14.4, emphasis added). The local party will be asked to provide evidence of the efforts made to find other applicants if they wish to proceed without a standard shortlist (Clause 14.6).[12] Sensitive to the charge of selectorate discrimination, Clause 17.7 notes: 'any wide variation in the scores between panel members may be examined by the RO' [Returning Officer] although it does so '... on the understanding that this does not necessarily make them incorrect'. If a shortlist fails to produce a list that meets the required sex balance, the RO 'will identify the scores associated with the male and female applicants ... and the shortlist will be drawn up accordingly. Where necessary the list will be increased rather than decreased to conform to the gender balance, provided all applicants meet the minimum standards'. At the hustings meetings it is permitted that questions to aspirant candidates are different. However, the RO 'must make it clear to the meeting' that there are questions they will not permit, such as those that make reference to financial contributions and those 'which discriminate against groups of applicants such as women ... from a particular geographical areas ethnic communities or applicants with disabilities'.

Despite the Liberal Democrats' refutation of a lack of party demand, Clauses 14.4 and 14.6 show that an artificial demand, is, in particular circumstances, created by the Party. An acknowledgement that the 'the key driver that makes local parties go out there and be proactive' in encouraging women to apply are the sex Short-listing rules – 'it makes the local parties do the work' – suggests that some local parties lack a sufficient demand for women. Indeed, when this process has been implemented it has identified approved women candidates in the particular constituencies.

The conservative party

David Cameron made clear his intention to tackle the under-representation of women in the Conservative Parliamentary Party just two minutes into his Leadership acceptance speech in 2005. Despite three sets of reforms, the party continues to reject equality guarantees. Equality rhetoric is peppered throughout the Party Rules for Selection: 'What the party needs most of all is people who can command respect locally and win over voters who are not always Conservative supporters ... this is why Associations will be selecting from a wide range of applicants, which includes both men and women, with different personalities, backgrounds and experience; 'It is important that the [selection] Committee recognize their responsibility to provide a list of applicants ... which displays diversity'.

Mechanisms for equality promotion are evident in the briefing of local Constituency Executive Councils by representatives of the Candidates Committee; the advisory role played by the Candidates Committee in the initial CV sift; the production of a selection DVD (see Case Study 3.3); the use of primaries or the non-voting, but advisory role, of local representatives in the non-primary selection model; the use of independent moderators, such as journalists to interview candidates, and the replacement of the traditional 'speech' with a 'Question & Answer' session in the interview.

The strongest example of Conservative equality promotion measures – and the central plank of Cameron's reforms – has been the creation of a category of priority candidates – often referred to in common parlance as the 'A list'. Vacant Conservative-held and target seats would be 'expected' to select from amongst these. The list of priority candidates itself would comprise at least 50 per cent men and women with a 'significant' percentage from BAME and disabled communities. The new selection procedures came into place after the May 2006 local elections with a commitment to a three month progress review. If insufficient numbers of candidates from diverse backgrounds (most notably, more women) were selected, 'further action' would be taken.

It was clear at the time that the reformed procedures were unlikely to *significantly* increase the numbers of women selected (Campbell *et al.* 2006). Under the first set of rules 32 per cent of the newly selected candidates were women, and 9 per cent BAME. What was not foreseen, at least to the extent that subsequently became clear by the Summer of 2006, was the impact of a proviso relating to local candidates. Although the priority list was intended to be of 'sufficient size', 'breadth and talent' that it would only 'rarely' be necessary to add a particular individual for a 'specific selection', this was, nonetheless, permitted. It turned out, however, there were rather a lot of 'exceptional men'. This created, in effect, a list of 'local' male candidates perceived to be in direct competition with priority list candidates. In such cases, selection manifestly became a question of local party autonomy versus central party control. And in a context of party competition that makes much of local versus non-local candidates, this preference tapped into a rich seam of support for the idea that a local candidate is always, and inherently, better than a non-local one.[13] Neither was the strategy of primaries – which extends the selectorate beyond the local activist party members – as popular as had been envisaged. Local constituencies were fearful of the cost and reportedly unhappy about giving the power to select candidates to non-party members, and in open primaries, even to non-Conservative voters.

Although there was no public target set, the review's conclusion looked to be an admission that the reforms fell short. It is possible that the review was merely symbolic, in which case the percentage of women selected in the first tranche would be irrelevant. However, against such an interpretation, one senior party gender equality activist claimed that Cameron was trying to avoid 'picking a fight with the party' – something which they thought was a mistake. In August 2006 a second set of reforms were announced: (1) Constituencies Associations with fewer than 300 members are expected to hold a primary; (2) where Associations choose not to employ a primary model, Members will draw up a shortlist of three or four candidates from a list of 12–15. The shortlist would be sex balanced: two women and two men; the final decision would be made by the EC on the basis of in-depth interviews; and (3) if the EC shortlists an AWS, the existing model of selection could be retained. A third set of reforms were announced in January 2007. These permit Associations to choose from the full list of approved candidates, with a requirement that at each stage of the selection process at least 50 per cent of the candidates have to be women. Associations could still choose to select solely from the Priority list.

The collective impact of these reforms is, as yet, unclear. As Cameron was proud to admit, the new measures stop short of equality guarantees, or in his words, 'positive discrimination'. Many of the new procedures are limited and beg further questions: quotas at the Short-listing stage are limited to ensuring that local Associations consider more women candidates – it cannot guarantee that they will ultimately select them; reversing the role of Executive Committee and party members relies upon the assumption that the EC will be more likely to look fairly on women candidates – which cannot be assumed; neither is it clear how many *target* seats have constituency parties with fewer than 300 members. Only the newly emphasized possibility of an AWS – sweetened by local associations being allowed to keep to the existing role for party members in selection – directly addresses the lack of party demand. But there is little confidence amongst party gender equality activists that AWS will occur in more than a handful of seats, if at all. Moreover, the issue of candidate selection remains dogged by the charge of party centralization; the media saw the third set of reforms as a victory for the Party's grassroots.

The UK Parliament in comparison

The percentage of women Members of the House of Commons places the UK Parliament in 51st position in the global League Table. The world average is just 17 per cent and nowhere do women constitute half of all members of a national parliament – the National Assembly for Wales is not classified as a national parliament for the purposes of such comparisons. In ten countries women have no representation (www.ipu.org). As Table 3.5 shows, the Nordic region tops the

Table 3.5 Women in single or lower houses, by region

Region	Percentage
Nordic	40
European OSCE countries (excluding Nordic)	17
Sub-Saharan Africa	17
Asia	15
Pacific	11
Arab	8

Table 3.6 Women's numerical representation in National Parliaments: select cases by rank

Position	Country	% women
1	Rwanda	48.8
2	Sweden	43.0
3	Costa Rica	38.6
8	Cuba	36.0
8	Spain	36.0
9	Argentina	35.0
10	Mozambique	34.8
14	South Africa	32.8
24	Uganda	27.6
32	Australia	24.7
42=	Pakistan	21.3
42=	Portugal	21.3
45	Canada	20.8
51=	UK	19.7
51=	Dominican Republic	19.7
67	US	15.2
70	Sudan	14.7
84	France	12.2
96=	Russian Federation	9.8
102	Brazil	8.6
118	Jordan	5.5
131	Kuwait	1.5

Source: Inter-Parliamentary Union.

League Table, followed by the European OSEC[14] countries (excluding the Nordic countries), Sub-Saharan Africa and Asia, and the Pacific region, and finally the Arab region. Yet, with women constituting between 15 and 17 per cent of national parliamentarians, the European OSEC, Sub-Saharan African and Asian regions are pretty similar. A country-by-country comparison, as shown in Table 3.6, reveals that, whilst the 'top ten' includes a fair share of Nordic countries (Sweden 2nd, Norway 4th, Finland 5th, and Denmark 6th), it also includes two African countries (Rwanda, which tops the table and Mozambique in 10th place), three countries from Central and South America (Costa Rica 3rd, Cuba joint 8th, and Argentina 9th), and one from Southern Europe (Spain joint 8th). In sum, the top ranking countries for women's descriptive representation include a number of countries which have only recently made the transition to democracy, others that are 'developing' and yet still others which are arguably less than democratic.

Observations that countries with widely differing economic, social, cultural and political structures can have similar numbers of women representatives whilst countries with similar economic, social, cultural and political structures can have widely differing numbers of women representatives, strongly suggest that there is no single explanation for women's descriptive representation that holds for all times and places. There are a large number of hypotheses that purport to explain the variations in women's descriptive representation. These can be broken down into cultural, socio-economic and political factors, as Box 3.1 summarizes.[15] None, in themselves, have been found to be sufficient. For example, Pippa Norris found that electoral system effects are strongest in post-industrial societies and weakest in developing countries (Norris 2004), while the use of sex quotas in some countries in Africa, for example, in Rwanda, Mozambique and South Africa, help explain their position amongst the top ranked countries.

In terms of cultural factors, it is widely held that societies which are more egalitarian and secular, and where women have been able to vote for a long period of time, will see higher numbers of women elected to Parliament. In such countries, traditional gender roles should be less inhibiting and a cultural of political equality more established. Similarly, where women's participation in the public sphere is normalized, and where women's employment is relatively high in the professions from which legislators are recruited, the expectation is that greater numbers of women will acquire the necessary political resources to participate in politics. Where the state takes greater responsibility for the work of the private sphere – through the provision of childcare, for example – women's participation is likely to be enhanced yet further.

Political factors point to the role of the electoral system and political parties. In the case of the former, proportional representation is widely correlated with higher numbers of women representatives. This is especially the case where the number of seats in the district is high. Here, parties do not have to select a single candidate to represent them – they can choose both women and men; in multi-member constituencies, the absence of women also makes a ticket look 'unbalanced'. Where there are higher numbers of parties competing, women's participation is also greater – selecting women candidates may be a vote winning strategy. In contrast, in majoritarian systems the imperative is to select the 'safest' candidate, that is the candidate who is most likely to win votes in a two horse race. Despite little evidence of electorates' discriminating against women candidates, the tendency is to choose the candidate who looks like existing representatives. In single-member constituencies this choice is a zero sum game of either a male or a female candidate.

Research has also observed that parties with women in top leadership positions have higher levels of women representatives. The assumption here is that such women, at least when pre-disposed towards women's descriptive representation, can act as role models for, and act to, enhance women's selection and election. Left-wing parties, because of their greater emphasis on equality, are also associated with higher levels of women representatives. Where party selection is centralized, and where party leaders seek to increase the numbers of women, then the selection processes themselves can aid, sometimes by imposing, women's selection. Finally, where a party recognizes the electoral benefits of having significant levels of women's representation, then it is likely that they will have higher numbers of women representatives.

Box 3.1   Hypotheses for women's descriptive representation

Cultural factors:

1. The more egalitarian the culture, the higher the number of women elected to parliament
2. The higher the degree of secularization, the greater the number of women elected to parliament
3. The longer the time since women's enfranchisement, the higher the numbers of women elected to parliament

Socio-economic factors:

4. The greater the participation of women in the public sphere, the higher the numbers of women elected to parliament
5. The greater the participation of women in the professions from which politicians are recruited, the higher the number of women elected to parliament
6. The greater the role given to the state (i.e. where the state is social-democratic, rather than neo-liberal), the higher the number of women elected to parliament

Political factors:

7. The presence of proportional representation electoral systems increases, and the presence of majoritarian electoral systems decreases, the number of women elected to parliament. (This is because in majoritarian systems the dynamic is to select the 'safest' candidate, that is the candidate who is most likely to win votes in a two horse race; in single-member constituencies it is also a zero sum game of either a male or a female candidate).
8. The higher the district magnitude (number of seats), the higher the number of women elected to parliament. (This is because parties do not have to select between a woman or a man; and the absence of women makes a ticket look 'unbalanced').
9. The higher the party magnitude (number of parties competing in the electoral system), the higher the number of women elected to parliament. (This is because of party competition).
10. The use of positive discrimination increases, and its absence reduces, the number of women elected to parliament
11. The presence of women (pre-disposed towards women's numerical representation) in top decision making bodies within a party increases the number of women elected to parliament
12. The more left-wing a party, the greater the likelihood of the selection of women as parliamentary candidates

(and in party democracies):

13. The more centralized the party selection process, the greater the ability of party Leaders, when willing, to encourage the selection of women as parliamentary candidates
14. The higher the salience of the 'women's vote' to a particular party, the higher representation of women amongst that party's representatives

Quotas

The UK – through the use of equality guarantees by some parties at Westminster and in the devolved institutions – has joined the growing number of countries that favour the 'fast' rather than the 'incremental track' to women's descriptive representation (Dahlerup and Friedenvall 2003). On the incremental track, women's descriptive representation improves gradually in a linear fashion over time as a consequence of changes in women's social, economic and cultural position; attitudes and prejudice towards women decline whilst their resources are enhanced. In contrast, and impatient for change, the advocates of fast-track approach identify women's exclusion from politics as the 'problem' and supports the use of measures, such as sex quotas,[16] that deliver women's inclusion. This emphasis on equality of results or outcomes further distinguishes fast-trackers from incrementalists; it also acknowledges that gender inequality is not historic but may be reproduced in 'modern settings', as well as the possibility of a backlash against women, as their descriptive representation increases. Finally, the fast track's discourse of exclusion shifts responsibility for women's under-representation from women themselves to political institutions, most importantly political parties.

Some form of sex quota is employed in over 100 countries: they are used in long-established European democracies as well as in newly democratic, transitional and post-conflict countries, and in developed and developing nations, and are employed by parties of the left and right (Guadagnini 2005, Norris 2004). They are also used in proportional and majoritarian electoral systems, and in countries with high, medium and low levels of women's descriptive representation (Krook 2006; Matland 2006). There are different types of quota systems, as Box 3.2 details. Approximately 40 countries employ constitutional or election law quotas and in more than 50 countries party quotas are used (Dahlerup and Freidenvall 2005). Particular quota systems map loosely onto particular regions and types of state. Election law quotas are characteristic of Latin America; reserved seats are more evident in semi-democratic states, and in the Arab region, South Asia and in some African countries; whilst in the West the preference is for party quotas. This reflects, in part, particular political systems and traditions. Krook *et al.* (2005) identify a relationship between models of political citizenship and quota systems (although they recognize that particular political parties, because of their own ideological heritage, might favour alternative types of quotas). Liberal polities, because they are concerned about definitions of equality, prefer targets or 'soft quotas', although, in some cases, such as the British Labour party, party quotas are adopted; consociational and corporatist polities see quotas as a means to 'acknowledge and promote group-based identities and interests', and will employ party and, in some cases, legal quotas; republican polities, because of their concerns about the nature of political representation, favour legal quotas.

Quotas function at three different levels. The first level relates to aspirant candidates (the supply pool). The second level relates to candidates standing for

---

Box 3.2   Different quota systems

Quota type	Definition	Illustrative examples
Constitutional quota	Quota provisions that are mandated in the constitution of the country	Burkina Faso, Nepal, the Phillipines and Uganda
Election law quota	Quotas that are provided for in the national legislation or regulations of the country	Latin America, Belgium, Bosnia Herzegovina and Sudan
Political party quota	Rules or targets set by political parties to include a certain percentage of women as election candidates	Argentina, Bolivia, Ecuador, Germany, Norway, Italy, Sweden, South Africa, UK
Reserved seats	A percentage of seats are formally reserved for women[17]	Bangladesh, Botswana, Pakistan, Taiwan, and Tanzania

Source: http://www.quotaproject.org/system.cfm#constnational and Lovenduski 2005a.

---

election – the selected candidates; while the third level is the level of members of parliament (Dahlerup 2006, 19). Quotas that operate at the first level are severely limited because they only address the very first step of the recruitment ladder (Matland 2006, 280). Most quotas function at the second level.

More important than the type of quota system is the precise detail of the quota. It is not the case that the different types of quota system can be straightforwardly ranked in respect of their capacity to increase women's descriptive representation. To deliver quotas must be robustly designed, fully implemented and fit well with the electoral and political system in question. Implementation failures character-ized initial quota use in France, for example (Murray cited in Childs *et al.* 2005). In the UK the permissive rather than prescriptive legislative framework means that the decision to adopt quotas is devolved down to individual parties. As in other party quota systems, only some of the UK's political parties have chosen to adopt equality guarantees.

Conventional explanations for the diffusion of quotas across the world draw on four 'basic stories' (Krook 2005): (1) women mobilize for quotas; (2) political elites recognize strategic advantages in supporting quotas; (3) quotas are consis-tent with existing or emerging notions of equality and representation; and (4) quotas are supported by international norms and spread through transnational sharing. The latter occurs through direct involvement in quota debates, some-times, but not always, in cooperation with local women's movements; where demonstration effects spur quota campaigns via transnational information sharing across national and transnational women's movements; where international events act as catalysts to domestic debates already in progress; and where international actors are pivotal to the rejection of quotas, despite mobilization by local women's groups and transnational NGOs.

The discourses that surround sex quotas are 'surprisingly similar around the world' (Dahlerup 2006, 296) as Box 3.3 demonstrates. The adoption of AWS in the Labour party – described in Case Studies 2.1 and 5.5 – shows that, in terms of getting quotas adopted, it is likely that gender equality advocates will frame their arguments in strategic and pragmatic, read electoral, terms.

Advocacy of quotas for women begs the question of the level at which the quota should be set: 30 per cent has widespread global currency. This was the desired percentage established at the UN conference in Beijing in 1995 (Tinker 2004, 531). Normatively speaking, there are, however, no grounds for accepting anything less than parity – as the justice arguments outlined in Chapter 4 make clear. Moreover, the likeliest rationale for international acceptance of a 30 per cent sex quota relies upon a particular reading of the concept of critical mass, which is heavily criticized in Chapter 5 of this book (Childs and Krook 2006c). Of course, the motives of gender equality advocates demanding 30 per cent quotas are likely to be honourable: 30 per cent is a minimum and not a maximum requirement, and one that may be more practically achievable, at least in the short to medium term. Nonetheless, quotas set significantly below 50 per cent can have unintended consequences, not least in creating an artificial 'good enough representation' glass ceiling (Trimble and Arscott 2003). Here, women representatives in excess of the quota are regarded as unnecessary. Fortunately, there is an observable shift (Lovenduski 2005a; Daherlup 2006) in the discourse of women's descriptive representation, from talk of 'greater representation' towards 'parity' or 'gender balance'.

Conclusion

The poverty of women's descriptive representation at Westminster might, on first reflection, seem surprising. The UK is a long-standing democracy in which women have made economic and social gains in the public sphere. Yet, as the fast track approach suggests, significant advances in women's descriptive representation in politics is unlikely to happen in an evolutionary fashion in the foreseeable future. Women's greater political presence is more likely to be secured through specific measures for inclusion. The experiences at Westminster, as well as in the devolved institutions in Scotland and Wales, bear this out. The impressive (relatively speaking) improvements over the last three elections in Parliament – or more accurately in 1997 and 2005 – owe much to the Labour party's decision to adopt equality guarantees for both of these general elections. The asymmetric representation amongst the main political parties at Westminster reflects the Conservatives and Liberal Democrats' failure to accept demand side explanations for women's descriptive representation and/or the logic which leads ultimately to equality guarantees. Equality rhetoric and equality promotion may make some difference, but they are unlikely to deliver equal representation in the short, or even the medium, term. Only equality guarantees, properly designed and fully

Box 3.3   Discourses of quotas

Proponents

Women are half the population and should have the right to half the seats in a parliament (justice argument).

Women's experiences should be represented; women and men have different interests on some issues and therefore women need to be represented by women (substantive representation of women argument).

Women in parliament act as role models for women in politics and in the public sphere more widely (role model argument).

Discrimination and exclusion account for women's under-representation (fast-track argument).

Merit is 'smokescreen'; quotas are compensation for discrimination against women rather than women's deficiencies.

Quotas can prevent tokenism and 'queen bee syndrome' because they enable women to enter parliaments in large numbers.

Sex balance is important, or even necessary for, the process of democratization.

Quotas can open up electoral choices: sections of the electorate will for the first time be able to vote for women candidates.

Opponents

Traditional: Politics is male business[18]	Post Communist opposition	Liberal opposition	Feminist opposition
Women's involvement will have negative impacts on families; women are under-qualified; quota women will be stigmatized; women politicians' femininity will be questioned	Quota women are associated with western feminism and Soviet style 'forced emancipation'	Quotas violate the principle of equality of opportunity and competitive equality; critique of group-based representation; gender should not play role in politics (gender-blind discourse); women's under-representation reflects women and men's different priorities; quota women will become token women and met with a lack of respect; quotas undermine the principle of merit	Fear of tokenism, especially under certain forms of reserved seats; 'puppet parliamen-tarians'; may create glass ceiling; is a 'sticking plaster solution' that addresses the symptoms and not the root cause of women's under-numerical representation; the advocacy of quotas is underpinned not by principled reasons but by vote maximizing calculations

Source: Dahlerup 2006, 296–300 and Lovenduski 2005a; Kittilson 2005.

implemented, negate the negative impact of the various socio-economic, cultural and political factors that configure to limit women's descriptive representation in a particular country or institution. At fewer than 20 per cent of all Members of Parliament, women's presence at Westminster in 2005 falls far short of parity of representation.

It is too early to precisely evaluate the effectiveness of the various measures adopted by the three main political parties to enhance women's descriptive representation at Westminster for the forthcoming general election. The fourth Hansard Society *Women at the Top* Report (Childs *et al.* 2005) made a number of recommendations which constitute one set of criteria against which to judge both the government and the political parties' efforts, as Box 3.4 outlines. Recommendation 8 has been partially addressed: as Prime Minister, Gordon Brown has announced his intention to 'extend the period of time during which parties can use AWS'. Whilst this stops short of prescribing that all parties adopt equality guarantees it, nonetheless, extends the life of the legislation that permits parties to adopt them.

Whilst Labour's commitment to equality guarantees looks to have become an established feature of its parliamentary selections, the other two parties are yet to be persuaded. If either opposition party fails to significantly enhance the number of its women MPs at the next General Election, it is likely that the House of Commons overall will have fewer women present. If the Conservative party fails to make gains –selecting more women candidates but leaving them languishing in unwinnable seats – there is, however, likely to be a reassessment by Conservative gender equality advocates of their historic antipathy towards equality guarantees. Women like Fiona Hodgson, Chairman of the CWO, would be prepared to support equality guarantees, and many more across the party's professional, parliamentary and voluntary parts, will demand the full and proper implementation of the strongest possible equality promotion measures. What form the Liberal Democrats' response will take is less clear. Although their previous leader, Charles Kennedy, was a belated convert to the equality guarantee cause, neither his successor, nor Menzies Campbell, nor the group tasked with improving women's descriptive representation, the Campaign for Gender Balance, are persuaded. There is little evidence of a wider grass-roots campaign either. Those individuals in the party who favour equality guarantees appear not to have sufficient power in the party to deliver them.

Whilst the task of translating women aspirant candidates into selected candidates and then into elected members of the UK parliament points to the importance of creating demand in all of the political parties, there are, in addition, remaining questions about supply that gender and politics scholars should revisit. The normative claims for women's descriptive representation demand that different types of women and not a homogeneous group of women are present in politics. To get these different kinds of women into our Parliaments they will need to form part of the supply pool and there has to be a party demand for them. Recall that only two of the 118 women in the 2005 Parliament are BAME women and not one sits in either Scotland or Wales. And whilst race has a higher profile,

Box 3.4 *Women at the Top* **Recommendations**

1. Political parties should support the principle of equal political representation of women and men (equality rhetoric); they should encourage women from a diversity of socio-economic and ethnic backgrounds to seek political office;
2. Political parties should ensure selection processes are non-discriminatory; to this end they should employ equality promotion measures, for example, gender and Black, Asian and Minority Ethnic (BAME) sensitive training for party selection committees and party members;
3. Political parties should operate internal sex quotas for party positions which helps to deliver a larger pool of potential candidates for election;
4. Political parties should act to eliminate sexual harassment in their parties and set a good example in terms of sex-balanced staff appointments;
5. Political parties should act to ensure, not only the selection, but also the election, of equal numbers of women and men by selecting women for winnable contests;
6. Political parties should employ measures that *guarantee* parity of representation and recognize that, in the absence of these, there will be only limited and incremental change and that this is unacceptable;
7. Political parties should monitor their selection procedures using equality trained monitors and produce reports on the outcomes of their selection processes after each election;
8. The government should consider introducing prescriptive rather than permissive legislation; at the minimum, the Government should, along with the other political parties, actively support the extension by secondary legislation of the Sex Discrimination (Election Candidates) Act that permits the use of equality guarantees and which expires in 2015;
9. The Government should implement international protocols and treaties requiring equality of women's representation;
10. The Government should provide funding for political parties to institute, operate and monitor equality selection procedures;
11. The Government should fund research on equal representation;
12. Westminster should learn the lessons from Scotland and Wales and reform itself to be more family-friendly and take more seriously work-life balance as one factor that determines who seeks elected political office in the UK; and
13. Arguments of justice and fairness should be used in support of women's political representation; although women can make a difference and act for women, their political presence should not be dependent upon so doing.

Source: Childs *et al.* 2005.

issues of class, education, disability and sexuality are also relevant. If gender equality advocates are concerned about women's descriptive representation, they should also be concerned about the kinds of women who are our representatives. Long-standing supply side arguments are likely to provide part of the reason for their under-representation Accordingly, the differential distribution of resources – whether they are political, economic, social, racial, or attitudinal – amongst women in the 'supply' pool should be monitored and efforts put in to minimize their effects. Specific mechanisms to guarantee the selection and election of particular types of women candidates should also be considered.

Case Study 3.1

Women's descriptive representation in the Scottish Parliament and The National Assembly for Wales, 1999–2003[19]

Following the 2003 devolved elections women constituted half of the National Assembly for Wales and 42 per cent of the Scottish Parliament – a highly favourable comparison to Westminster. The most obvious candidate for explaining these differences in women's descriptive representation is proportional representation. Both Scotland and Wales use a mixed electoral system. However, closer analysis suggests that this is too simplistic: women's gains were made not in the PR seats but in the SMSP seats, as Tables 3.1.i and 3.2.ii show. And here, it was the use of equality guarantees, especially by the Labour Party, that made the difference. The use of equality guarantees, in turn, reflected women's activism in the devolution process (Mackay *et al.* 2003, 85). In Scotland, for example, this brought together a wide coalition of women's organizations over a period of ten years, who argued that 'new politics' could not be 'new' if Scotland's institutions merely reproduced male domination.

Table 3.1.i Members of the Scottish Parliament (MSPs), 2003

Party	Constituency women	Constituency men	Regional women	Regional men	% women
Labour	26	20	2	2	56
SNP	2	6	7	10	36
Conservative	0	2	4	13	19
L. Democrat	1	11	1	4	13
Other	1	1	6	9	40
Total	**30**	**40**	**20**	**38**	**42**

Table 3.1.ii Members of the National Assembly for Wales (AMs), 2003

Party	Constituency women	Constituency men	Regional women	Regional men	% Women
Labour	19	11	0	0	63
Plaid Cymru	1	4	5	2	50
L. Democrat	2	1	1	2	50
Conservative	0	1	2	8	18
Other	0	1	0	0	0
Total	**22**	**18**	**8**	**12**	**50**

By the time of the 2003 elections, the more systematic strategies used in Wales to increase women's representation outflanked the Scot's reliance on 'luck' (Mackay 2003). A commitment to sex parity and to equality guarantees had slipped down the political agenda in Scotland (Mackay 2004c, 156). In Wales, it became more entrenched: with Labour and Plaid Cymru employing equality guarantees inter-party competition created contagion effects.

Table 3.1.iii Equality guarantees at the 1999 and 2003 devolved elections

	1999	2003
Scotland	Labour: Twinning	
Wales	Labour: Twinning	Labour: AWS
	Plaid Cymru: Sex Quota for Regional Lists	Plaid Cymru: Sex Quota for Regional Lists

Labour

Labour's decision to 'twin' constituency seats in both Scotland and Wales in 1999 reflected the acknowledgement that it was most likely to win constituency rather than regional seats. In Wales, twinning was only agreed to on a 51.95 per cent vote (Russell et al. 2002, 57–9) whereas in Scotland it was widely supported by grassroots Scottish women and Labour women MPs. The Scottish Party Leadership also recognized the possibility for electoral advantage. Greater numbers of women would: signal modernization; distinguish the new institutions from (tarnished) Labour local government; help counter electoral competition from the SNP; and preempt the establishment of a women's party. At the second elections, Labour in Scotland relied on incumbency, although women were placed in first position in the two regions where it stood the greatest chance of being successful (Mackay 2004c, 151–2). In contrast,

Welsh Labour took advantage of the Sex Discrimination (Election Candidates) Act 2002 and used AWS in six constituency seats.

Scottish National Party

It was expected that the SNP would use zipping for the first devolved elections. The party had been supportive of the principle of a sex-balanced Scottish Parliament in the run up to the first election, and its electoral successes were likely to come in the regional lists. Yet, this did not happen. Instead, the party relied on leadership exhortation (equality rhetoric). In 1999, this proved successful – women were selected near the top of their regional list but in 2003 this strategy was less successful.

Plaid Cymru

Facing a Labour Party committed to twinning and under pressure from senior women, Plaid's Leadership was persuaded to implement a 'gender template' in the regional lists, where it was expected to be electorally successful: women were guaranteed first and third place on each of the five regional lists. In 2003, the party again placed women in the first two places on each regional list.

Liberal Democrats and Conservatives

The Conservative Party made 'no serious moves to adopt' equality guarantees for any of the devolved elections (Russell *et al.* 2002, 65). The Liberal Democrats used sex 'balanced shortlists' in Scotland in 1999, an example of equality promotion, but took no action in Wales in 1999. In 2003 it focused on enforcing its shortlisting rule. In Scotland in relied more on exhortation (Mackay 2004c, 152).

Source: Childs *et al.* (2005).

Case Study 3.2

'This is what you get when you don't listen': AWS at the 2005 General Election

Blaenau Gwent, a safe Labour seat with a 19,000 majority, was lost at the 2005 General Election on a swing of 49 per cent to the ex-Labour

Assembly Member, Peter Law. Law had stood on an explicit anti-AWS ticket. Critics of AWS were adamant that the policy had unravelled, as seven other AWS candidates were similarly beaten at the ballot box. The electoral facts are, though, very different. Blaenau Gwent was the exception rather than part of a wider pattern. Elsewhere AWS candidates suffered not from any anti-AWS effect but from being *new* candidates.

Once levels of Labour support are taken into account there is no evidence of sex effect when women non-AWS candidates and AWS candidates are compared against all male candidates (incumbents and new). However, Labour did slightly worse in constituencies where it selected AWS candidates. Both new non-AWS candidates (new candidates in vacant seats) and AWS candidates (new candidates selected by AWS) are compared against all Labour incumbent non-AWS candidates: new candidates performed worse than incumbent candidates. Importantly, there are no statistically significant differences between non-AWS candidates and AWS candidates.

These findings suggest that at the 2005 General Election there was no significant anti-AWS effect which proved detrimental to Labour; being a new candidate was a far more important factor and one masked by AWS. Of the seven lost AWS seats in 2005, taking account the exceptional circumstances in Blaenau Gwent, Labour losses occurred in the more vulnerable AWS seats, with only Hove and Stourbridge bucking the trend. Notably, six of the seven AWS losses were late retirement seats, with selected candidates having little time to 'work' their constituency.

These results should not, perhaps, have been surprising. The enormity of Law's swing always suggested that there was probably something more than a simple anti-AWS factor at work. Whilst it is possible that local party members might not choose to vote for Maggie Jones, tens of thousand of Labour voters would also need to be conscious of, and sufficiently troubled by, AWS to do the same. An equally plausible explanation is the perception of an imposition of a 'New Labour' and London-based candidate, alongside internal Welsh Assembly/Labour Party politics relations and the long standing popularity of Law. At the same time, the behaviour of the Blaenau Gwent constituency party suggests that they were trying to subvert the AWS policy. Because the sitting MP announced his intention to retire before December 2002, Law and his supporters 'thought they had had an assurance that an AWS would not be imposed'. Yet Labour Party rules state otherwise: if there were insufficient numbers of voluntary AWS in the seats where sitting MPs were retiring, Labour's National Executive Committee (NEC) would impose AWS to ensure at least 50 per cent of vacant seats had women candidates. In any case, Labour decided to delay the selection process in Wales, which led to Blaenau Gwent being included as one of the late retirement constituencies.

Source: Cutts *et al.* forthcoming.

Case Study 3.3

Equality rhetoric and promotion: the Conservative selection DVD

Change; Hope; Optimism; Making the Change;
Change to Win; Win for Britain.

These are the words that open the Conservative Party's selection DVD. 'Making the Change' is self-consciously Cameron's DVD: he both opens and closes it. Throughout, he is presented as the Party Leader who has 'turned the fortunes of the party' and who has the authority to reform: 'no one will stop us', he declares, 'if we have the courage and the bravery to fight for "modern compassionate conservatism" with every ounce and vigour and passion in our bodies'.

Other talking heads in the DVD look to have been chosen to refute any charge that the issue of candidate diversity is a partial or metropolitan concern. Not only are there women and men, they are younger and older, white and minority ethnic, traditionally and more contemporarily dressed, and some speak with regional accents. Similarly, local party activists sit alongside MPs in supporting Cameron's reforms. High profile gender equality activists are absent.

The nature of the Conservatives' electoral problem is presented as two-fold. Its 'image' is stopping those who support its policies from voting Conservative, and it has lost its historical advantage amongst women voters. In 2005 'the Conservative Party was the third choice party for women aged 18–34' and its share of 'professional women dropped five points'. The DVD's message is clear: electing a more descriptively representative group of Conservative candidates is the key to the party's electoral success. For too long, Conservative candidates have been unattractive to the '95 per cent of our voting supporters who are not [party] members': 'we have to look for candidates' with 'appeal much wider than our own supper clubs and social functions'. Cameron's reforms will ensure that selected candidates 'relate naturally to people' and 'talk in straightforward language about the issues that concern us all'. In the final frame, Cameron asserts: a 'better balance between men and women' is 'about responding to all the concerns that people have got in this country'.

That the reforms might appear 'radical, even a little startling' is acknowledged, but quickly, and quietly, refuted – others in the party find them 'refreshing'. The reforms are not, it is emphasized, about political correctness. 'None' of the new Conservative women MPs are 'keen' on that; they won their seats because 'they appealed beyond the traditional party member and activists'. Past selectorate discrimination against women candidates is implied: in 2005 women constituted 42 per cent of the party's 50 least winnable seats compared to 12 per cent in the 50 most winnable.

Meritocratic criticisms are directly contested. The new selection processes are 'open and transparent'. Every full member of the approved list could apply to become a priority candidate. Each applicant had 'to face a rigorous interview' and would be tested against the six 'key competencies', including, 'of course', conviction. Fears that the new reforms might lead to the selection of centrally approved rather than local candidates is addressed by Justine Greening MP. She admits that she 'didn't live' in Putney when first selected. But she '*became* a local candidate'. In making such a statement, Greening challenges party critics who depict priority list candidates as distinct from, and in competition with, local candidates. In sum, the Party can be 'perfectly relaxed about' which priority candidate is selected, because, as Cameron reminds local associations, the priority list identifies the 'best and the brightest'.

To further counter charges that the new selection procedures are a threat to intra-party democracy it is made clear that the reformers have been working in conjunction with the 'voluntary, party and professional sides of the party'. Cameron explicitly acknowledges the role played by local Associations: it is 'your decision who you select'. But he hopes 'we can have more women selected in winnable seats'. And he lavishes praise on his party: 'we've got brilliant MPs, we've got a great voluntary party and we've got a real army of supporters out there'; he closes the DVD with a plea to his party to: 'please help us to do it'. Elsewhere, though, the selection of parliamentary candidates is represented as a 'massive responsibility' – rather than a right – for local associations which must be taken 'very seriously'.

Notes

1 This figure includes Sylvia Heal, First Deputy Chairman of Ways and Means and Rachel Squire (Labour), who has since died.
2 Updated following the 2003 by-election.
3 This figure includes the late Patsy Calton.
4 This figure does not include the constituency of South Staffordshire, where the election was suspended due to the death of the male Liberal Democrat candidate.
5 This apparent contradiction can be explained in the following fashion: in a centralized party a leader seeking to increase women's representation may 'have the power to persuade local constituencies to implement standard policies to promote women' (Kittilson 2006, 127).
6 See Case Study 5.5
7 *Guardian*, 23 August 2006.
8 *Guardian*, 25 February 2005.
9 If there are fewer than three candidates and/or if there are too few women or men, then the Returning Officer consults with the regional Candidates' Chair as to whether the selection proceeds. In certain cases a shortlist of one is acceptable – the rules do not identify, but the implication is that this is most likely in unwinnable seats.
10 At the time of writing just ten Labour selections had occurred. Of these – and they were all in non-Labour-held seats where no existing MP had a geographical claim – three were AWS.
11 As a federal party, the following section relies upon the English Liberal Democrat's rules for the Selection of Parliamentary Candidates (excluding by-elections).
12 Prior to this stage local parties are only allowed to exhort in general terms, for example by stressing that they welcome applications from under-represented groups; individuals cannot be directly asked to apply.
13 As Philip Cowley suggests, such a claim begs all sorts of normative and empirical questions.
14 Organization for Security and Cooperation in Europe.
15 The following draws on Norris and Lovenduski 1995; Squires and Wickham-Jones 2001; Norris 2004; Kittlison 2006; Studlar and McAlister 2002; Childs *et al.* 2005; Inglehart and Norris 2003.
16 Despite the overwhelming tendency by gender and politics scholars, gender equality advocates, and political practitioners more generally, to use the term gender quotas (Krook 2006), the term sex quota is preferred in this instance. This is not pedantry. If feminists are right to insist that socially constructed differences between women and men are gender and not sex differences, and that gender exists along a continuum whilst sex is understood as an (largely) oppositional dualism (male-female) (Lovenduski 2005a), then it must be right to acknowledge that quotas aimed at securing the presence of biological females, rather than more femininely gendered women or men, are sex quotas and not gender quotas.
17 Dahlerup (2006, 20) contends that reserved seats should be regarded as quotas.
18 Women's representation remains a live issue in an era of post-communism and fundamentalism (Dahlerup 2006).
19 See Appendix E for women's descriptive representation in the Scottish Parliament and National Assembly for Wales following the 2007 elections.

Section II

Substantive and symbolic representation

4 Representation

Why women's presence matters

Introduction

Descriptive representation, the notion that political institutions should reflect the major social characteristics of society, historically had little purchase in British Politics. Geographic representation was prioritized: elected representatives 'represent' members of a specific spatial entity – whether that is a local election ward, the parliamentary constituency, or regions for devolved and European elections. Once elected, the representative would act as a trustee. On top of geographic representation – although arguably cross-cutting it – is the tradition of party representation. Since the late-nineteenth century political parties have been the dominant means through which political interests are aggregated. At an election, voters vote for a particular candidate because they are standing for the party the voter supports, or, at the minimum, because the candidate is best placed to defeat the voters' least preferred party (Phillips 1995). Once in the legislature, it is accepted that party cohesion is likely to influence representatives' behaviour.

Such accounts of political representation render the fact that Westminster is overwhelmingly populated by middle-class, middle-aged, white men unproblematic. Feminist political science, in contrast, calls attention to the *under* representation of women in politics. Accordingly, the lack of women's equal descriptive representation in parliaments is regarded neither as natural nor just. Feminist conceptions of representation further contend that women's descriptive representation matters over and above arguments of justice; for symbolic and, more contentiously, substantive reasons. Arguments on the basis of substantive representation hold that women's concerns and perspectives will be imperfectly considered in political institutions where women representatives are absent or under-represented.

The starting place for any serious discussion of women's political representation is the work of Hanna F. Pitkin, whose *The Concept of Representation* (1967) structures subsequent mainstream and feminist discussions. Too often, though, Pitkin's ideas are summarized in a paragraph or two – an approach that belies the comprehensiveness and sophistication of her theorizing. Here, her work is considered in greater detail and subject to the following question: what do her differing conceptions, and especially her preferred definition of representation as 'acting for', offer to discussions of women and politics? A discussion of Anne Phillips' *The Politics of Presence*, the key feminist text on representation, follows. This has underpinned much contemporary empirical research on women in politics – particularly in the UK, but also throughout the world. The different arguments advanced for women's political presence have not gone unchallenged, particularly in respect of substantive representation – the claim that women representatives are more likely, albeit not guaranteed, to 'act for' women. Reflecting on Phillips' argument and contemporary responses to it, the case is made for a conception of substantive representation that acknowledges the complicated rather than straightforward nature of the relationship between women's descriptive and substantive representation.

Hanna F. Pitkin, *the concept of representation*

Pitkin defines representation, drawing upon the word's etymological origins, as making present again. But, she acknowledges, 'except in its earliest [Roman] use ... this has always meant more than a literal bringing into presence, as one might bring a book into the room' (Pitkin 1967, 8). Representation means, then, 'the making present *in some sense* of something which is nevertheless *not* present literally or in fact' (Pitkin 1967, 8–9, emphasis in the original). Even this more expansive definition remains problematic. To state that 'something is simultaneously both present and not present' is paradoxical, as Pitkin admits, and begs additional questions, namely, in what sense can the 'something' be considered present when 'in fact it is not'? And, 'who is [doing the] considering'? (Pitkin 1967, 9).

Choosing to explore the concept of representation through looking at its ordinary usage – considering the family of words on the root 'represent', and its close synonyms – Pitkin develops a four-part typology of representation:

1   Formalistic representation
2   'Standing for': descriptive representation
3   'Standing for': symbolic representation
4   Representing as 'acting for'

Formalistic representation

Formalistic representation refers to the formal bestowing of authority (the right) onto a person to act for others. In this conception the represented (those for whom the representative is acting) become responsible for the consequences of the representatives' actions, as if they had done them themselves (Pitkin 1967, 38–9, 42–3). Pitkin, however, finds the authorization definition inadequate because it assumes that 'as long as he has been authorised *anything* that a man does is representing' (Pitkin 1967, 39, emphasis added). In a similar fashion, she rejects 'accountability theories' of formalistic representation, where the representative is 'someone who is to be held to account ... for what he does' (Pitkin 1967, 55). Once again, there is no guarantee that the representative will act *for* the represented; that they might be removed from office at the end of their term cannot guarantee the quality of representation as it occurs.

'*Standing for*': descriptive representation

Descriptive representation refers to a notion of correspondence between a representative's characteristics and the represented: the representative 'stands for' them, by virtue of a correspondence or connection between them (Pitkin 1967, 61). This conception is particularly troubling for Pitkin. First, she considers the apparent transparency of descriptive representation misleading. Representative art is 'never a replica', neither is a map absolutely accurate – some depict 'land', others 'topography' or 'economic trade regions'; mirrors reflect 'only visual features' (Pitkin 1967, 66–72). In a similar vein, Pitkin asks the question, whom should our political fora represent – 'the one who is typical and average in every conceivable respect, including intelligence, public spiritedness, and experience'? (Pitkin 1967, 76) The characteristics that warrant representation are not always self-evident and constant either (Pitkin 1967, 87). Second, Pitkin questions the link between characteristics and actions and concludes that there is 'no simple correlation' (Pitkin 1967, 89). Third, a man can 'only be held to account for what he has done' and 'not for what he is'. This means that neither representation as 'acting for', nor representation as accountability, is possible within descriptive representation (Pitkin 1967, 90). Finally, Pitkin worries that descriptive representation 'almost inevitably' means that there is a concentration on the composition of our political institutions (who is present), rather than its activities (what they do) (Pitkin 1967, 226).

'*Standing for*': symbolic representation

Symbols represent something or someone because they 'stand for' and 'evoke' their referent – the flag representing the nation, for example. But symbols are, in Pitkin's view, often arbitrary, with no obvious connection to what is being symbolised (Pitkin 1967, 97). This means that the only criterion of what constitutes a symbol is 'peoples' attitudes and beliefs' (Pitkin 1967, 100). Thus, in politics, the criterion of symbolic representation is whether the representative is believed in. This, however, renders the basis for symbolic representation 'emotional, affective, irrational psychological responses' (cited in Squires 1995, 16). Once again, there is no room in symbolic representation for representation as 'acting for' the represented. With no rational criteria for judging it, Pitkin thus finds this conception wanting; it is open to manipulation as the representative can simply make the represented *feel* represented.

Representing as '*acting for*'

In everyday language, representatives are said to act 'on behalf of others', 'in their place' and 'in their interest' (Pitkin 1969, 17). Moreover, Pitkin asks us to acknowledge both that people behave differently when they are acting on behalf of someone else and that we have expectations of how a person will act if they are acting on our behalf (Pitkin 1967, 118). Distinguishing between mandate (under explicit instruction) and independence (acting in the best interests of the represented) theories of representation, Pitkin considers the proper relationship as one in which the represented is 'logically prior' – the representative must be 'responsive to' the represented 'rather than the other way around' (Pitkin 1967, 140). This implies that 'normally' the wishes of the represented and the action of the representative will converge, but that when conflict occurs the representative should provide an explanation for their actions (Pitkin 1967, 163–5).

A feminist reading of Pitkin

'Acting for' representation is, for Pitkin, the true meaning of representation: the representative system must look after the public interest and be responsive to public opinion, except insofar as non-responsiveness can be justified in terms of the public interest (Pitkin 1967, 224). However, her confidence that this is the true and only definition of representation has not gone unchallenged, even in the mainstream literature (Birch 1971; Judge 1999). And with sex and gender added into the mix, the limitations of Pitkin's conceptualizations become clear.

Formalistic representation

Pitkin's rejection of formalistic theories of representation as an adequate notion of representation stands the test of time. In both its authorization and accountability forms it fails to permit an evaluation of the activity of representation – the relationship between the represented and the representative – as it occurs. For this reason, formalistic representation has little to offer discussions of women's political representation. Whilst it might be the case that particular representatives (men or women) claim that they *will* act, or *have* acted, in particular ways in respect of women's concerns, in party democracies it is difficult to hold representatives to account for one particular issue amongst all the others they are associated with (Voet 1992, 397). To be sure, a representative's position on, for example, abortion (either pro- or anti-) might 'trump' other policy positions, enabling voters who feel strongly about abortion to give or deny them their vote on that basis. But what if the represented have to choose between apparently contradictory policy positions on women's concerns, for example a representative who is both pro-state funded childcare provision and against the minimum wage (which, in practice, disproportionately benefits women). For whom should they vote?

There is, though, one redeeming feature of formalistic representation: it reveals the identity of our representatives – here the sex of our representatives. In this way it supports the important activity of counting and recording the numbers of women in our political institutions (Trimble and Arscott 2003). Even if this is limited in what it can tell us about why women are numerically under-represented, or why their numbers increase or decline in particular places and at particular times, it is important for feminist political scientists and activists that the numbers of women elected to parliaments around the world are documented and monitored.

Representing as 'acting for'

Representation as 'acting for' – Pitkin's preferred conception – looks to resolve feminist concern with the relationship between women's descriptive and substantive representation. For the representative relationship to be operating, representatives must be responsive to women. If they are not – irrespective of whether they are male or female – then they are failing in their (acting for) representation. However, there is little agreement as to what Pitkin's notion of the representative being 'logically prior', and responsive to, the represented actually means in practice (Pitkin 1967, 140; Birch 1971, 15–16; Rao 1998, 29, 31). Moreover, with party representation cross-cutting 'acting for' representation it is likely that individual representatives' desire to act for women will be circumscribed. So, this conception seems unable to account for the actions of a representative who, forced by party discipline, votes neither in the apparent interests of the represented, nor with their own judgement, but with their party (Judge 1999, 71; Birch 1971, 97). It might be argued, of course, that the represented should have been aware of their representative's party identity when they voted for them and should not feel aggrieved at their actions (Pennock 1968, 24). In any case, women can, subsequently, and like all electors, act to try and vote out any representative who has not acted for them. Nevertheless, something remains unsatisfactory in these contentions.

'Standing for': symbolic representation

If symbols can be arbitrary it should not matter if our political representatives are disproportionately male, for they can still symbolically represent women. Yet, the form a symbol takes may be more important than Pitkin allows. Could the British Union Jack be transformed into one constituted of pink and green butterflies, as it was by the British fashion designer Paul Smith in his 2004 collection, and still represent the UK? Similarly, can a political institution constituted of men really symbolically represent women in their absence? Note further that, according to Pitkin, the criterion of symbolic representativeness is *feeling* represented, and that she was highly critical of this (Squires 1996, 86). A conclusion that women are symbolically represented when they believe they are, even if all the representatives are men, is surely as unconvincing now as the general principle was for Pitkin in the late 1960s.

'Standing for': descriptive representation

Although descriptive representation has become highly fashionable (Phillips 1991, 63) Pitkin's criticism continues to resonate. The case against is pretty straightforward. It might be unfortunate that the bodies in our parliaments are overwhelmingly male. But this does not really matter: with universal suffrage, individuals choose to vote for representatives that best represent their views – views which are neither determined by, nor contained in, particular sexed bodies. And even if one accepts the principle that our political institutions should reflect our societies, critics ask (just like Pitkin) how is it possible to determine which characteristics should be represented? (Judge 1999, 45) The case for descriptive representation on the basis of sex might hold, but what about other, more questionable (at least in the critics' view) characteristics? (Phillips 1991; Voet 1992) Designing electoral mechanisms to deliver descriptive representativeness is also said to be problematic (Judge 1999, 45). Sex quotas may be workable but, again, critics assert, what about other mechanisms for other characteristics? (Duerst-Lahti and Verstegen 1995, 221; Phillips 1995). Are all-black shortlists possible *in practice*?

Pitkin's conclusion that an over-emphasis upon the composition of political bodies prevents a proper focus upon the activity of representation also remains a strong criticism of descriptive representation. However, a careful reading of *The Concept of Representation* shows that Pitkin herself chose to downplay the idea that elected bodies are determined to some (unsubstantiated) degree by those who constitute them, even while she was aware that advocates of descriptive representation are concerned about ensuring descriptive representation 'precisely because they expect the composition [of a political forum] to determine the activities' (Pitkin 1967, 63, cited in Judge 1999, 22). Indeed, concepts of descriptive representation played a part in the extension of the franchise to previously excluded categories of people – which begs the question of why it was thought necessary to extend the franchise to the working classes and women if rich white men were representing them in the first place (Birch 1993, 72; Voet 1992).

A distinction between two forms of descriptive representation, the microcosmic and the selective is helpful here (Mansbridge 1999). The concern that microcosmic representation, 'achievable only by lottery or another form of representative selection', might throw up 'legislators with less ability, expertise' and 'possibly commitment to the public good' than those selected through election is acknowledged. However, selective descriptive representatives 'need not be significantly less skilled' than other representatives because they are as likely to have 'chosen politics as a calling', been selected through competitive mechanisms and have demonstrated the necessary skills (whatever they may be) for politics (Mansbridge 1999, 631). Furthermore, to argue that the presence of women will be deleterious for our politics is on very weak ground: sex is *not* a determinate of ability (Darcy *et al.* 1994). Thus, even if the argument holds (and it may not) that small farmers are better represented by politicians than small farmers, it does not hold for women. In short, women selected to fulfil particular legislative quotas need not be the less able or expert women that Pitkin or other critics of descriptive representation fear.

Even so, and again following Pitkin, advocates of women's presence must contend with the criticism that women's descriptive representation is in fact illusory (Voet 1992, 392); women who become representatives will be, by definition, different from those they represent – at the minimum by dint of their being representatives, but also because they are likely to be more educated, more middle-class and members of the dominant ethnic group (not least because women who are less qualified or atypical are less likely to be selected as candidates and elected as representatives) (Parry *et al.* 1992). This argument is not specific to women's representation, though. All representatives are, on these terms, distinct from those they represent. In any case, this should cause us to investigate the diversity of our women representatives and put in place measures to ensure that women's heterogeneity is represented in our political institutions – a call for more and not less descriptive representation.

The most damning critique of descriptive representation remains, however, Pitkin's conclusion that there is no simple correlation between representatives' characteristics and action. If women representatives cannot be trusted or made to act in a way that is responsible and responsive to women (Rao 1998, 25) – remember there is no room in descriptive representation for representing as 'acting for', nor means of holding representatives to account (Voet 1992, 393) – there will have to be other grounds on which to argue for women's political presence, ones that are not linked to substantive representation.

Anne Phillips, the politics of presence

The argument for women's political presence is one example of a wider claim for a politics of presence made by other disadvantaged groups. The normative case is argued on four grounds. First, in terms of symbolic representation; second, it is premised upon the need to tackle exclusions that derive from party representation; third, on the basis that disadvantaged groups need more aggressive advocates; and finally, presence is said to be needed to ensure a transformation of the political agenda.

In symbolic terms, the presence of the formerly excluded demonstrates that they are the equals of those who were previously included because, contra traditional understandings of symbolic representation, particular bodies need to be physically present to symbolize their equality. Their inclusion is also likely to have the effect of enhancing the legitimacy of political institutions as more people identify with, by seeing themselves in, particular political spaces. The second argument for a politics of presence looks to the limitations of party representation. Here, the represented must choose between limited numbers of parties. Inevitably, certain issues will be left out of the parties' agendas (packages). In addition, a particular party's position on one policy area, for example privatization, may well be a poor indicator of another, say, sexual or racial equality (Phillips 1995, 41–2). At the same time, and even where party cohesion is strong, representatives still have some room to act independently of their party identify. For this reason (and to ensure that women's and other groups' concerns are strongly articulated), it matters who our representatives are. The third argument – disadvantaged groups' need for aggressive advocates – is not a claim that no one ever acts on behalf of others, but rather, as Phillips makes clear, that the presence of the previously excluded may be necessary to ensure the assertive articulation of their concerns. The fourth argument for the politics of presence refers to the idea of a broadening of the political agenda and builds on the previous case. The politics of transformation focuses upon the realm of preferences not yet formulated, articulated or legitimated on the political agenda and therefore unable to be part of the packages of political ideas (Phillips 1995, 44). In such circumstances it is important that representatives with different perspectives and concerns are present.

The case for women's political presence is made on four related bases. First, principles of justice. Now rarely contested, women's absence from our political institutions is increasingly regarded as prima facie evidence of injustice (Phillips 1995, 65). Second is the role model effect. The presence of women representatives (just like women in any other hitherto male-dominated occupation) should engender women's greater descriptive representation as women see representatives who look like them 'doing politics'; some may even gain direct experience working for women representatives (Clark 1994, 100). Third is the realist argument that women's interests are discounted in the absence of women's political presence;[1] and fourth, is a claim that women have a different relationship to politics, one in which women will introduce a different set of values and concerns.[2] These latter arguments are two sides of the same coin – suggesting a relationship between descriptive and substantive representation, although they also cover the argument that suggests that women prefer a more consensual rather than confrontational style of politics.

The claim that women should be present in politics because of a relationship between descriptive and substantive representation is the most contested argument for women's political presence. This might be a useful, if not necessary, argument to employ in order to secure women's enhanced participation in electoral politics, as it has the power to mobilize women to seek selection. However, the argument that women should be present in politics because, once there, they will act for women, especially when crudely portrayed, seems to be both reductive (reducing women representatives' attitudes and behaviour back to their bodies) and essentialist (presuming that women are a category who share a set of essential attributes) (Mackay 2001a; Young 1990).

In *The Politics of Presence*, Phillips turns away from such a strong interpretation and advocates, as an alternative, 'gender parity'.[3] She rightly does this because there is no 'empirical or theoretical plausibility' to the idea that women share experiences or that women's shared experiences translate into shared beliefs or goals. Neither does Phillips consider it likely that women will organize themselves into a group with group opinions and goals that can be represented (Phillips 1995, 53–5). Women, in short, are too diverse. At the same time, Phillips maintains that women do have concerns that derive from their gendered experiences and that these will be inadequately addressed in political forums dominated by men. Consequently, her argument claims that women should be present in politics because they are more likely to act for women but, crucially, this is not a guarantee that they will.

Contemporary feminist debates

Arguments for women's presence, even when premised on gender rather than sex, as in Phillips' case, still need to contend with a number of complicating counter-points. The first derives from the theoretical and practical problems thrown up by feminist understandings of women's differences. If women have multiple identities and experience the world in different ways, the basis upon which women can act for other women seems by necessity either to succumb to essentialism or be underpinned by a denial of women's differences. The second derives from post-modernism. When the universal subject has been declared dead, the very possibility of representing women is questioned (Baker 2005). The third questions the basis upon which women substantively represent women in practice (and is addressed in the next chapter).

Laurel Weldon (2002, 1156) renders the difficulties associated with reconciling substantive representation and women's differences easily explicable in the following fashion:

> If she is a white, straight, middle class mother, she cannot speak for African American women, or poor women, or lesbian women on the basis of her own experience, any more than men can speak for women merely on the basis of theirs ...'

Accepting that women are heterogeneous rather than homogenous means that one cannot contend that a group perspective 'resides completely in any individual from that group' – it is the product of the interaction between women – a 'collective phenomenon' (Weldon 2002). Moreover, if one contends that women's differences reflect not just differences between women, but a hierarchy of differences with dominant and minority sub-groups, it makes even less sense to argue that an individual woman can know the interests of, and act for, other women on the basis of her own experience. In short, Weldon is arguing that women's perspectives are created when women interact with other women 'to define their priorities'. Thus, only when women participate in group activities will they acquire 'deeper knowledge of the issues and concerns that members share with others of their group' and be able to legitimately speak for the group (Weldon 2002, 1157). Even then – when women come to share a group perspective – this does not mean that there will be an agreed set of women's policy positions or recommendations; 'group perspective' refers to is an 'agenda of topics for discussion or list of problem areas' (ibid).

Accordingly, women may, indeed are likely to be, divided over women's concerns. Take the example of childcare: those seeking care for their children might prefer lower wages whilst those women providing the care would prefer higher wages and better working conditions. In providing this example, Weldon recognises that both groups of women 'confront the issue of the relationship between motherhood and work'. In this they share in, if not create, childcare as a women's concern that can, and needs to be, represented. Furthermore, and despite arguing that women's perspectives come from women interacting with one another, Weldon admits that an individual woman representative can 'articulate a truncated version of the group perspective' 'without interacting' with other women '*if* she is so inclined' (Weldon 2002, 1158, emphasis added). Although this 'truncated version' is clearly inadequate, her statement, nonetheless, implies that there is some kind of (albeit it imperfect) relationship between a woman's identity and her actions; between women's descriptive and substantive representation. Otherwise, how can one explain why some women representatives are '*so* inclined' to act for women?

For these reasons, Weldon's position is, arguably, not so distant from other feminists who maintain that the substantive representation of women remains possible, even if it cannot be guaranteed. First, it makes intuitive sense that women constitute a social group. Looking outside, there appear to be 'women' who are distinct from 'men', despite their recognizable differences in terms, at the very least, of social class, race, ethnicity and sexuality.[4] Second, propositions that there really are no women's interests *per se* confound those who seek to count and measure women's interests as politically articulable and salient (Trimble 2004, 9). Furthermore, as Cynthia Cockburn (1996, 17) notes, it is important that differences between women are not 'read as delegitimating' the claim for women's political presence based on women's gendered differences from men. It is also somewhat ironic that women's 'representational claims are declared inauthentic' (Vickers 1997, 41–2) precisely at the moment when women are increasingly recognized and accepted as 'subjects' and therefore able to demand political presence.

The work of Jane Mansbridge, the late Iris Marion Young and Suzanne Dovi are particularly instructive in furthering our understanding of women's political representation, and particularly, substantive, representation. In her 1999 article, 'Should Blacks Represent Blacks and Women Represent Women'? Jane Mansbridge argues that, 'yes', women should represent women (and Blacks, Blacks). Crucially, though, her 'yes' is contingent – descriptive representation is 'not always necessary'. There are four contexts in which disadvantaged groups may seek to, and 'constitutional designers' should, 'institute policies to promote selective descriptive representation'. These are in the contexts of:

1   Mistrust between disadvantaged and advantaged groups;
2   Uncrystallized, not fully articulated, interests;
3   Where the social meaning of 'ability to rule' has been seriously questioned for members of disadvantaged groups; and
4   Past discrimination against disadvantaged groups

Of the four functions of representation that Mansbridge identifies – communication; innovative thinking; the creation of a social meaning of 'ability to rule'; increasing the polity's de facto legitimacy – only the first two engender substantive representation. The third and fourth provide non-substantive, albeit significant goods. In the former case, this confers political equality on all citizens by ending the distinction between those who are and are not present in our political institutions (between those considered able and unable to rule).[5] Importantly, this function is less a question of whether a particular individual 'feels' included, or identifies with descriptive role models, than a question of how the psychology of the advantaged group is transformed. In respect of de facto legitimacy, the presence of descriptive representatives causes the previously excluded to feel included – 'as if they were present in the deliberations' (Mansbridge 1999, 650) – not least because of the enhanced communication and the articulation of their concerns that follows.

Mansbridge's understanding of the communicative dimension of the relationship between descriptive and substantive representation reflects an acknowledgement of both the deliberative and aggregative functions of democracy. Whilst aggregation does not require descriptive representation, deliberation is enhanced by it:

> Although a representative need not have shared personally the experiences of the represented to facilitate communication and bring subtlety to a deliberation, the open-ended quality of deliberation gives informational and communicative advantages to representatives who are existentially close to the issues (Mansbridge 1999, 635–6).

Furthermore, where interests are uncrystallized and/or new to the political agenda, 'the best way to have one's most important substantive interests represented' lies with descriptive representatives: as issues arise the descriptive representative is more likely than the non-descriptive representative to 'react more or less the way' the represented would have were they present (Mansbridge 1999, 644). Drawing on experiences garnered from constituents and speaking 'with a voice carrying the authority of experience', descriptive representatives also engage in horizontal communication with other representatives. Empirical examples include: a black woman member of the US Senate who acted in respect of the confederate flag (though there are no comments on the role of gender here); and women members of the US House of Representatives in the case of Anita Hill versus Judge Clarence Thomas (where a charge of sexual harassment was levelled at Thomas).

Sensitive to charges of essentialism and of 'balkanization', Mansbridge presents three questions by which to identify those groups that warrant descriptive representation:

1 What are the features of the existing electoral process that have resulted in lower proportions of certain descriptive groups in the legislature rather than in the population?
2 Do members of that group consider themselves able adequately to represent themselves?
3 Is there any evidence that dominant groups in the society have ever intentionally made it difficult or illegal for members of that group to represent themselves?

If the answer to the first question suggests discrimination and the suppression of interests, and answers to the second and third questions are positive, then the group 'appears to be a good candidate for affirmative selective representation' (Mansbridge 1999, 639). The proportional representation of descriptive representatives, although in theory unnecessary for deliberation, is highly desirable. Greater numbers and a greater diversity of representatives from a particular group are more likely to produce more and better information and insights as a consequence of synergistic deliberation; they may be necessary to constitute a 'critical mass' (defined here as a situation where they are 'willing to enunciate minority positions') and are able to 'convince the dominant group' of the 'widely-shared, genuinely felt and deeply-held' views; to ensure that there are sufficient representatives to be present in all the deliberative spaces within a particular political institution; and to reflect the internal diversity of the group (for example, differences of opinion, including those caused by intersectionality). According to this schema the case for women's descriptive representation is well-made on the basis of 'past historical' processes. Yet, because of Mansbridge's (1999, 639) commitment to avoid basing the claim on women's essential nature, once 'systemic barriers' to women's participation 'are eliminated' the need for 'affirmative steps to insure [sic] descriptive representation will disappear'.

The relationship between women's descriptive and substantive representation is understood then, in a similar fashion to Phillips, as based on gender (women's shared experiences) rather than sex (visible characteristics). In recognition of the reality of women's heterogeneity, it must be said that not all women will have shared the same particular experiences. Nonetheless, women representatives share 'the outward signs of having lived through' the same experiences. This gives them 'communicative and informational advantages' and enables women representatives to 'forge bonds of trust' with the women they represent (Mansbridge 1999, 641) – creating vertical communication between women representatives and the represented women.

The concept of 'surrogate representation', highlighted by Mansbridge, further illustrates a dimension of women's substantive representation. Surrogate representation refers to the substantive representation of individuals by descriptive representatives with whom the represented have no formal electoral relationship, although in the UK convention prevents this form of relationship happening at the individual-MP level. Furthermore, surrogate representation risks reduced vertical communication between descriptive representatives and the represented. This is likely to be caused by an assumption on behalf of the represented that their descriptive representatives will act for the represented by dint of their shared characteristic. Such an assumption of 'blind loyalty' can be, according to Mansbridge, minimized by comparison between descriptive representatives, although how this might function in practice, especially in party democracies and in electoral systems with single member constituency systems of election, remains unclear.

To counter critics of group representation – not least the assumption that social groups share a set of common interests (what affects or is important to the life prospects of individuals) and opinions (principles, values and priorities) – Iris Marion Young argues in favour of the concept of 'social perspective' when she makes the case for women's political inclusion. Social perspective 'consists in a set of questions, kinds of experience and assumptions with which reasoning begins'; 'two people may share a social perspective and still experience their positionality differently ... however, [it] gives each an affinity'. One's social perspective derives from group members being 'similarly positioned' and 'attuned to particular kinds of social meanings' and causes members to have affinity with one another (Young 2002, 123, 136–7). This does not rule out the possibility that someone not from a particular social group can represent another's social perspective, but it is unlikely and would require 'more work'. In a similar fashion to Mansbridge, Young illustrates women's social perspective through the example of US women Senators and Members of the House of Representatives coming together to demand an enquiry into allegations of sexual harassment. Although the women legislators agreed that the issue should be addressed, this did not mean that their views on sexual harassment per se, and/or the guilt or innocence of the Senator in question, were shared.

Recognition of intra-group differences leads Young I. M (2002, 123) to conclude that that 'no single representative could speak for any group'. Thus, representation is conceptualized as a 'differentiated relationship among political actors engaged in a process extending over space and time' (ibid). Here, the representative 'speaks for' the represented even though they cannot 'speak as' they would (Young I. M 2002, 127). The key to good representation lies, then, in the quality of connection between representatives and represented, by which she means the extensiveness and continuity of communication over and above the formal moments of election and re-election.

Such qualifications and contingencies that run through much of the feminist literature on substantive representation are addressed head on by Suzanne Dovi (2002) when she asks, 'will just any woman do?' She answers in the negative: substantive representation requires the presence not of *any* women representatives but the presence of 'preferable descriptive representatives'. Preferable descriptive representatives experience a sense of belonging to, have strong mutual relationships with, and share aims with other women – they want to see women's 'social, economic and political status' improved – and experience a 'reciprocated sense of having [their] ... fate linked' with women (Dovi 2002, 736–7). They also recognize differences between women and acknowledge that women may have 'different conceptions of what is necessary' to achieve women's aims. Women representatives who do not share 'policy preferences' or 'values' with women cannot be said to share their aims (Dovi 2002, 737–8). Like representatives generally, women representatives should sometimes act as trustees and at other times act as delegates.

Preferable descriptive representatives should also possess 'strong mutual relationships with dispossessed subgroups of historically disadvantaged groups' (Dovi 2002, 729); be judged by whom they know and interact with. The reasoning behind articulating a criterion to judge between descriptive representatives is straightforward: some descriptive representatives 'fail to further, and can even undermine, the best interest' of those they represent (Dovi 2002, 742).[6] Not recognizing this possibility risks entrenching certain group interests – Dovi writes of privileging heterosexual Latinos at the expense of gay and lesbian Latinos. A more explicit illustration is the African–American representative 'who grew up in a primarily white neighbourhood, attended primarily white private schools, has a white spouse, *and has shown no demonstrable interest in the problems of other African Americans'* (Dovi 2002, 737, emphasis added). In such a scenario, whether the descriptive representative satisfies the normative reasons for political presence advanced by theorists like Phillips (1995) is questioned. In particular, the representative lacks the relationships that could enable them to 'achieve mutual recognition' with the represented; the likelihood that she would voice their concerns and mobilize the community is reduced, and were she to disavow her relationship to them – as Dovi suggests she might, not least for electoral reasons – the trust African–Americans place in her is likely to be limited. For these reasons, it is important to look at what descriptive representatives do as well as who they are.

Conclusion

Feminist theorists have spent considerable time and effort reconsidering the concept of representation over the last decade or so. The limitations of mainstream conceptions of representation are clear: classic typologies are gender blind. In particular, Pitkin's preference for representation as 'acting for' belies an appreciation that liberal democracy has, thus far, proved resistant to any substantial representation of women (Phillips 1991). Such insights would have been unimaginable without a feminist reworking of the concept of representation.

That political institutions should better reflect our society, at least in terms of sex, has become more widely accepted. Indeed, such demands are being made around the world. The case for measures that would guarantee women's political presence, remain, however, more contested. In terms of both feminist theory and empirical analysis, it is the acclaimed link between women's descriptive and substantive representation that has garnered the lion's share of attention. This is not to say that the symbolic dimension of women's representation is unimportant nor that it should be treated as unrelated to women's descriptive and substantive representation.

An appreciation of the theoretical challenges thrown up by contemporary understandings of identity, as well as an acknowledgement of women's differences, reminds us that sex cannot be the basis upon which substantive representation is premised. Employing gender, as Phillips and Mansbridge do, or women's social perspective, as Young does, to underpin the relationship between women's descriptive and substantive representation is more theoretically defensible. An appreciation of women's differences implies that the relationship between women's descriptive and substantive representation will be less predictable – electing more women to our political institutions may not automatically deliver

Dovi's preferable women representatives. It is quite possible that our Parliaments will be filled with women representatives who choose either not to identify with women, or even if they do, may not interpret this identification in feminist terms. Should this trouble us? Most gender and politics scholars are likely to be seeking the *feminist* substantive representation of women – that is, gender and politics scholars' 'preferable descriptive representatives' will be feminist women acting in feminist ways; but other women's 'preferable descriptive representatives' may well not be. Add into the mix analysis of the wider political contexts within which women representatives act 'on the ground', and the idea that simply ensuring women's presence will engender women's substantive representation of women becomes untenable; the relationship between women's descriptive and substantive representation is far more complicated than that.

Notes

1 On the concept of interests, see Sapiro (1998), Diamond and Hartsock (1998) and Jonasdottir (1990).
2 In her later work, Phillips reframes the fourth point and refers to a revitalization of democracy that bridges the gap between representation and participation (Phillips 1998b).
3 As in the case of sex versus gender quotas, the term sex parity rather than gender parity would be more accurate here.
4 This is not to say that these map automatically or completely on to sexed bodies.
5 The claim for presence should be based on the concept of reparations rather than disadvantage, not least because the latter creates the impression that the previously excluded are in some way ill-suited/equipped for governing (Mansbridge 1999, 650).
6 Dovi (2002, 733) acknowledges that this risks questioning the 'authenticity' of some descriptive representatives' identities.

5 The substantive representation of women

Sarah Childs and Mona Lena Krook

Introduction

Many contemporary gender and politics scholars accept that there are theoretically coherent and defensible grounds for maintaining that, whilst undoubtedly a complicated one, some kind of relationship exists between women's descriptive and substantive representation. The conceptual framework that has been commonly employed to hypothesize this relationship in practice is critical mass. Borrowed from physics, the term is usually understood to hold that, once women constitute a particular proportion of a parliament, 'political behaviour, institutions, and public policy' will be transformed (Studlar and MacAllister 2002, 234). As an argument for women's descriptive representation, the concept has held great sway amongst feminist activists and gender and politics scholars over the last two decades or so. Recently, however, critical mass has come under sustained criticism.[1] 'Critical mass theory' – the uncritical usage of the concept – posits a straightforward and simplistic relationship between women's descriptive and substantive representation, one that is dependent upon a particular proportion of women being present in a political institution. Yet, empirical studies, in the UK and elsewhere, reveal multiple relationships between the proportions of women present in political institutions and the substantive representation of women; something which critical mass theory struggles to explain.

The profound reconsideration of the relationship between women's descriptive and substantive representation – what the substantive representation of women means – has brought different, and hitherto rather distinct, literatures together: mainstream political conceptions of representation, feminist literature on representation as well as state feminism[2] and feminist comparative policy[3] (Celis *et al.* 2007). Accordingly, contemporary gender and politics research increasingly acknowledges the multiple, rather than single, sites and actors involved in women's substantive representation. This suggests that our conceptual framework needs to shift away from a focus on *when* women representatives 'make a difference' – the precise percentage of women representatives necessary for political institutions to experience change – to the study of *how* the substantive representation of women occurs. A second shift, necessitated by the first, addresses issues of method – how gender and politics scholars might best capture, empirically, women's substantive representation.

Kanter and Dahlerup

The limitations of 'critical mass theory' lie, at least in part, in the failure to adequately reflect the totality of the contributions of Rosabeth Moss Kanter (1977a/b) and Drude Dahlerup (1988). A close reading of the former reveals not a *single* claim about the impact of the proportion of women, as much of the gender and politics literature suggests, but *three claims*; whilst Dahlerup, who popularized the term critical mass in the study of gender and politics, advances the concept of critical acts, which is all too often lost in secondary accounts of her work.

Kanter's work examines women's token status in a large American corporation in the 1970s. She observes that the 'relative numbers of socially and culturally different people in a group' – differences which derive from 'salient master statuses' like sex, race, and ethnicity are 'critical in shaping interaction dynamics' in group life (Kanter 1977a, 965–6). Kanter constructs a typology consisting of four distinct majority–minority distributions:

1. Uniform groups with one significant social type at a ratio of 100:0;
2. Skewed groups with a large preponderance of one social type, at a ratio of perhaps 85:15;
3. Tilted groups with a less extreme distribution of social types, at a ratio of perhaps 65:35; and
4. Balanced groups with a more or less even distribution of social types, at a ratio of 60:40 to 50:50.

Based on her study of a skewed group, Kanter argues that the numerically many, or 'dominants', 'control the group and its culture', while the numerically few, or 'tokens', are reduced to symbolic representatives of their social category. Tokens are subject to greater visibility within the group, leading dominants to stress intra-group differences in ways that compel token women to conform while also suffering stereotypes in line with these perceived differences. These tendencies in turn generate three particular challenges for token individuals: performance pressures, which require them to overachieve or limit their visibility; token isolation, which forces them to remain an outsider or become an insider by being a 'woman-prejudiced-against women'; and role entrapment, which obliges them to choose between alternative female stereotypes like the 'mother', the 'seductress', the 'pet' or the 'iron maiden'. As a consequence of these dynamics, token women – even if there are two together – find it difficult to 'generate an alliance that can become powerful in the group' (Kanter 1977a, 966). Thus, in the absence of greater numbers capable of creating a 'counterculture', token women are left with 'little choice about accepting the culture of dominants' (Kanter 1977b, 231).

Tokenism in this manner is self-perpetuating: rather than paving the way for others, it reinforces low numbers of women.

Reflecting on how inter-group dynamics might change in the transition from a skewed to a tilted group, Kanter makes three claims regarding women's behaviour:

1. With an increase in relative numbers, minority members are potentially allies, can form coalitions, and can affect the culture of the group;
2. With an increase in relative numbers, minority members begin to become individuals differentiated from each other;
3. Despite a lack of change in relative numbers, the presence of feminist or 'women-identified-women' can reduce performance pressures, token isolation and role entrapment if the particular women involved form coalitions.

The first of Kanter's claims is the one widely interpreted as *the* definition of critical mass (that upon which 'critical mass theory' is premised): as the proportions of women increase their ability to effect change is consequently increased. Yet, her second claim, which stresses the possibility of differences between women, warns against a presumption that greater proportions of women will necessarily translate into collective action – different kinds of women may have alternate and/or competing goals. Moreover, Kanter's third claim suggests that a concern with numbers may, in fact, matter less than the presence of 'women-identified-women'. Thus, even when women are few in number, 'feminist' women can effect change: token performance pressures, isolation, and role entrapment are reduced and, just like in balanced groups, personal and structural factors become key to group dynamics (Kanter 1977a, 966).

Despite the importance of acknowledging all three of Kanter's claims, limitations remain in applying her analysis to the study of women's substantive representation. First, her study examines women's token status in a large American corporation. Consequently, her research does not actually speak to the question of whether or not women political representatives will seek to 'act for' (substantively represent) women, but focuses on whether women in a big corporation are able to fulfill their roles as employees (Bratton 2005). Secondly, Kanter is unclear about the precise 'tipping points' between skewed, tilted and balanced groups. Do the dynamics between dominants and tokens change continuously as their relative proportions change – so the performance pressures are less for tokens in groups of 80:20 than they are at 85:15, or do they change only at the particular 'tipping points', when, for example, the ratio is 65:35? These questions are not unimportant: the level of women's descriptive representation in many of the world's parliaments places them in Kanter's skewed and tilted groups.

Kanter's analysis also underplays the role of gender. In particular, and although she recognizes that it is women's sex, and associated gender roles, that differentiate women and men within society, she maintains that women's tokenism reflects their 'rarity and scarcity, rather than femaleness per se' (Kanter 1977b, 207): relative numbers 'can account for any two kinds of people regardless of the category from which the token comes' (Kanter 1977a, 972). At the same time, she relies upon gendered analysis to make sense of her observations: her description of the dynamics of tokenism stems from an appreciation of how women's gender 'master status' is displayed and reproduced on and through women's bodies, especially where she points out how sexual innuendos serve to exclude and demean female tokens (Kanter 1977a, 968). Moreover, and despite her acknowledgement that some men are more likely to be hostile towards, and others merely confused by, women's presence – she notes several men who are 'openly angry' and simply do not know how to interact with a woman who is not their wife or their secretary because they went to 'all-male technical schools' (Kanter 1977b, 42). These reactions cannot be understood without a prior theory of patriarchal gender relations. In glossing over them, Kanter underplays the potential for backlash against women in occupations 'normatively defined as men's work' (Yoder, 1991).

If Kanter's analysis is the starting place for the use of the concept of critical mass by gender and politics scholars – even though she did not herself employ the term – it is the work of Dahlerup (1988) which did much to popularize it. Dahlerup contends explicitly that 'politics is not physics'. Rather, factors beyond numbers, especially those that are impossible to isolate or control, like broader shifts in societal attitudes, might go further in explaining both change, and lack of change, following the advent of greater numbers of women in politics. Six areas are identified where women representatives might have an impact: (1) changes in the reactions to women politicians, with a decline in sexist treatment and sexual harassment; (2) changes in the performance and efficiency of female politicians, with fewer women leaving politics; (3) changes in the social climate of political life, with the arrival of a more consensual style and family-friendly working arrangements; (4) changes in political discourse, with a redefinition of 'political' concerns; (5) changes in the policy-making agenda, with a feminization of the political agenda; and (6) increases in the influence and power of women in general, with the broader social and economic empowerment of women. However, her empirical study of Scandinavian politics, where women at the time constituted some 30 per cent of representatives, leads her to conclude that only in respect of changes in the social climate does it seem relevant to talk about a kind of 'automatic' change.

Consequently, Dahlerup (1988, 296) puts forward the concept of 'critical acts' – initiatives that 'change the position of the minority and lead to further changes'. Examples include the recruitment of other women, the introduction of sex quotas, new equality legislation and equality institutions. Crucially, critical acts depend on '*the willingness and ability of the minority to mobilize the resources of the organization or institution* to improve the situation for themselves and the whole minority group' (ibid, emphasis in the original). Further, these acts precede but do not necessarily lead to, nor are they dependent upon, critical mass. In this respect, Dahlerup's notion of critical acts implicitly revives Kanter's third claim, namely that feminist women can have an impact above and beyond their token status if they form alliances with one another, and despite small numbers.

In many ways, Dahlerup's contribution represents a significant improvement on Kanter's. In particular, she adopts an explicitly gendered analysis that emphasizes how women's minority position in society relates to their minority group status in politics. Thus, particular performance pressures experienced by women – what she describes as over-accommodation, sexual harassment, lack of legitimate authority, stereotyping, lack of consideration for family obligations and exposure to the double standard – are revealed as the *combined* consequences of women's status in a patriarchal society and their minority position in politics. Men would not therefore experience these pressures even if they were in a similar minority (Dahlerup 1988, 279). Furthermore, and as importantly, Dahlerup makes a distinction between the performance pressures on women politicians *as politicians* – to be 'just like' and 'just as able' as men – and the pressure on them to prove that it *makes a difference* when more women are elected.

Nevertheless, Dahlerup's analysis unintentionally provides subsequent gender and politics scholars with an account of Kanter that allows for a misrepresentation of the latter's work and a range of interpretations about whether – and in what ways – numbers matter. Take for example the following assertion:

> In the *tilted group* ('with ratios of perhaps 65:35', Kanter writes, from her figure, however, from 15 to about 40), the minority is becoming strong enough to influence the culture of the group, and alliances between minority group members become a possibility (Dahlerup 1988, 280).

Here Dahlerup transforms the 'critical mass' debate in two ways that have important implications for subsequent research. First, by focusing exclusively on the opportunity for women to form supportive alliances when there is an increased number of women, she overlooks both the possibility that women as a group will grow more diverse as their numbers grow (Kanter's second claim), and the chance for women to have an impact even when they constitute only a very small minority of all political representatives (Kanter's third claim). Second, Dahlerup inserts a new definition of tilted groups as those where the proportion of women ranges between 15 and 40 per cent, meaning that they occupy all the space between Kanter's skewed (85:15) and balanced groups (60:40). Note that elsewhere in her article, Dahlerup defers to the common usage of the term 'critical mass' and identifies 30 per cent as the crucial cut-off point, even though a strict reading of Kanter would categorize such a group as skewed, rather than tilted or balanced.

Finally, Dahlerup's argument easily fosters a range of distinct interpretations about whether – and in what ways – numbers matter. When she discusses changes in the reaction to female politicians, for example, she writes that 'the presence of women politicians in great numbers does make it seem rather hopeless to try to remove women from the public sphere today. So numbers do count'. Dahlerup (1988, 285) elaborates by explaining that 'following the growing number of women in politics, stereotyping decreases, because so many different types of women now occupy the political arena'. She then adds, however, that 'it is not possible to conclude that these changes follow from any fixed number of women, such as 30 per cent.' Rather, 'the example of just a few successful women in top positions ... may have contributed substantially to the change in the perception of women as politicians'. This leads Dahlerup (1988, 287) to conclude that 'in such cases it is not numbers that count, but the performance of a few outstanding women as role models'.

Mapping the substantive representation of women

As argued above, the relationship between women's descriptive and substantive representation is, in practice, more complicated than critical mass theory would suggest. As Box 5.1 outlines, a number of assumptions about the dynamics of women's substantive representation, as well as alternative findings, can be discerned from empirical studies.

Box 5.1   Mapping the substantive representation of women

1. **Anticipated effects of increased proportions of women**
   - Women will form strategic coalitions with other women
   - Women will influence men's behaviour in a feminist or women-friendly policy direction
   - Women will provoke a backlash among male legislators
   - Women will be less effective than at smaller proportions of female legislators
   - Women will become increasingly more diverse as a group, leading some to lobby on behalf of women and others to pursue other policy interests
2. **Constraining and enabling characteristics of legislative contexts**
   - Institutional norms, especially in legislative practices
   - Positional power, especially in legislative committees
   - Political parties, especially in terms of party ideology
   - Political climate, especially in terms of its relation to women's empowerment
   - Legislative arenas, especially in terms of varying distributions of women and men in distinct legislative spaces
3. **Identities and interests of female and male legislators**
   - Similarities and differences among women, especially race, age, party affiliation, and feminist identity
   - Similarities and differences between women and men, especially alternative conceptions of 'similarity' and 'difference' as the measure of women's impact
4. **Feminist and non-feminist definitions of women's issues**
   - Feminist definitions focused on role change for women, often through increases in autonomy and scope for personal choice
   - Non-feminist definitions focused on women's traditional roles in family and society
   - Context- and time-bound features of these definitions
5. **Stable and contingent features of policy-making processes**
   - Stages in the policy-making process
   - Legislative policy cycles and demonstration effects
   - Impact within and outside the policy-making process

Anticipated effects of increased proportions of women in political office

Although the most common assumption in the gender and politics literature is that, as women grow more numerous in parliaments, they will increasingly be able to form strategic coalitions with one another in order to promote legislation related to women's concerns (Thomas 1994), existing research presents at least four other scenarios: (1) a rise in the number of women may influence men's behaviour in a feminist direction, causing both male and female legislators to pay more attention to women's issues (Bratton 2005; Flammang 1985); (2) the increased presence of women may provoke a backlash among male legislators, who may employ a range of tactics to obstruct women's policy initiatives and keep them outside positions of power (Hawkesworth 2003; Heath *et al.* 2005); (3) a lower proportion of women may be more effective than a higher number because women legislators may be able to specialize in women's concerns without appearing to undermine male domination (Crowley 2004; Dodson and Carroll 1991); and (4) a rise in the overall number of women may result in the election of an increasingly more diverse group, who may or may not be interested in pursuing women's issues, either because their priorities lie elsewhere or because they believe that other women legislators will continue to lobby on behalf of women (Carroll 2001; Schwindt-Bayer 2004).

Constraining and enabling characteristics of legislative contexts

Here the literature is critical of the assumption that numbers are all that matters in the substantive representation of women and identifies a multiplicity of factors that influence representatives' opportunities to act for women. Much of this research focuses on institutional rules and norms that reflect a bias towards men's experiences and authority (Hawkesworth 2003; Kathlene 1995), and as such, compel women to conform to existing masculinized legislative practices in ways that undermine their ability to advance women's concerns and effect policy change (Carroll 2001). Representatives' impact, both individually and collectively, are likely to be influenced by their relative positions within the institution as well as its wider norms and practices (Trimble and Arscott 2003). The impact of party affiliation and ideology on women's legislative activities is also noted. For example, candidate selection processes, combined with pressures for party discipline, determine what kinds of women are selected and elected, as well as the specific policy positions that they are likely to take once present (Gotell and Brodie 1991). Where party cohesion is high and single party government the norm (such as in the UK Parliament), representatives may be more constrained; at the same time membership of the ruling party is likely to be more conducive to changing policy than membership of a marginal oppositional party. Similarly, being a member of the government, rather than an ordinary representative (backbencher), might enhance an individual's opportunity to voice their concerns and influence decision-making, although frontbenchers may well find themselves constrained by norms or conventions such as collective responsibility which limit their actions. Membership of a particular parliament's key institutional positions, such as being chair of an important committee or chair of a cross-party group, might also provide extra opportunities to act for women (Dodson 2001). Other researchers (Chaney 2006) draw attention to institutional norms, the presence of women's caucuses and women's policy machineries (Thomas 1994; Weldon 2002), and some party ideologies that offer greater opportunities for the substantive representation of women (Reingold 2000; Swers 2002).

Identities and interests of female and male legislators

While some feminists, especially in the past, sought to discern or define a shared perspective among women as a group, most empirical researchers stress divisions among women – like race, class, age, and party affiliation – that prevent the formulation of a collective agenda (Dodson and Carroll 1991; Swers 2002). Others (such as Carroll 2001), argue that identity categories like 'women' are inherently exclusionary and serve to reify one difference while erasing and obscuring others, or contend that 'gender' is not a pre-political and fixed identity that women bring with them when they enter politics, but one that is partially produced and reproduced within the context of particular legislatures (Towns 2003; Whip 1991). The danger of eliding women's bodies with feminist minds is also remarked upon (Childs 2004); being female may matter less than 'gender consciousness' for achieving feminist substantive representation (Reingold 2000).

Feminist and non-feminist definitions of women's issues

Researchers have adopted various definitions of women's issues. These include policies that increase the autonomy and well-being of women (Bratton 2005; Wángnerud 2000); concerns that belong to the private sphere, as traditionally understood (Meyer 2003); areas where surveys discover a gender gap in the population (Schwindt-Bayer 2004); and any issues of concern to the broader society (Dolan and Ford 1995). Some prefer feminist definitions that focus on role change for women through increases in autonomy and the scope for personal choice (Dodson and Carroll 1991; Reingold 2000), while others opt for more inclusive ones that capture a broader range of issues affecting women's everyday lives (Swers 2002). Yet others favour definitions based on the concerns articulated by women's movements at various moments in time. This allows for women's issues to remain a priori undefined, context-related, and subject to evolution (Celis 2004). Women's issues have also been defined as the collective product that emerges as women interact with other women to identify their priorities (Weldon 2002).

Stable and contingent features of policy-making processes

The possibility to achieve substantive gains for women depends closely on the policy making process, which influences how and when women's concerns are put on the table (feminizing the agenda) and are passed into law (feminization of legislation). There is evidence that women as a group have the greatest impact – or, more specifically, tend to differ most in their behaviour from men – in terms of setting the parliamentary agenda and proposing bills that address issues of concern to women (Swers 2004). For this reason, gender and politics scholars (Tamerius 1995) often criticize studies that focus exclusively on legislative voting, and argue that it is better to examine the entire legislative process rather than privileging the 'end point' (Carroll 2001; Swers 2002). Others point out that policy-making often involves numerous elements of contingency: complex combinations of actors – often in series of chance events – are responsible for moving an issue onto the agenda and into legislation (Childs and Withey 2006). At the same time, policy cycles and demonstration effects strongly condition which issues enter and are kept off legislative agendas (Bratton and Ray 2002).

From 'when women make a difference' to 'how the substantive representation of women occurs'

Moving beyond existing studies and conceptualizations of women's substantive representation, we posit two new means for rethinking women's substantive representation. First, a reformulation of the central research question from *when* women make a difference to *how* the substantive representation of women occurs, and second, a refocusing of the investigation from the macro-level (i.e. what do 'women' do?) to the micro-level (i.e. what do specific actors do?).

Central to this approach, is the concept of critical actors – a concept which resonates with much in the original formulations of both Kanter and Dahlerup, who, as already noted, point to diversity among women and the importance of individuals who resolve to act on behalf of women as a group. Critical actors are those who put in motion individual and collective campaigns for women-friendly policy change: they initiate policy proposals on their own, even when women form a small minority; and embolden others to take steps to promote policies for women, regardless of the proportion of female representatives. Importantly, critical actors may not even be women. Their common feature is their relatively low threshold for action: although they may hold attitudes similar to those of other actors, they are much more motivated than others to initiate the substantive representation of women. Even so, whilst they may operate alone, they may stimulate others to act, setting in motion a momentum for policy change. Alternatively, they may provoke a backlash. As such, their effects are neither guaranteed nor unidimensional: smaller numbers may join together to promote common goals with great success, while larger numbers may enhance the opportunity for critical acts but may also engender resistance.

This new approach – shifting to analyzing how the substantive representation of women occurs – begs further questions (Celis *et al.* 2007): The first is, '*who* acts for women?' namely, who are the critical actors and with whom do they act? The second is, '*where* does the substantive representation of women occur?' The third is, '*why* is the substantive representation of women attempted?' And the fourth question is, '*how* is the substantive representation of women expressed?' This refers to the importance of exploring interventions at various points in political processes to identify the claims made in support of women's substantive representation, the actions taken to promote the substantive representation of women, as well as the outcomes of these attempts.

Addressing these additional questions allows us to ask '*what is* the substantive representation of women?' They also throw into relief the tendency, hitherto dominant, in gender and politics research to focus primarily on the analysis of the behaviour of women representatives within political institutions. In this way, the new approach resonates with state feminism and feminist comparative policy research that talk in terms of 'feminist advocacy coalitions' (Mazur 2002) and 'strategic alliances' (Waylen 2004). Such alliances often appear to be key to the feminist substantive representation of women (Mazur 2002, 177), even if sympathetic non-feminist allies in key decision-making positions are sometimes necessary.

Concerns about the research methods and techniques that are employed to investigate women's substantive representation underpin the second of the two shifts. When the question of women's substantive representation is framed in terms of 'critical mass theory' empirical research often focuses upon demonstrating that 'women make a difference' for women. In practical terms this usually translates into the search for *sex differences* in representatives' attitudes and behaviour. In short, the following is to be demonstrated (Lovenduski 1997 and 1990; Bochel and Briggs 2000): (1) there are distinctive women's perspectives and issues; (2) that women representatives share these perspectives and issue positions; (3) women representatives act decisively on the basis of such differences; (4) have a feminist commitment; (5) have different motivations; and (6) have a different political style.

Attempts to prove these assumptions have, until recently mostly relied upon surveys and interviews to establish representatives' opinions (answering questions 1, 2, 3 and 4, respectively). Too often, though, there has been a tendency to interview only women politicians (Childs 2004). Attitudinal data, based on self-reported claims, is also limited in that it does not permit close examination of their actual veracity (Lovenduski and Norris 2003); attitudes are no guarantee of behaviour. More recently, in part because circumstances now allow the application of such techniques in the UK – there are simply greater numbers of women to study – but also because of mainstream political science's preference for quantitative methods (Mackay 2004a), studies of political behaviour have been undertaken. These answer question 3, above. Moreover, skeptics who do not believe representatives' self-reported claims can be persuaded when hard behavioural data and quantitative analysis is presented. Some behavioural data – for example, about how MPs vote – is easy to collect, particularly since the advent of electronic records posted on parliamentary websites (Cowley 2002). But this type of data can itself be limited as a test for women's substantive representation. As argued above, analyzing how representatives vote in parliament suffers from a focus on the end point of legislation, where women may be less free to act in accord with their attitudes, particularly in institutions characterized by party cohesion and other constraining institutional norms. Analyzing other parliamentary behaviour, where the constraints are less determining, is often harder. There are particular difficulties gathering behavioural data in respect of activity that occurs 'behind the scenes', where representatives' actions and effects are neither observable nor measurable. While it may be possible in some instances to employ surrogate measures, these can only be suggestive.

Even with a range of research methods to choose between, the question of what constitutes proof of the substantive representation of women remains. Are sex differences in representatives' behaviour all that counts? (Lovenduski and Norris 2003) While many would agree that observable and measurable sex differences in representatives' behaviour (with women being more concerned with, and acting on, women's concerns) would demonstrate that the presence of women engenders women's substantive representation, their absence does not necessarily prove the opposite (Reingold 2000). A lack of sex differences in representatives' behaviour may be caused by a number of factors: it may reflect a convergence in gender roles that are hidden because studies employ sex as a proxy for gender (Swers 2002, 10): maybe men and women's attitudes and behaviour have converged as a result of changes in gender roles over time. Alternatively, it may reflect the institutional norms that reduce the spaces in which women can act for women (Lovenduski and Norris 2003, 90). The very presence of women in politics may cause men to become more aware of and active on with women's concerns, leaving no observable or measurable sex differences in their attitudes or behaviour (Reingold 2000, 50). Here, women are having a feminized effect but not one that is visible. An absence of sex differences may also be an effect of the choice of research method adopted: for example, quantitative methods testing for sex differences reveal similar behaviour at one level (for example, in how women and men vote in legislatures) but might hide differences at another level (in women's and men's levels of support for, or feelings towards, that act (Tremblay 1998)). A careful reading of particular studies should identify how individual researchers have conceived of women's interests, concerns and perspectives, whether they have imposed a definition of substantive representation (and according to what definition), and the type of research techniques employed.

To avoid essentializing women and their interests, concerns and perspectives, it is best to leave the concept of women's substantive representation as an 'empty' category. It is precisely because feminization refers to the 'integration of women, both in terms of numbers and ideas' (Lovenduski 2005a, 12), that what constitutes women's substantive representation must become part of – be discovered during – the research process rather than assumed a priori (Celis 2005). The acts and processes involved in the substantive representation of women will be illuminated during the research. Here, it is useful to emphasize once again the distinction between a feminization of the political agenda (where women's concerns and perspectives are articulated) and the feminization of legislation or policy (where output has been transformed). Operationalizing women's substantive representation in this dual way should capture the articulation of women's concerns and perspectives, even if this has little or no effect in terms of legislative output. Finally, contemporary empirical research should more explicitly acknowledge the recent institutional turn in feminist political science (Mackay 2004a, 111): empirical research must explore what is involved in 'real political institutions' – the procedures and culture in which decision-making takes place and of the everyday activities and behaviour (Lovenduski 2005a, 13, 149), not least to identify the ways in which institutionally sexist institutions can resist feminized change.

In order to better capture, empirically, how the substantive representation of women occurs (acknowledging, of course, the multiple sites and actors of women's substantive representation) future research should, at least in the first instance, engage in post-hoc analyses, process-tracing, and then comparison, to uncover the identity and actions roles of 'critical actors' (Celis *et al.* 2007; Mackay 2004a). Process tracing allows the researcher to 'follow the unfolding of a particular set of policy decisions over time', identifying the actors and events that explain the particular outcome (Mazur 2002, 33). Such studies are likely to reveal to a much greater extent than before the contextual environments in which representatives act and the wider features of particular policy-making processes. This is unlikely to be discovered by large scale quantitative studies. Subsequent comparison should then provide more generalizable insights to help better theorize the role of critical actors in the substantive representation of women.

The substantive representation of women in britain: a 'substantial amount of circumstantial evidence'

The inclusion of a substantial number of Case Studies in this chapter had two main aims. The first is to present in a single place a summary of published research on women's substantive representation at Westminster and in the Scottish Parliament and National Assembly for Wales. Many of these Case Studies were designed using different research methods – some of which have been qualified in the preceding discussion of how best to research women's substantive representation. For example, studies of single parliamentary sessions or parliaments, in particular, cannot tell us whether patterns of behaviour are similar to, or different from, those that preceded or come after it. Nonetheless, taken together these Case Studies provide the best snapshot of women's substantive representation to-date. Second, the Case Studies illustrate something of the complexity of the relationship between women's descriptive and substantive representation. Indeed, lessons learnt from the empirical research upon which the Case Studies are based, informed the conceptual analysis that gave rise to the critique of critical mass theory and the shift to critical actors advocated here. In simple terms, it began to seem as if the likelihood of women representatives acting for women was dependent upon such a range of factors, and that the focus on the behaviour of women representatives was too narrow to capture the multiple actors and multiple sites where women's substantive representation might be occurring.

The first, and arguably most important, finding in a number of the Case Studies is that of behavioural sex differences between women and men. To be sure, the 'search for sex differences' as *the* test for women's substantive representation has been, and should be, questioned. Even so, it has been strategically very important for feminist political scientists to be able to demonstrate behavioural as well as attitudinal differences between women and men (as evident in the pioneering British Candidate Studies (BCS) and British Representation Studies (BRS) (Norris and Lovenduski 1995;). In this respect, the Early Day Motions (5.1), Parliamentary Questions (5.2), National Assembly for Wales Plenary Debates (5.3), Parliamentary Hours (5.4) and Sex Discrimination (EC) Act (5.5) Case Studies demonstrate, especially to those who are suspicious of claims that the sex of our representatives matters for substantive reasons, that women representatives have *in practice* acted for women. Moreover, the distinction between feminist and women's substantive representation is also evident in these Case Studies: not only do women representatives voice women's concerns, their understanding and interventions are often in a feminist direction. This is not to claim, of course, that this will always be true; rather that, in these reported cases, many of the women's actions are in a feminist rather than neutral or anti-feminist direction.

The importance of representatives' party identity is also evident in many of the Case Studies: inter-party differences remind us that any straightforward assumption that the sex of the representative is all that matters in determining representatives' behaviour is highly questionable. The findings in the Parliamentary Questions Case Study (5.2), which demonstrates a lesser tendency for Labour women MPs to make reference to women in their questions compared with either Liberal Democrat or Conservative women, highlights the lack of a singular relationship between numbers and substantive representation. In line with Kanter's second and third claims, it suggests that the responsibility to act for women may be more keenly felt by a small number of elected women who may act for women when they are strongly identified with women and women's concerns. Conversely, as the numbers of women increase, not only may women representatives become more differentiated, they may also feel less responsible individually, and they may find themselves facing a backlash.

Despite these broad findings of women acting for women, this is not the same thing as finding that British politics has become 'saturated' with women's concerns as a consequence of women's greater political presence since 1997. As the EDM (5.1) and Parliamentary Question (5.2) Case Studies reveal, women's concerns constitute a small fraction of the questions or parliamentary activity under scrutiny. Acting for women looks to be only a small part of what representatives do. The imperative to recognize the particularity of institutional contexts and gender regimes is illustrated through the National Assembly for Wales Case Study (5.3). Here, sex differences are reduced in respect of interventions in terms of 'equality' and 'equal opportunities' – this is linked to the legal requirement to promote 'equality' for all persons contained with the Assembly's statutory duty.

Whilst a number of the Case Studies focus on the feminization of the political agenda three Case Studies (the Sex Discrimination (EC) Act (5.5), Domestic Abuse (5.6) and the Reduction of VAT on Sanitary Products (5.7)) provide evidence of the feminization of legislation. All three also constitute examples of research approaches which seek to explain an outcome by tracing the actors and actions involved in bringing about changes favourable to women – the research approach advocated in this chapter. Case Study 5.7 is instructive in two main ways: first, the analysis of EDM signatures demonstrates that Labour's women MPs were more likely to act for women by signing the VAT sanitary products EDMs, thereby establishing behavioural sex differences. Second, by providing thick description of the actions that gave rise to the policy change, the critical actors involved in the policy change are identified. The critical actor here was a woman representative, one of the 1997 in-take of Labour women MPs, Christine McCafferty. It is the case that the Treasury had considered reducing the VAT just after the 1997 General Election; it is also the case that the Treasury Minister concerned, Dawn Primarolo, was in favour of the reduction. But, it was McCafferty's efforts that put the issue onto the political agenda in advance of the 2000 budget. This Case Study leaves, however, a number of other, more specific, questions begging: in particular, why did McCafferty not seek to create a strategic alliance involving a sympathetic woman Minister in the Treasury, the Women Ministers, whose job is to act for women and/or women's civil society groups? The former might be explained by the distance the Treasury keeps from other departments, but it was almost certainly also a reflection of McCafferty's newness. Not only did she lack the confidence to take the issue up with the Minister, she did not have an established reputation which might have made the Minister bring her on board at the earlier moment. The lack of substantive response from the Women's Ministers implies that their focus was at this time elsewhere, for whatever reason. Finally, whilst it is possible that the absence of a wider feminist coalition made little difference in this instance, this is not necessarily true when an issue is less 'stand alone' and/or where government is less supportive. The National Assembly for Wales Case Study (5.3) also supports the notion of critical actors: in an institution where women constitute more than 40 per cent of all members, a significant amount of interventions in parliamentary debates were linked to a small number of women representatives and ministers.

In both the Domestic Abuse (5.6) and the Sex Discrimination (EC) Act (5.5) Case Studies, the important role of wider strategic alliances are evident: women representatives, women ministers, WPAs and women in civil society groups acted together and, in the Scottish case, took hold of the opportunities provided by devolution, to first advocate, and then implement an avowedly feminist policy. In Scotland the political agenda was transformed over time as women's civil society groups placed the issue onto the political agenda; the institutional form of the Scottish Parliament provided for greater civil society and individual women's participation. The presence of greater numbers of women in the Parliament and in the Executive sympathetic to the issue, coupled with the secondment of a domestic violence specialist in the Executive, proved fertile ground. Moreover, this Case Study charts a successful feminist policy change in which the link between women's descriptive and substantive representation is evident within a wider context of women's mobilization and the establishment of both vertical and horizontal accountability between women.

The possibility that women and men representatives experience a particular political institution in differently gendered ways is raised directly by the Parliamentary Questions Case Study (5.2). Here, men appear to be more comfortable gendering their written questions but less likely to *ask* questions containing the terms women, men and/or gender. Such apparent unease reminds us that our institutions are not single spaces; that nominally similar political activities may be differently perceived and undertaken by women and men.[4] Furthermore, dominant gender regimes may restrict men's opportunities to act in particular ways. The National Assembly for Wales Case Study (5.3) further reveals how the institutional framework of a particular institution mediates substantive representation: there is suggestive evidence that the institutional presumption in favour of equality enshrined in the founding statute of the National Assembly for Wales constitutes a more conducive environment for both women and men to articulate gendered and equality concerns. These findings suggest that masculinities scholars might wish to turn their attention to the relationship between descriptive and substantive representation. Whilst women's gender is widely accepted as part of the discourse of political representation, men's gender has rarely surfaced. There is greater discussion about the representation of working class or black men, but here it is often their class or ethnicity which is privileged.

The EDM Case Study (5.1) similarly highlights the particularity of different forms of parliamentary activity: EDMs are an example of a parliamentary activity which is relatively cost free. The findings in such studies may indicate how representatives would behave if they could act without incurring costs. Of course, in many instances representatives' actions are likely to be constrained, not least by institutional norms. It would, therefore, be mistaken to extrapolate strongly from studies of relatively safe parliamentary activity. Moreover, whilst it is claimed that well-supported EDMs may influence government, this is rarely demonstrated (Blackburn and Kennon 2003, 537). Although EDMs did play a role in the campaign to reduce VAT on sanitary protection, as Case Study 5.7 reveals, voicing women's concerns through EDMs may, on many occasions, be more symbolic than substantive.

In contrast to those cases which show the possibility of feminized change, the Parliamentary Hours Case Study (5.4) provides an example of institutional resistance. Reformers' efforts were ultimately overturned by a House which preferred its old way of doing things. Women representatives did not act uniformly in respect of the House's hours. A number of Labour women were, nonetheless, vocal in arguing for retaining hours that were more in tune with 'family life' and in line with those established for the Scottish Parliament and National Assembly for Wales. That these women were advised not to employ gendered or feminist accounts in their arguments supporting modern hours reveals, moreover, the inhospitable climate of the institution.

Conclusion

This chapter offers a critique of critical mass – hitherto the analytical framework most often employed in the study of women's substantive representation. Whilst it has been shown that, in many cases, the apparent limitations of the concept are actually the failings of 'critical mass theory', rather than a refutation of the ideas and arguments articulated by Rosabeth Moss Kanter and Drude Dahlerup, the preference here is for a re-conceptualization of women's substantive representation. Two shifts are advocated. First, the shift away from a focus on *when* women 'make a difference' – the precise percentage of women representatives necessary for political institutions to experience change – to *how* the substantive representation of women occurs. Together with a new focus on critical actors, this shift acknowledges insights gained from more than twenty years of gender and politics research into women's substantive representation, as well as insights drawn from mainstream political theory, state feminism and feminist comparative policy literature. It recognizes that critical actors – those who either initiate reforms themselves or play a central role in mobilizing others for policy change – can exist in the absence of 'critical mass,' and that there are likely to be multiple sites of substantive representation. The second shift – from the macro to the micro – proposes that future empirical research should identify and examine, through process-tracing and comparison, the critical actors and events that engender women's substantive representation. Subsequent research will need to investigate the actions of male legislators, members of executives, women's policy agencies (WPA) and femocrats, as well as civil society groups (Mackay 2004a; Lovenduski 2005b) to see if they act in addition to, or in the place of, elected women representatives.

This chapter's focus on legislatures is understandable given the sub-discipline of gender and politics research: originally research centred on whether women representatives were attitudinally predisposed to act for women, because that is what feminist political theory suggested; then the question became whether these attitudes translated into legislative behaviour. The key question next became whether women representatives were able to transform both the political agenda *and* policy outcomes; subsequently, research focused on the means by which political actors achieved this – under what conditions, acting with whom, and recognizing that critical actors might not be women – who the actors are in particular cases, what actions are undertaken, and to what effect. Finally, however, it became apparent that the overall research question itself might need to be redefined, as in the ways explained in the body of this chapter. It was, in short, time for feminist political scientists to walk away from critical mass theory. Neither this statement, nor the recognition of multiple sites of substantive representation and multiple actors, necessarily undermine the examination of legislatures as *one* of the possible sites for the substantive representation of women.

Case Study 5.1

'Parliamentary Graffiti'[5]: Early day motions in the 1997 UK Parliament

Labour women MPs' disproportionate signing of 'women's' Early Day Motions (EDMs) during the 1997 Parliament constitutes precisely the kind of hard behavioural evidence demanded by skeptics of women representatives' self-reported claims to act for women. Moreover, in a context of strong party cohesion, like at Westminster, analyzing EDMs represents a particularly good means to reflect on how women representatives might behave in the absence of party and institutional constraints. With little cost or effort involved, MPs should feel free to sign particular EDMs. In the 1997 Parliament Labour's women MPs, evidently, felt so moved to sign 'women's' and particularly feminist 'women's' EDMs.

Women's' EDMs are those which have women and/or their concerns as their 'primary subject matter' (Reingold 2000, 166–67), with 'women's concerns' referring to those 'issues that bear on women' for either 'biological' or 'social' reasons (Cockburn 1996, 14–15; Lovenduski 1997, 708). In the 1997 Parliament 'Women's' EDMs constituted 4.5 per cent of all EDMs. Over the whole Parliament, backbench Labour women signed an average of 43.3 'women's' EDMs compared with 38.6 for men. Whilst the sex difference is just outside of the 5 per cent significance level (p = 0.058), analysis of the percentage of 'women's' EDM's signed from the total number of all EDMs signed, reveals highly significant sex differences (p = 0.000). For 95.9 per cent of men, the proportion of 'women's' EDMs that they signed constituted fewer than 10 per cent of all EDMs signed; the comparable figure for women was 53 per cent.

When 'women's' EDMs are coded for direction, these pro-women sex differences are even more apparent. Feminist 'women's' EDMs are motions that seek to expand women's opportunities. During the 1997 parliament, women signed an average of 28.7 feminist EDMs compared with 23.4 for men (p = 0.009). The proportion of feminist EDMs signed is also higher for Labour women – a difference that is statistically significant (p = 0.000). Overall, 78.5 per cent of Labour's women MPs signed at least 5 per cent of the feminist 'women's' EDMs. This compares with just 15.7 per cent of the men.

Of the 189 'women's' EDMs suitable for individual analysis, 30 had statistically significant sex differences at the 5 per cent level; in 26 women demonstrated a greater propensity to sign than men – 81 per cent were coded feminist and 19 per cent neutral. There were no anti-feminist 'women's' EDMs that were disproportionately signed by Labour's women. The largest sex differences in women's favour are found in respect of EDM 1292 (97/98), which is concerned with better standards of cancer care and, in particular, ovarian cancer (a sex difference of 45.2 percentage points); EDM 119 (99/00), which congratulates the Women's National Commission on '30 years of ensuring that the views of women in this country are made known to government' (a sex difference of 45.2 percentage points); and EDM 101 (97/98), which calls for a review of rape law with the 'removal of the defendant's right to cross-examine the victim' (a sex difference of 36.7 percentage points). In total, there are ten individual 'women's' EDMs signed by more than half of all Labour's permanent backbench women MPs – this was true for men on only one occasion.

Sex differences are not, however, always found when analyzing groups of 'women's' EDMs. They are, for example, absent from many of the 'neutral' EDMs, including those concerning women's imprisonment, widows, women's experiences in the Second World War, those referring to the sailor Ellen MacArthur and women's health EDMs – although when this latter category is broken down sex differences are found in relation to ovarian and breast cancer. More surprisingly, sex differences are absent from EDMs concerning the establishment of a crèche at Westminster, and regarding lone-parent allowance, both of which are coded feminist. Nevertheless, on 'women's' EDMs concerned with women's bodily integrity – those that were pro-abortion, pro-emergency contraception and against violence against women – significant pro-women sex differences are, once again, evident.

Source: Childs and Withey 2004.

Case Study 5.2

Women asking questions for women; Men asking questions for men: Parliamentary questions at westminster

As a percentage of the total number of parliamentary questions in the 1997/98 Parliamentary session (more than 59,000) just 1 per cent – 85 oral questions and 562 written questions – contained any of the following terms: 'women', 'men' and 'gender'. In total, 27 per cent of all MPs posed a parliamentary question, either written or oral, that contained at least one of these. But, nearly half of all women MPs (48 different women MPs) compared to one fifth of men (128 different men MPs) asked such questions. Women asked 35 per cent of all these questions despite constituting only 18 per cent of the House of Commons.

Men and women use different types of questions, as Table 5.2.i shows (significant $p < 0.001$). Similar percentage of women, around 30 per cent, include 'women', 'men' and/or 'gender' in both their written and oral questions; men are much less likely than women to use these terms in oral questions – 4 per cent compared with 20 per cent.

Table 5.2.i Number of MPs who asked a question including 'women', 'men' and/or 'gender'

	No. male questioners	% of male MPs	No. of female questioners	% of female MPs	Total
Oral	21	4	34	29	55
Written	108	20	36	30	144

Analyzing the propensity of MPs to ask multiple written questions containing any of the research terms also reveals that women MPs are more likely than their male colleagues to ask three or more gendered questions, as Table 5.2.ii shows.

Table 5.2.ii Number of written Questions asked by each MP including 'women', 'men' and/or 'gender'

No. of questions	No. male questioners	No. of female questioners
1–2	75 (69%)	20 (56%)
3–4	17 (16%)	8 (22%)
5–6	5 (5%)	4 (12%)

Table 5.2.ii Number of written Questions asked by each MP including 'women', 'men' and/or 'gender'—cont'd

No. of questions	No. male questioners	No. of female questioners
7–8	2 (2%)	0
9–10	2 (2%)	2 (5%)
11+	7 (6%)	2 (5%)

Sex differences are again found when the search terms are disaggregated. The total number of written questions containing the term 'women' is 423; the number containing the term 'men' is 105; and those containing 'gender', 34. Women made 53 per cent of the references to 'gender' and 35 per cent of the references to 'women' – both higher percentages than their presence in the House – but only 10 per cent of the references to 'men' in written questions. Intra-party sex differences are also apparent. For example, 38 per cent of Conservative women, compared to 11 per cent of Conservative men, include the term 'woman' in a written question. The figures for the Labour Party are 33 per cent and 19 per cent, compared to the Liberal Democrats at 100 per cent (three MPs) and 28 per cent, women and men respectively.

Analysis of oral questions finds similar differences. Once again, higher numbers of oral questions contain the term 'women', compared to either 'men' or 'gender': seventy-one, eight and six respectively. Women's propensity to ask oral questions, including one or more of the research terms, is again higher than their numerical representation in Parliament, at around 30 per cent; and women MPs are responsible for the majority of such questions, some 75 per cent. Disaggregating the research terms in oral questions also establishes, as Table 5.2.iii shows, sex differences in MPs' tendency to include the individual research terms: men constitute nearly 90 per cent of those MPs including 'men' in their oral question; none of those who mentioned 'gender' and 33 per cent of those MPs who made reference to 'women'.

Table 5.2.iii Number of oral questions including 'women', 'men' and/or 'gender'

	No. of questions including 'women'	No. of questions including 'men'	No. of questions including 'gender'
Male MPs	24 (33%)	7 (88%)	0
Female MPs	47 (66%)	1 (12%)	6 (100%)
Total	71 (100%)	8 (100%	6 (100%)

Inter and intra-party sex differences are again evident in oral questions: Labour MPs ask more than twice the number of oral questions including the term 'women', 'men' and/or 'gender' than either Conservative or Liberal Democrat MPs. Furthermore, in respect of questions containing the term 'women', fewer than 5 per cent of men MPs include this term in their oral questions. The relevant percentage for women MPs are 29 per cent, 46 per cent and 100 per cent (Labour, Conservative and Liberal Democrat parties, respectively).

Source: Bird 2005.

Case Study 5.3

'Hot air' or substance: Plenary debates in the National Assembly for Wales

The plenary sessions of the National Assembly for Wales are wide-ranging; the Assembly's Standing Orders and its founding statute hold that 'the Assembly may consider, and make appropriate representations about, any matter affecting Wales'. More than three million words of text were generated during plenary debates in the Assembly's first term (1999–2003). In total, some 48 per cent of these included discussion of' women's issues' – domestic violence, childcare, and 'equal pay for work of equal value'. Just over half of the debates included references to 'equality', 'equal opportunities', and 'women'. As Table 5.3.i shows, women AMs exhibited a greater propensity to engage in these debates than men AMs (P = 0.001).

Table 5.3.i The incidence of key terms featuring in political debate recorded in the Official Record of the first term of the National Assembly for Wales 1999–2003

Debating term	Female % all references to topic	Male % all references to topic
Childcare	64.7	35.3
Domestic violence	70.2	29.8
Equal pay	68.0	32.0
'Women's issues'	77.8	22.2
Equality	52.2	47.8
All	59.8	40.2
N	532	358

These significant differences are most pronounced in respect of 'women's issues' where, overall, women make approximately two-thirds to three-quarters of all interventions. Reflecting the legal imperative on each AM to promote equality for 'all persons' and in respect of all governmental functions, there is a less pronounced pro-woman sex difference in respect of interventions employing the terms 'equality' and 'equal opportunities'. Women had, though, a significantly greater propensity to initiate debate on gender equality – approximately two-thirds to three quarters (P = 0.001). Women AMs can also be seen to advance the substantive representation of women across a significantly broader range of policy areas than their male colleagues, as Table 5.3.ii demonstrates.

Table 5.3.ii Interventions in political debate to promote interests of women: by policy area

Policy area	Female	Male
Agriculture	2	1
Arts and culture	0	1
Asylum seekers	1	0
Carers	1	0
Economic development	10	0
Education	3	2
Employment	4	4
Families	1	0
Health	22	6
Homelessness	2	0
Peace campaigners	1	0
Policing	3	0
Political participation	4	0
Political representation	4	0
Sport	10	4
Welfare	0	1
Women's rights	6	2
Miscellaneous	4	0
Totals (N)	78	21

In terms of the direction of AMs' interventions, women are significantly more likely – almost twice as likely – than the men to make feminist interventions in the discussion of women's issues: women made 85.9 per cent of feminist interventions compared to just 14.1 per cent made by men. Furthermore, male AMs are more likely to make 'neutral' interventions: 9.1 per cent of all interventions, compared to 5.4 for women, and make all of the overtly anti-equality interventions (six in total).

Sex differences are again evident in respect of the extent to which the tendency to articulate 'women's issues' in plenary debates is shared amongst AMs. Although not significant, and with some variation by issue, an average of 67 per cent of women AMs engage in debate on 'women's issues', compared to 36.4 per cent of male AMs: approximately one half of all women participate in debates on domestic violence and equal pay and over three-quarters do so in relation to childcare and other 'women's issues'. A more modest difference (8.6 per centage points) is evident in respect of AMs' references to 'equality' in debates. Overall, when all references to equality and women's issues are combined, the sex difference remains pronounced with 73.6 per cent of the female AMs engaging in debate compared to 47.4 per cent of male AMs. At the same time, the presence of women critical actors is also evident: three women AMs account for between, approximately, a third and a half of all women's interventions.

Looking at the contributions by ministers in the plenary debates reveals, as Table 5.3.iii shows, that women ministers typically account for two-thirds to three-quarters of all such interventions.

Table 5.3.iii Ministerial interventions in debate on key topics recorded in the Official Record of the first term of the National Assembly for Wales 1999–2003

Debating term	*Female % all ministerial interventions on topic*	*Male % all ministerial interventions on topic*
Childcare	67.0	33.0
Domestic violence	76.5	23.5
Equal pay	77.3	22.7
'Women's issues'	77.4	22.6
Equality	60.5	39.5
All	66.2	33.8
N	198	101

Source: Chaney 2006.

Case Study 5.4

'We are not just changing the hours of the House':[6] Reforming Westminster

'What sort of Parliament do we want? the MP Julie Morgan, one of Labour's 1997 intake of women MPs, asked in the House of Commons in 2005. By a margin of 292 to 225, the House voted for the status quo ante: Tuesday night sittings would return to 2.30 pm–10 pm. Since January 2003 they had been 11.30 am–7 pm.

The predominant framing of the debates surrounding reforms to the Chamber's sitting hours highlighted MPs' concerns with democracy and accountability, cross cut with concerns about institutional continuity, professionalization and representation. Traditionalists argued that shorter working days and a shorter working week would make MPs look lazy, create a 'metropolitan elite' of MPs with constituencies close to Parliament, marginalize Parliament, diminish the effectiveness of parliamentary committee work and 'curtail' Parliament's 'vibrant social life'. In contrast, advocates argued that the reforms would symbolize a modern institution – by 'aligning its hours with those kept by society' – opening it up to the electorate, and improving media coverage and Parliament's agenda-setting abilities. Key votes, for example, would occur in time for the evening news bulletins and the early morning newspapers.

Reform of the hours was also regarded as an issue of gender equality: the new Parliamentary hours should be more compatible with childcare responsibilities. Yet, those responsible for organizing the 2002 vote, which brought in the revised hours for a trial period, believed that explicit reference to gender might cost them parliamentary support. Hence, they tried to ensure family-friendly arguments were down played and enjoined women MPs not to make their case in feminist terms. However, and despite facing accusations that they were selfishly seeking to improve their own working conditions, some Labour women MPs denounced the masculinized style and practices of the House and raised the issue of domestic responsibilities. Caroline Flint said 'she did not wish to return to her family at the weekends too exhausted to be a good mother'; Oona King 'drew attention to the need for MPs to fulfil their family responsibilities'.

Such gendered concerns were revisited in the 2005 debates. Critics, of both sexes and from both sides of the House, noted that what constituted 'family-friendly' hours differed according to whether one lived in London or not. The Conservatives' Richard Shepherd and Oliver Heald saw in the discourse of 'family friendly' hours an inappropriate concern for personal convenience and rubbished arguments that looked to employment practices beyond Westminster. Their colleague, Eric Forth, contended that MPs should be prepared to be present in parliament 'as long as necessary to do our job properly', whilst the Liberal Democrat, Paul Tyler, agreed that 'family-friendly' or, in his terms 'MP-friendly' hours, were less important than improving legislation, scrutiny and communication with the electorate. Personalizing her contribution, Labour's Alice Mahon MP sought to 'lay the myth that everyone who comes here has always worked from nine-to-five', and added: 'I worked two nights a week when my children were little'.

These perspectives were, though and as before, directly challenged by some Labour women MPs. Anne Campbell asked whether it was 'right to deny those who live near London' the possibility of seeing their family midweek? Advancing a more substantive feminist counter-argument, Julie Morgan and Joan Ruddock raised the issue of the symbolism of any repeal of the new hours: 'the public would view it as a return to the jolly hours in the Smoking Room'. Morgan also linked the debate to women's under-representation in Parliament: in her view the 'clubby portrayal of life in Westminster' influences party selectorates to 'think that they should select male candidates'.

When it came to the vote there was no absolute division by sex, although men voted disproportionately on the winning side. Women, in contrast, were more likely to vote against the amendment and for a continuation of the reformed hours: accounting for just under 20 per cent of voting MPs, women constituted 12.7 per cent of the 'Ayes' but 28.9 per cent of the Noes (37 out of the total of 292 compared to 65 out of 225, respectively).

Source: Brazier *et al.* 2005; Lovenduski 2005a/b.

Case Study 5.5

Strategic alliances and the Sex Discrimination (Election Candidates) Act

The Sex Discrimination (Election Candidates) Act 2002 introduces a new section (42A) to the Sex Discrimination Act (SDA). It dis-applies the anti-discrimination rules in Parts 2 to 4 of the Act from arrangements which 'regulate the selection by a political party registered under the Political Parties, Elections and Referendums Act 2000 of candidates in an election for Parliament' and 'are adopted for the purpose of reducing the inequality in the numbers of men and women elected, as candidates of that party, to be members of the body concerned'. The Act's remit includes elections for Westminster, the European Parliament, the Scottish Parliament and National Assembly for Wales and local government elections. Clause 3, a 'sunset' clause, causes the provisions of the Bill to expire at the end of 2015, unless a statutory instrument is passed to ensure its continuation.

The inclusion of the Bill in the first Queen's speech of Labour's second term reflected a strategic alliance between Labour's women parliamentarians and government ministers, women in the wider party, officials and special advisers in the Women's Unit and Department of Transport, Local Government and the Regions, non-partisan women's civil society groups and campaigning organizations outside Parliament such as the Fawcett Society, and feminist academics. It also required Blair to overturn his earlier antipathy and give leadership on the issue in Cabinet.

The Sex Discrimination (Election Candidates) Act was passed with little opposition – there was no division in the Commons or the Lords. Women Members across all parties and in both Houses took disproportionate interest in the debates accompanying the Bill. In the Commons' Second Reading 61 per cent of Labour speakers, 63 per cent of Conservatives and 33 per cent of Liberal Democrats were women. The relative percentage of women in each of the parliamentary parties at that time was 23, 8 and 10 per cent respectively. In the Commons' Third Reading, two of the four Labour MPs (50 per cent) and four of the five Conservative MPs (80 per cent) were women, although the lone Liberal Democrat was male. This pattern was reflected in the Lords: 80 per cent of Labour speakers at Second Reading were women, though they constitute only 22 per cent of their party in the Lords; 40 per cent of

Liberal Democrats were women compared to their percentage in the Lords of 24 per cent; and one of the two Conservative Peers was a woman (50 per cent), while they constitute a mere 15 per cent of the Conservative Party in the Lords. The one crossbencher was also a woman.

The reason for the men's conspicuous absence in these debates is unclear. Ann Widdecombe lamented: 'hon. Gentlemen welcome it as a great step forward. It is a massive step towards inequality for men, and the poor souls just let the women walk over them'. Perhaps they considered the Bill an example of 'women's legislation' which, for either honourable or dishonourable reasons, should be debated by women. Alternatively, they might have been too embarrassed to speak out publicly against a Bill that was aimed at securing greater levels of women's descriptive representation, as Baroness Dean in the House of Lords suggested. Or they might have thought that because the Bill was permissive rather than prescriptive, they should not waste their time on it in Parliament – the real battles would come later within their parties.

Support for the principle of women's greater presence in politics was evident across the parties: 'our democracy is deformed', 'a men's democracy,' declared Labour MP Fiona Mactaggart. For the Liberal Democrats, Patsy Calton added that this is 'the supreme example of the failure on the part of a parliamentary democracy to achieve true representation of the people'; and from the Conservative backbenches Andrew Lansley asserted that the MPs 'do not represent the society that we wish to serve'. Party differences became apparent as the debate shifted to what mechanisms would be necessary to deliver higher numbers of women MPs. On the Labour benches, women were adamant that their party would have to return to AWS: 'no other measure – we have tried all the others that I know – will work for Westminster selections and elections'; 'it is only through AWS that progress has actually been made'.

Source: Childs 2002, 2003.

Case Study 5.6

Acting together: Domestic abuse in Scotland

Action against domestic abuse is widely recognized as the most concrete gain for the women's agenda of the first session of the Scottish Parliament. The issue has a higher profile in Scotland than elsewhere in the UK and spending is proportionately greater; substantial improvements have been made in service provision for survivors of domestic abuse: new legislation has been passed – The Protection from Abuse Act (Scotland) 2001 – and government prevention initiatives, such as media campaigns and educational work in schools, have been undertaken.

Domestic abuse was put onto the pre-devolutionary political agenda by women's organizations, such as Scottish Women's Aid, who had been campaigning, lobbying and providing services for survivors of domestic violence, for more than 30 years. Devolution opened up new opportunities to act: the Parliamentary Public Petitions Committee, the Executive-sponsored Civic Forum, the Scottish Executive Women in Scotland Consultative Forum and the Gender Reporter of the Parliamentary Equal Opportunities Committee. There would also be opportunities to feed into policy at the pre-legislative stage through open consultations, on-line consultations and video-conferencing. A National Group to Address Domestic Abuse in Scotland was established in June 2001, with a remit to oversee the implementation of the National Strategy and a specialist Violence Against Women policy unit was also established inside the Scottish Executive.

In analyzing the responsiveness to the issue of domestic abuse in Scotland, researchers examined the extent to which institutions and politics recognized (1) women as full citizens – as legitimate political actors with differentiated interests and concerns; (2) the gendered implications of policy; (3) gender-based barriers to full citizenship; (4) whether the increase in descriptive representation of women parliamentarians impacted upon the promotion of women's concerns; (5) the number and nature of mechanisms that hold government and other state actors to account; and (6) whether any outcomes were concrete or merely declarations of good intent.

In terms of recognition, the issue of domestic violence against women, rather than being at the margins of the political agenda, has been accorded the same national priority status as 'health or education'.

Moreover, it is a feminist understanding of domestic abuse that has been accepted. Such abuse is not considered the actions of a few aberrant or psychopathic individual men but the more systematic and systemic 'male abuse of power'. Links between domestic violence and gender inequality and between different forms of violence against women are also recognized.

With regard to accountability, there are examples of both vertical and horizontal accountability. In respect of the former, there is the institutionalization of women's organizations (which means that on a day-to-day basis women's organizations are part of the policy making process) and regular reporting mechanisms, seminars and consultation. In respect of the horizontal accountability, there are regular reports to parliament and annual debates on violence against women.

In respect of substantive representation, domestic violence is clearly an issue that female ministers and parliamentarians took a personal interest in, as interviews with women MSPs and ministers revealed. Women's predisposition to act on this issue was translated into action – domestic violence was the subject of the first parliamentary committee legislation. As one woman former member of the Cabinet stated: 'men might have got around to tackling domestic abuse eventually – but women did it right away'.

Connections between women in Parliament and women's organizations outside provide evidence of vertical substantive representation: female MSPs are more likely than their male counterparts to have past or current links with women's organizations. In the Labour party the majority of women reported such links. In addition, women activists are institutionalized within the policy process as part of the National Group; they were also party to the parliamentary committee discussions, regularly providing evidence; and a feminist domestic violence abuse expert was seconded to the Executive. Nonetheless, 'acting for women' was not, on this issue, limited to women. The actions of individual men, such as the male convenor of the Cross-Party Parliamentary Group on Men's violence Against Women, suggest a positive reaction from men to the actions of their women colleagues.

Source: Mackay and Kenny 2005; Mackay 2005, 2004b.

Case Study 5.7

The tax cut that 'dare not speak its name': The reduction of VAT on sanitary products

Until the Budget of 2000, sanitary protection – an essential item for millions of women – was treated by Her Majesty's Treasury as a luxury item, liable to VAT at 17.5 per cent. 'Me too claims' was one of the reasons the Treasury was against reducing the VAT; any such reduction would apply to equivalent items for men, a list which the Treasury argued included, razors, shaving cream and, incredulously, lawnmowers. In an answer to a written question in 1997, and reiterated two years later, the Treasury made clear that 'it is not possible to single out sanitary protection for special treatment'.

The subsequent, and surprising, reduction 'might not have happened', a Treasury insider conceded, had there 'been a different group of people and different events'. The 'critical actor' was the backbench Labour woman MP, Christine McCafferty. Her motivation reflected discussions in the Parliamentary Labour Party's women's group soon after the 1997 General Election. Reducing VAT on sanitary products was considered an achievable policy goal – it was relatively cost free in monetary terms – approximately £35 million. An element of mischief was also involved with the women feeling that they could embarrass the then Chancellor Gordon Brown into action.

McCafferty tabled three EDMs in 1997/8, 1998/9 and 1999/2000:

> That this House believes that sanitary products should be classed in the category of 'essential to the family budget', just as food, children's clothing and books already are, and that, like such products, they should be classed as VAT-free under the EC Sixth Directive; notes that Britain currently has one of Europe's highest rates of VAT on sanitary products and that 15 million British women spend in excess of 300 million a year on products that are necessary to personal hygiene; further notes that removing VAT from sanitary products would only cost the Treasury one penny a year for every woman in the country using them; calls on the Government to reduce the VAT on sanitary products to the EU minimum of 5 per cent; and ask the Government to support a change in the European law so that such products can be zero-rated.

McCafferty's EDMs constituted the 38th, 31st and 6th most signed motions in their parliamentary sessions, receiving, 174, 188, and 247 signatures, respectively. Labour MPs comprised more than three quarters of all signers on each occasion – 78 per cent, 80 per cent and 82 per cent respectively. McCafferty proved to be largely successful in her goal of 'get[ting ... the] support of every woman MP!'[7] The first time the EDM was tabled 59 per cent of Labour women MPs signed, compared to 50 per cent of Labour's men. In 1998/9, 71 per cent of Labour women, compared to 55 per cent of Labour men, signed – a significant sex difference – and on its final outing, 84 per cent of women compared with 73 per cent of men, had signed. Sex differences are also evident in MPs' reasons for signing. A survey of the MPs who signed the EDMs found that almost 30 per cent of the women signed because it was a 'women's concern', compared to just under 12 per cent of the men. The men preferred to talk in terms of equity or to call attention to the fact that sanitary products are not 'luxury items'.

Despite overwhelming support from Labour backbenchers, and especially women in the PLP, there was, though, no observable or immediate reaction to the EDMs; being widely supported is neither a necessary nor sufficient condition to translate an EDM into legislation. Nor was there any observable effect when McCafferty raised the issue personally with either the Prime Minister (in late 1999 or early 2000) or the Chancellor (March 1999 and February 2000), or when she stood outside the House of Commons with a poster publicizing the issue. The immediate trigger in advance of the 2000 Budget appears to have been McCafferty's decision to speak on BBC Radio 4's Woman's Hour. One of Brown's special advisers heard the interview and spoke to the Chancellor. Despite continued civil service concerns – and these remained strongly worded – the Treasury Minister, Dawn Primarolo, took the issue off her shelf, dusted it down and finalized the detail. Even so, Brown made no mention of the reduction in his Budget speech – it was slipped out in a press release.

Notes

1 See, for example, *Politics and Gender,* 2006, 2, 4.
2 State feminism refers to the advocacy of women's movement demands inside the state (Lovenduski 2005b, 4).
3 FCP considers women's descriptive and substantive representation in 'the pre-formulation, formulation, implementation and evaluation of a specific policy' (Mazur 2002, 4).

4 These Case Studies support other research that finds – on the basis of interview data with MPs and Members of the Scottish Parliament – a shared perception that women and men have different styles of politics (Mackay 2005; 2004b). It is also suggested that women's style may be more harshly judged by their male colleagues (Childs 2004).
5 Flynn 1997.
6 Julie Morgan MP.
7 A handwritten note on a fax dated 22 January 1998 – the exclamation mark is in the original.

6   Women politicians, the media and symbolic representation

Introduction

Without doubt, the most ubiquitous media representation of British women politicians in recent years has been 'Blair's Babes'. This moniker has been widely used to refer collectively to Labour's women MPs, but especially to those first elected in 1997. It was part of a deliberate strategy on behalf of the right of centre *Daily Mail* newspaper to set Labour's new women MPs up to fail. The now infamous photograph of many of the new women MPs surrounding Tony Blair taken just after the election has since been interpreted as proof of their sycophancy, even if at the time many women MPs saw it as celebratory. What women politicians wear is also much remarked on in the British press. The following parliamentary sketches are illustrative of this: Ann Treneman, writing in the *Times*, was reflecting on Tessa Jowell's performance in the Commons' Chamber. In the spring of 2006, the Secretary of State for Culture, Media and Sport was facing calls to resign over allegations of financial impropriety against her husband:

> Tessa was clearly nervous and, like so many stars, she really does owe a great deal to her stylist. She did not look like the same distraught woman of the past few days. Her hair, make-up and clothes (charcoal trouser suit with trendy necklace) looked entirely natural and therefore wildly expensive. It was crisis dressing at its very best.[1]

Or take Simon Hoggart's musings in the *Guardian* on the Opposition Leader of the House, Theresa May, speaking in the Parliament, in autumn 2006:

> Mrs May was not wearing a veil. She was dressed entirely in black but, far from covering up her body, her clothing revealed a great deal more of it – more, to be frank, than I can recall any woman MP showing before ... a quantity of cleavage that would not have disgraced a Page 3 Stunner opening a nightclub ... The top of her dress was horizontal, so it looked as though she might have been wearing the niqab, but it had slipped south, by about 18 inches.[2]

It is not difficult to find such examples. And it is not just political journalists. Women's magazines periodically turn their attention to women and politics, especially in general election years. This is true of the high-end fashion magazine *Vogue*, younger women's magazines such as *Cosmopolitan*, as well as the celebrity magazine *Hello*, and the best selling woman's weekly *Take a Break* (Deacon *et al.* 2007). Often their reports are accompanied by highly stylized photographs of women politicians. At the time of the General Election in 2005, Harriet Harman MP was photographed in a number of different outfits in *Hello*. Plus ca change. At the inaugural meeting of the Ladies Grand Council of the Primrose League in April 1885 (Maguire 1998, 34) reporters were invited from both the fashion and political sections of the *Morning Post*.

Reflecting on the media representation of women politicians, two main questions come to the fore: the first enquires about the extent to which, and ways in which, women politicians are symbolically represented in a gendered fashion in the media – do journalists systematically and routinely focus on women's sex and gender – emphasizing less what they do and more what they look like? And when they do evaluate what women politicians do, is it the case that British women politicians are always negatively compared to male politicians? Do they come in just 'five lurid shades'? (1) 'Not up to it' (all of them at some time or other); (2) 'Nanny – fussy do-gooder, obsessed with trivia' (all of them at some time or other); (3) 'Blair Babe – obedient clone, too dim to think for herself' (all except Clare Short and Mo Mowlam); (4) 'Charming maverick, outspoken loner, lovable but going nowhere' (Short and Mowlam); (5) 'Terrifying termagant – but don't you love a flame-haired hand-bagging?' (Margaret Thatcher and Barbara Castle).[3]

The second question asks what the effects of such representations might be – asking, in short, whether gendered representations of women politicians matter and, if so, in what ways and in respect of whom – the individual woman representative themselves, women politicians more widely, or women in society more generally? Back in 1981 Virginia Sapiro (1998, 183) drew attention to the link between women's descriptive and symbolic representation: 'women and men' she declared, 'continue to think of politics as a male domain because the empirical truth at this moment is that politics *is* a male domain' (emphasis in the original). Greater numbers of women in office would '*increase* the acceptability of women in government and change the cultural impression of politics' (emphasis added). This would be particularly true for women: women representatives would act as role models, encouraging other women to seek political office. Women represented by women representatives might also have higher levels of political efficacy, competency and participation (High-Pippert and Cromer 1998; Norris *et al.* 2004).

Such optimistic readings of the symbolic effect of women's greater descriptive representation are by no means certain. It is possible that women representatives' presence might not be normalized but, rather, rendered suspect and 'other' through gendered media representations. More specifically, representations which focus on women politicians' appearance, clothing, and familial relations, or depict women politicians as unable to cope with the politics and pressures of Parliament or the Hours of the House, re-present and reinforce, rather than challenge, widely accepted assumptions about the suitability of women and politics. In short, such representations point up the distinction between the *male–politician–norm* and the *female–politician–pretender*.

The study of gender, politics and the media: three approaches

The study of gender, politics and the media usually takes one of three forms. The first – symbolic annihilation – examines whether women politicians receive less media coverage than their male peers (Norris 1997b). The second explores stereotypical representation – where the media draw on conventional stereotypes of femininity and politics, such as the public man/private woman, or focus on women's appearance (Norris 1997b; Lee 2004; Considine and Deutchman 1996). Here a distinction is drawn between stereotyping, in which individuals are evaluated on the basis of characteristics 'assumed to be shared by social groups, irrespective of the individual's personal qualities, abilities or experience' and gendered frames, which are the 'broader narrative within which sex stereotypes may be located' (Norris 1997b). The third approach considers 'sex specific narrative frames' (Gidengil and Everitt 2003a, 561). This is where women's sex is the frame (Trimble 2006). For example, women might be depicted as 'agents of change' (Carroll and Schreiber 1997). Gender biases may also be present when women are not being framed in stereotypically feminine terms (Gidengil and Everitt 2003a/b). In this case, bias is likely to take the form of more 'subtle conventional wisdom about women', the use of 'gendered news frames', and the harsher evaluation of women's capabilities (Norris 1997b; Trimble (2006, 7). For this reason, the concept of gendered mediation is often preferred (Sreberny-Mohammadi and Ross 1996; Ross and Sreberny 2000, 93). This acknowledges a male-orientated agenda that privileges the practice of politics as an essentially male pursuit.

Whether these three different approaches are discrete and/or whether they reflect chronological stages is debated (Fountaine and McGregor 2002). Similarly, there is no agreement as to whether particular assumptions hold across different media (in both print and broadcasting media, for example), between journalists of both sexes, in respect of women in different political offices (Kahn 2003), or for all women (Ross 2002). For example, Pippa Norris (1997) found little evidence of gender role stereotyping of world leaders, whereas Kim Kahn (1994, 2003) discovered an overemphasis on US women Governors', but not Congresswomen's personalities. Iva Deutchman and Anne Ellison (1999) contend that the Australian politician Pauline Hanson was often denied agency in media coverage, with her first name used more frequently than her male comparator's. American studies (Kahn 1994, 155) also show that the amount of coverage of women and men politicians varies by political office, and may well not always be in men's favour, as women's novelty value may garner women greater media attention. Other research (Gidengil and Everitt 2003a/b; Sampert and Trimble 2003) reveals that women politicians do not always 'win' even when they conform to the norms of political behaviour. Finally, more recent research

(Ross 2003; 2000) suggests that women politicians are not simply passive recipients of media representations but can also participate in their construction – women politicians may seek to cultivate relationships with particular women journalists, agree to 'lifestyle' magazine articles in an attempt to transform perceptions of who can be a politician, or opt for live interviews and studio discussions rather than pre-recorded programmes, in which producers might edit what they say.

Expectations about the role of women journalists in the media representation of women politicians in the extant literature also point in different directions. On the one hand, and similar to some feminists' assumptions about the relationship between women's descriptive and substantive representation in politics, it is assumed that women journalists – because of their own gender identity and gendered experiences – are more likely to adopt a different (read feminist) perspective and approach than their male colleagues (Norris 1997b). On the other hand, the culture and political economy of the newsroom is said to constrain women journalists' freedom to report – comparable to the constraints faced by women representatives' when seeking to act for women (Weaver, cited in Helmand *et al.* 2000, 2). Women politicians frequently claim that women journalists are the worst offenders (Sones 2005; Sreberny-Mohammadi and Ross, 1996). Yet, such criticism might be misdirected if the sex of the reporter reflects a sexual division of labour within the media (Ross 1995) – so that it is women who are more likely to be the writers or broadcasters of feature style reports rather than 'straight' news or political journalists. It would also be misplaced if women journalists perceive they must act to counter institutional performance pressures (Kanter 1977a). Another complicating contention (Sones et al) is that the media's coverage of women's looks and fashion may simply reflect women readers' greater interest in these areas.

British research

Research on gender, politics and the media in British politics is less comprehensive than studies elsewhere, especially North America. This reflects, in part, the smaller number of academics working in this area in the UK. The most common British approach examines women politicians' perceptions of their representation by the media, although more recently studies have begun to examine how women politicians seek to mediate that representation (Ross 2002; 2003). British women politicians, like others, contend that 'their appearance is the focus of both more column inches and airtime than anything they might say' and that the media expects better standards of behaviour and higher moral values from women politicians. Women MPs also perceive that they are described in gendered ways (Sreberny-Mohammadi and Ross 1996): one contended: 'I don't know how many times I've been described as having my claws out ... who would describe a man's claws being out'.

A few studies (Stephenson 1998; Campbell and Lovenduski 2005) document the relative absence of women politicians, women journalists, the female public and/or 'women's issues' from the media's coverage of General Election campaigns. Loughborough University's analysis of the 2001 General Election campaign found that only one sitting woman MP, Ann Widdecombe, made it to the top ten most visible politicians – the other woman in the list was Margaret Thatcher (Lovenduski 2001, 184). Appearances by politicians in election news saw men outnumber women by a factor of about nine to one. The same is true of the 2005 General Election campaign (Deacon *et al.* 2006, 235): the gap between the coverage of men and women politicians was 91 per cent to nine percent; men appeared ten times more frequently than the women.

The British literature lacks, in particular, extensive empirical studies employing systematic quantitative and qualitative content analysis. Karen Ross's (1995) analysis of the Labour Party Leadership election in 1995 noted that a 'cursory reading' of newspaper articles reveals 'a strong bias towards Blair from the very beginning'. Illustrative evidence is presented of various ways in which the representation of Margaret Beckett, then acting Party Leader, was mediated by gender. Beckett's age was routinely cited (she was post-menopausal compared to the youthful 40-something Blair); her appearance and fashion sense was critiqued (she was compared to a gargoyle); her sexuality was questioned (she had 'stolen another woman's husband'); and her first name used when her rivals were *Mr* Blair or *Mr* Prescott.

The new research which constitutes the core of this chapter is a single Case Study. This was designed to provide systematic analysis of the gendered representation of two women politicians in the 1997 Parliament – Estelle Morris and Clare Short. These Cabinet Ministers were the only two women to resign from Blair's Cabinet. Against a backdrop of widespread media criticism of Labour's women MPs, especially the 1997 intake, it was unclear how these Labour women, who were by no means parliamentary virgins, would be represented. As members of the Cabinet, both women were very much already under the media spotlight. Ministerial resignations are, moreover, by their very nature, newsworthy. Rather than investigating how *much* coverage they received it was more important to analyze the *nature* of their media representations. The intra-sex comparison enables exploration of whether the media relies on a singular notion of femininity in its representations (van Acker 2003; Greco Larson 2001).

The analysis looks at (1) stereotypes; (2) gendered adjectives/traits in newspaper article headlines and articles, in particular, for the use of positive, negative, neutral *and* gendered adjectives/traits; and (3) gender frames: that is where the article foregrounds the resigning Cabinet Minister's sex/gender as either a reason for the resignation or as basis for the media representation of the resignation. The first research technique takes up Sreberny-Mohammadi and Ross' (1996) challenge to systematically study women politician's perceptions. It is possible that women MPs misperceive how they are represented in the British media. The second approach considers the ways in which the behaviour of the resigning Cabinet women is informed by notions of appropriate behaviour for both politicians and women (the *male–politician–norm* vs *female–politician–pretender*). Further, comparing headlines with the body of the reports enables comparisons between the journalists responsible for the articles and the newspaper's ideological position – it is editorial staff who write the headlines (Timble and Sampert 2004, 56). The third technique recognizes that gender can itself be the 'peg' upon which a particular story is hung. Here, the concern is with the ways in which both Morris' and Short's resignations are presented as peculiarly about women and politics. Five gender frames are identified. Three – the 'politics as male', 'not their own woman' (agency) and the 'all women' frames – are employed in respect of both Estelle Morris and Clare Short. The 'women's resignation' frame is applied only to Morris and the 'love' frame only to Clare Short.

All articles published in UK national daily and Sunday newspapers were gathered for a one-week period either side of the two women Ministers' resignations. In the first instance, all of the articles were read to determine whether the article had *as its primary subject* matter the Cabinet Minister's resignation (Reingold 2000, 166–7), although this rule was relaxed in respect of 'omnibus articles'.[4] The second coding stage established whether articles also contained evaluative and analytic sentences, that is sentences that provided interpretations of the resignations rather than merely descriptive sentences (Everitt and Gidengil 2003). Unmediated contributions, those that reproduce mediated analysis published elsewhere, and readers' letters were excluded. Of the original 377 Estelle Morris articles, 166 were subject to in-depth analysis; the numbers for Clare Short are 352 and 114 respectively.

On the basis of this particular Case Study – of just two ministerial resignations – it is not possible to conclude that all women ministers or all women politicians are represented by the media as 'not up to the job'. Further, and despite the perception held by many of Labour's women MPs (and women politicians more widely), there is little evidence of the extensive and routine representation of these women Ministers in terms of their appearance, fashion, or familial and personal relations. It might be that an inter-sex comparison would reveal disproportionate coverage but, at this stage, the evidence suggests that the media did not systematically and explicitly foreground these issues. This is not to say that the media's representations of Morris and Short's resignations are not saturated with gender. The range of gendered adjectives used to describe the Ministers is extensive; adjective after adjective describes the women in gender specific terms. Both are also criticized in terms of the expected behaviour of politicians. This includes the use of adjectives that are normally considered positive in respect of women but which are considered negative in respect of the political sphere. Moreover, the analysis of the gender frame articles shows the dominance of particular 'gender frame' stories.

The media's ability to distinguish between women politicians – to acknowledge different forms of femininity – was found most explicitly in the analysis of gendered headlines, but it was also evident in their use of adjectives and in those articles that were wholly framed by gender. This suggests that the media's representation of women politicians is determined, at least in part, by their perception of the extent and different manner in which individual women transgress gender norms (Deutchman and Ellison 1999). Morris, to be sure, is considered as a *bad*

Cabinet Minister but she, nonetheless, remained a *good* woman. And for this she was given credit. Clare Short, in contrast, was both a *bad* Cabinet Minister and a *bad* woman. For this, she was damned.

Some interesting sex differences in the representations by women and men journalists were also forthcoming in the Case Study, though by no means are all women journalists sympathetic and all men hostile. One notable difference was that far fewer men wrote articles that used gender as the frame upon which the resignations were hung. Yet, it was precisely in the gender frame articles where the gendered nature of politics was most acutely problematized. These journalists, many of whom were women, were keen to question the masculinized norms of political behaviour and valourize women's different political style, either implicitly or explicitly underpinned by an assumption of women's shared gender identity. At the same time, some apparently felt obliged to name women politicians who could cope with parliamentary politics as currently practiced – as if they were concerned that if they did not also make such statements then the charge that all women are 'not up to it' would prevail.

The single Case Study presented in this chapter can but only fill a small gap in the British literature on gender, politics and the media. As stated above, inter-as well as intra-sex comparisons must be undertaken before strong conclusions can be drawn about the wider gendered mediation of British politicians, male and female, in the media. Future research must also examine the gendered representation of women and men politicians across different forms of media and over time. There is also the question of politicians' agency to be explored, not least the ways in which representatives play an active role in their own media representations. The relationship between the gendered representation of women representatives and the sex of journalists also invites greater investigation; in what ways does the sex of the journalist matter and how does the sexual division of labour with the newsroom, or newsroom norms themselves, influence media representations? It might, for example, be unfair for gender and politics scholars to pick on the parliamentary sketch writers, when it is in the nature of what they do to exaggerate particular politicians' personalities and proclivities – you should see what they have to say about some male MPs.[5] Finally, gender and politics scholars need to return to the conceptually and methodologically complex question of whether, and in what ways, gendered media representations matter – symbolically and substantively – and, in particular, whether it impacts on women's descriptive representation and representatives' ability to act for women, the substantive representation of women.

Case Study 6.1

'Not up to the job': Women's resignations from Blair's Cabinet

Estelle Morris, Secretary of State for Education, resigned in October 2002 and Clare Short, Secretary of State for International Development, resigned in May 2003. In both cases the British media agreed that the Ministers were, albeit for different reasons, 'not up to the job'. The media happily concurred with Estelle Morris' own consideration that she had not 'been as effective' as she 'should have been' in the top job;[6] Clare Short's cabinet career was, apparently, always 'destined to end in tears'. Both resignations apparently caught the media by surprise. In Morris' case, this was despite the Conservative party calling for her to resign the previous week over a promise, initially made by her predecessor, David Blunkett, to resign if particular levels of achievement were not reached by school pupils. And this was just the latest in a series of difficulties Morris had faced during an 'autumn of crises': the 'debacle' of A level grading; the contested role of teaching assistants in the classroom; school (ill)discipline; and University tuition fees. There were also reports that documented Morris' apparent unease and unhappiness with 'media intrusion' into her private life and stories about conflict with Andrew Adonis, an unelected special adviser. Clare Short's resignation was a surprise to the British media and political classes because it was widely expected that she would be sacked by Tony Blair. On BBC Radio 4's 'Westminster Hour', Short had threatened to resign if there was no mandate from the UN for the war in Iraq, and she had claimed that Blair had acted in a 'reckless' fashion.[7] Her resignation, some eight weeks later, garnered unfavourable comparisons with the 'principled' and 'timely' resignation of the former Foreign Secretary and Leader of the House of Commons, the late Robin Cook.

The two Ministers' resignations were unevenly covered by the different parts of the British print media. Overall, the broadsheets contained 56 per cent of all the articles, compared to the mid-market and tabloid newspapers, which both contained 21 per cent.[8] Of the daily newspapers, the *Times* and *Guardian* led the others, closely followed by the *Mirror, Daily Mail* and *Independent*. The *Observer* headed up the Sunday newspapers. In terms of distribution by partisanship – defined in a 'common sense' fashion – there were more articles in the right-wing press: 57 per cent as compared to 40 per cent. When partisanship is defined as the 'political party of choice at the 2001 general election', this pattern is reversed, with 66 per cent of the articles published in pro-Labour newspapers. Most of the articles were published in the news section of the papers (41 percent), although a significant minority were published in the 'features' and 'leader' sections (19 percent and 21 per cent respectively). In terms of authorship, women wrote 24 per cent of the articles whilst men wrote 72 per cent, and mixed-sex teams 4 per cent. Disaggregating the newspapers by format shows that the broadsheet newspapers, perhaps unsurprisingly, offered more in-depth coverage, whilst the tabloids provided less extensive coverage with the mid range papers falling somewhere in between.

Contrary to women politicians' perceptions – tested by the first of the research techniques – the percentages of articles that refer to minister's personal and familial relations appears low (Table 6.1). Reporters do not seem to routinely mention the women Ministers' age, appearance and personal or familial relations.[9] Even the apparently ubiquitous 'Blair's Babes' label was rarely used in conjunction with these women, although this may reflect the fact that these women were not part of the new 1997 intake of women MPs.

Table 6.1 Percentage of articles that refer to the Ministers' personal and family relations

	Fashion	Appearance	Gendered personality	Marital	Age	Children	Blairs Babes
Estelle	7.8	18.7	30.7	8.4	10.8	0.6	3.6
Morris	(13)	(31)	(51)	(14)	(18)	(1)	(6)
Clare	7	8.8	43	7.0	3.5	12.3	0
Short	(8)	(10)	(49)	(8)	(4)	(14)	
Both	7.5	14.6	35.7	7.9	7.9	5.4	2.1
	(21)	(41)	(100)	(22)	(22)	(15)	(6)

Male journalists outnumbered women 158:52 in respect of the single-authored articles and there are nine articles written by teams of women and male journalists. There are no differences in the types of articles, by newspaper section, written by men and women journalists. Table 6.2 shows the distribution of articles mentioning personal information/attributes of the Ministers which shows, contrary to expectation, that higher numbers of references to the Ministers' personal attributes/situations were covered in the news section.

Table 6.2 Personal information mentioned, by newspaper section

	News	Features	Leaders
Fashion	3	4	4
Appearance	8	5	4
Age	7	0	0
Marital	7	1	1
Children	7	1	1
Blair's Babes	1	0	0

There is little evidence in this study that the sex of the journalist made a difference to the coverage of the Ministers' appearance, age, marital status and children, or the use of the term 'Blair's Babes'. 17 per cent of articles written by men and 17 per cent of articles written by women refer to appearance; 33 per cent of mixed sex authored; age was covered in articles written by 6 per cent women, 11 per cent men and 11 per cent mixed; 8.9 per cent articles by men mentioned the Ministers' marital situation compared to 11.5 per cent of those written by women, and 22.2 per cent of those written by women and men together; 13.5 per cent of articles written by women mention children, compared to 11.1 per cent of articles written by mixed-sex team (just one article) and 4 per cent of those written by men. Women journalists were, however, significantly more likely to discuss fashion than their male colleagues, as Table 6.3 shows ($p = 0.001$).[10]

Table 6.3 Mention of fashion by sex of author

	Not mentioned	Mentioned	Total
Male	95%	5%	100%
Female	79%	21%	100%
Mixed	100%	0%	100%

With respect to how the women were 'named' in the headlines there are some intra-sex differences (Table 6.4). Whilst the number of times the ex-Ministers' first names are used is similar, Short was much more likely to be referred to by her family name than was Morris, although this difference probably reflects the ability of headline writers to use 'Short' as a pun – 'Short n so Sharp'; 'Rebel who Deserves Short Shift'; and 'Vengeful Clare is Short on Integrity'.

Table 6.4 How the Ministers were named in the headlines

	First name	Family name	Both names	Not named	Other	Total
Estelle Morris	21%	23%	12%	36%	8%	100%
Clare Short	19%	38%	19%	16%	9%	100%

In terms of critical evaluations – examined here in terms of the number of negative and positive headlines – there is further suggestive evidence of intra-sex differences, as Table 6.5 shows.[11] Short receives many more negative headlines than does Morris, a situation which is reversed in respect of positive headlines. This differential representation may reflect the harsher evaluations given to women who transgress gender norms: as the qualitative analysis of the use of gendered headlines and adjectives demonstrates (see below), despite Morris' failings as a Minister (and these are extensively discussed in the press) she was, in the manner of her resignation, nonetheless perceived to be acting in line with traditional notions of femininity. In contrast, Short was both a 'bad' Cabinet Minister and a 'bad' woman.

Table 6.5 Headline evaluations of the Ministers

	Negative	Positive	Neutral	Not about Minister	Total
Estelle Morris	14%	13%	25%	49%	100%
Clare Short	29%	8%	33%	30%	100%
Both	*20%*	*11%*	*28%*	*41%*	*100%*

Despite expectations that left-wing newspapers might be more sympathetic to the resigning women Ministers, and right-wing newspapers more hostile, there is little evidence in the quantitative analysis of headlines to support the claim that partisanship played much of a role: left-wing newspapers were more likely than right-wing newspapers to contain more negative (23 per cent and 18 per cent, respectively) and positive headlines (13 per cent and 10 per cent, respectively).

Table 6.6 Use of gender frame by sex of author

	Gender frame	No gender frame	Total
Women	42% (22)	58% (30)	100% (52)
Men	27% (42)	73% (116)	100% (158)
Mixed authorship	56% (5)	44% (4)	100% (9)

Turning to the analysis of gender frame articles, just over 40 per cent of the articles written by women journalists employed a gender frame compared to just over one quarter of those written by men – differences that are statistically significant at the 0.05 level. Those articles with mixed authorship were more likely to employ a gender frame than not, although the number of cases here are very small. Whether these differences reflect the division of labour within the newspapers rather than sex is hard to judge because of the small number of cases: of the 19 gender frame articles in the news section ten are written by men and six by women, with three having mixed authorship. In total there are only 16 gender frame leader/opinion pieces and five in the features section. Sex differences are once again apparent in the news section: ten men compared to six women employed a gender frame (22 per cent and 35 per cent respectively); in the leader/opinion section of the newspapers the differences were smaller, eleven and five (73 per cent and 63 per cent) respectively, and in the other direction. However, none of these differences were statistically significant, though the small n makes significance less likely.

Estelle Morris' 'woman's resignation'

In her resignation letter to the Prime Minister, Morris was explicit about her reasons for resigning:

> I've learnt what I'm good at and also what I'm less good at ... I am less good at strategic management of a huge department and I am not good at dealing with the modern media

In short, Morris considered herself not to have been 'as effective as I should be or as effective as you need me to be'. That Morris chose to resign was less, according to media accounts, an indictment of her abilities than of her character – although there were of course many who criticized her performance. For some, it was more than this, it was, nothing less than a 'women's resignation' – a term attributed to the 'alpha male' interviewer of the BBC's Newsnight, Jeremy Paxman.[12] More specifically, the media representation of Morris' resignation took one of three forms: first, they made reference to her honesty. Second, they referred to her personality and character traits, of which her honesty was just one dimension. Finally, they adopted one of four specific gender frames: (1) woman's resignation (2) politics as male (3) 'all women' – the failure of one woman reflects on all women and (4) the 'not her own woman' thesis in which women politicians are denied agency.

The **women's resignation** frame suggests that only a woman would have resigned in the manner of Morris:

- 'how refreshing to hear a politician come clean and how typical that it took a woman to do it';
- '... in its harsh judgments of her own abilities and lack of self-belief, [Morris' resignation letter] would never have been written by a man';
- 'you can never imagine Gordon Brown or Alan Milburn saying anything like she did';
- 'from memory the only other notably gracious departures I can recall are Harriet Harman ... and Margaret Thatcher'.

The **all women** gender frame refers to statements that group women politicians together and, or, draw on notions of shared gender identity and characteristics. For example: 'So she wanted out. And let women down'. This category also includes statements that question this elision. For example, 'those who claim Estelle Morris' resignation last week represented a defeat for all women, fail to explain how her appointment ... marked a victory for all women'; or, as another newspaper put it: '[when] the England football manager Kevin Keegan resigned ... no one argued that this was a setback for footballers with feelings'.

The **not her own woman** thesis suggests that Morris was subject to the will of other men, either her junior Minister David Milliband, the special advisor Andrew Adonis, the Prime Minister Tony Blair, or other unnamed men in Downing Street. To illustrate: 'Ms Morris could never entirely shake off the impression that she was Tony Blair's creature and doing his bidding'; 'he never intended her to run education policy. That would be done from No. 10' while 'she mouthed platitudes and gave impressive performances at photo-calls'. One article went so far as to suggest that this was a reason for her inclusion in the Cabinet: Blair 'was so determined to appoint a puppet that he gave Morris her ill-fated promotion'.

The **politics as male** frame claims that women are unsuited for politics and implies that women's presence in politics transgresses gender norms: 'the tabloids presented her as a lonely 50-year-old single woman married to her job, going home to her flat every night and letting the drip, drip, drip of criticism keep her awake all night'. This frame also includes arguments that women and men have different styles of politics and that politics is, whether unfortunately or not, 'macho'. The argument runs that Morris lacked the aggressive 'bruiser instincts'; and needed to 'grow the armadillo skin'; '... advisers were still having to tell her to stop wrapping her arms protectively around her body and crossing her legs when being interviewed'.

Gendered adjectives: Estelle Morris, the 'hopeless' and 'hapless' Minister

More than 100 different adjectives were used to describe the Cabinet Minister that was Estelle Morris. The number of critical adjectives is larger and used more often than the positive ones, and the negative adjectives are also 'more negative' than the positive ones, some of which look like faint praise. On the positive side, Morris is regarded as 'passionate about education' and children – there is no doubting her 'commitment', 'dedication', 'competency' and 'earnest' 'hard work', although none of these comments speak of her abilities to deliver on her Ministerial responsibilities. In this respect, Morris is felt to be 'principled' and 'inspired' – a 'credible' politician who has 'spoken intelligently', and is 'likeable' and 'assertive'. On the negative side, as a Minister, Morris is 'less than sure footed', 'slow to take decisions' and lacks 'judgment', and 'authority'; in essence, she is 'hopeless', 'hapless' and 'accident prone'. Indeed, she was 'drowning', a woman who had been 'abused', 'grilled', 'battered' – a Minister who having needed to 'get a grip' but, with her 'confidence undermined', simply 'couldn't cope'; 'haunted' and ultimately 'hounded' out of office.

Nevertheless, Morris' resignation provided the media with the opportunity to lavish praise on the former Minister's 'refreshing' 'honesty' – the latter being the most frequent adjective used to describe Morris, employed more than 30 times. By resigning in such a 'candid' way, she demonstrated her 'candour' – how 'straight' and 'unspun' she was. Morris is an 'honourable' and 'decent' woman with 'integrity' – 'frank' in admitting her failing as a Cabinet Minister. Her resignation is therefore considered 'sincere' and 'noble', an act which shows her 'humanity' and 'humility'. For some, her action was 'brave' and revealed that she 'had guts' and 'character' – she has 'done the right thing' and gone with 'good grace'. However, her 'dignified' resignation also reveals her 'self-doubt'. Here is someone who is 'self-abasing' and 'selfless'. 'Timid' and 'meek', 'emotional' and 'sensitive', Morris suffers from a 'nervous' disposition; too 'thin skinned' she took 'everything personally'. She is, commentators deduced, too 'gentle', too 'sheltered' and 'private', even too 'nice' – and, for one commentator, even 'masochistic'. As such, she was overly 'self-critical' with 'low self-esteem' and with little 'self-respect'.

These attributes are only partially countered by more positive appraisals: she is 'open-minded', 'unaffected', 'well meaning', 'modest/unflashy', 'dutiful', 'sweet', and 'diffident' – in short 'normal' (like a woman). At the same time, she is regarded as somebody who 'bared' and 'opened her soul' – 'self-knowing'. More positive comments were few and far between: in one case she is considered 'eloquent' and another 'outspoken'. Representations which discussed her relationship with teachers and students – Morris had herself practised the profession for nearly two decades – find her 'empathetic' to both teacher and students. This is not necessarily a positive attribute for a Secretary of State for Education who, as one critical paper suggested, shared their 'producer' interest. But, for all the representation of Morris as weak, in a small number of cases when the papers were discussing the 'sacking' of the head of the Qualifications and Curriculum Authority (QCA), she was regarded as 'shrewd' and 'spiteful'. Her apparent shrewdness was also evident in the way in which she managed to negotiate the Blair–Brownite camps at the heart of the Labour Government – whilst she had secured from Brown extensive funding for education, she could also count on the support of Blair.

Morris' perceived personality traits were further evidenced in characterizations of her gendered political style – this Secretary of State did not 'play by the rules', preferring to 'work with' and 'listen and learn' from others; to 'negotiate', be 'pragmatic' and play the role of 'peace-maker'. With an 'emollient' style, she was 'caring' and 'self-effacing' – a Minister who brought an air of 'freshness' to the job. All of which might be to the good, except that such a style of politics is often considered less effective and less appropriate (Cowley and Childs 2003). Being a 'genuinely nice person' or a 'brilliant human being' is not a qualification for political office – neither is being compared to Mother Theresa.

The headlines: Downfall of the Cabinet golden girl who refused to play the political game

The headlines that accompanied Morris' resignation present a traditional view of what and who constitutes politics and politicians: Morris may have given politics 'a touch of class', but she was ultimately incompatible with political life. It is not enough to be considered a Saint, she could not take the pressure – one headline read 'I can't stand the heat: Estelle fails to make the grade as education chief but gets an A for honesty'. She did not even have the 'pungently individual style, call it sex appeal' of Nancy Astor, Margaret Thatcher or Mo Mowlam to save her.

The designation of Morris' resignation as a **'woman's resignation'** is evident in a headline that linked her honesty to her sex/gender: 'her lesson in honesty puts men to shame', while another paper baldly stated that Westminster was 'unused to such admissions of frailty'. That Morris was **not her own woman** is demonstrated in the depiction of her as 'being jerked on strings pulled from somewhere high above'; in head-lines that fore-grounded her 'feud' and 'clash' with Adonis; and in the injunction to her successor that the 'education system will benefit' if he 'is his own man'. That Morris' resignation might be symbolic of **all women** was explicitly stated in two headlines: 'Will admission of failure condemn women to political wilderness: fall out from Morris resignation opens debate about 'softer' style'; '[journalists ask] ... if her downfall will damage the high hopes of other Labour women'. Yes, was the answer in one newspaper: 'Estelle has let us down: the Minister's resignation was a bad day for all women'. Such views are, however, contested: her resig-nation demonstrates a bullying 'political culture that patronizes and pigeonholes women'. Indeed, the following examples show that women MPs acted in the aftermath of her resignation to ensure that the (perceived) sexism of the press was revealed to the public. The *Times* headline on the 26 October 'The weak in politics' is challenged by others: 'Ministers' fury at sexist jibes'; 'women MPs seethe over sexist tributes'. Nonetheless, and despite headlines acknowledging her brav-ery, dignity, and principled stance – again adjectives that whilst objec-tively positive may have more negative connotations when applied to politics – Morris was commonly depicted as somebody not suited to the cut and thrust of politics.

The contrast between the personality, characteristics and styles of the outgoing and incoming Secretaries of State for Education also fed into the depiction of **politics as male**. Her successor, Charles Clarke's 'bruiser' qualities were much remarked on: 'he's rough, he's tough'; 'A political heavyweight looking for a fight'. Moreover, that Blair would have wanted to, and should have, replaced Morris with such a politician was apparently self-evident: 'Only big guns need apply'. Yet for all the displayed hyper-masculinity of her replacement, there were headlines questioning more directly the maleness of politics – was the House of

Commons 'a woman's place?' – with the implication that it should be, and of whether those who 'refused to play the political game' could succeed.

A woman's resignation: Gender frames

Ten articles (out of the 45 that contained at least one reference to one of the four gender frames applied to Morris) were wholly framed in terms of gender. All bar one of these articles were written either individually by a woman journalist or women and male teams of journalists. Most were published in broadsheet newspapers (Table 6.7).

Table 6.7 Estelle Morris articles framed by gender, by sex of author, paper type and partisanship

Sex of author	Male	1
	Female	6
	Mixed	3
Newspaper	Broadsheet	7
	Midmarket	3
Partisan	Left-wing	4
	Right-wing	6

The overwhelming concern in the gender frame articles, even those that are less sympathetic overall, is that Morris' resignation would confirm 'every prejudice' against women in politics – even amongst 'perfectly decent, left-leaning men at Westminster'. In the words of Jackie Ashley:

> Up until this week, I had no idea there were so many different ways of saying 'I told you so', but the smugness I have seen among politicians is sickening. There's the sympathetic grin; the slight incline of the head with eyebrows raised; the knowing shrug of the shoulders – each and every one saying silently what only a few will dare to say aloud: 'Of course Estelle Morris couldn't stand the heat. We've known all along that women and politics just don't mix.'[13]

Here, then, was proof that the 'slow feminization of politics' was beating a retreat – there was no 'new deal for women'; it would now be harder for women to 'make their mark'. The gender of Morris' replacement – Charles Clarke – a man not noted for displaying his feminine side, was also widely remarked upon. It was a good day for macho qualities: 'hard men', 'big hitters' and 'bruisers'. In short, the 'football loving', male politician. In two articles, the coincidental timing of Morris' resignation and a Commons celebration for Harriet Harman's 20th Anniversary as a Member of Parliament was noted: the 'sisterhood, that loose mafia of well-connected, well-dressed Labour women, linked for years by their passion for female causes' were 'clutching their champagne flutes', 'appalled at Estelle throwing herself off the bridge'. Women MPs let it be known that they were 'angry and depressed' by Morris' resignation and media representations thereof.

Some women journalists evidently sought to identify women politicians who successfully practiced the masculinized art of politics, naming the 'fearless' Clare Short, the 'veteran', Margaret Beckett, and Patricia Hewitt – 'no shrinking violet'. They also named younger women in the government's junior ranks: Yvette Cooper and Ruth Kelly. More critical still is their accusation of 'bully boy tactics' by Blair's regime. Sue Cameron, writing in the *Mail on Sunday,* implies that the suggestion that Morris should have 'limited her ambition to being a home economics teacher' – was inspired by No. 10. Other victims of bullying were said to be Mo Mowlam and Harriet Harman. A defence of a 'women's style of politics' is also made: refusing to stand 'the heat' is a sign of 'sanity'; women are 'right' not to like the way politics works. This is, then, a systemic and not an individual failing. Hence, Morris was right to prefer a more cooperative style and to have rejected civil servants' advice to 'stir a public row and push her rival department'. She chose not to have a 'makeover', grow a thicker skin, or fight 'dirty'. Indeed, women's difference might form a basis for a better kind of politics. Stewart Steve, writing in the *Mail on Sunday,* commented:

> If the only reason for bringing women to Westminster is so that they can behave in exactly the same way as rough, unimaginative testosterone-fuelled, over-ambitious men, then that would seem to me to be pretty pointless.

For this reason, he rejects women MPs' fears that Morris' resignation has put back 'the cause of women in politics'. Yet, such conclusions sit uncomfortably alongside others' concern that Morris' behind-the scenes approach might be equated with 'dodging the real arguments'.

Two of the gender frame articles, both written by women (in the *Daily Telegraph* and the *Sunday Express*) are less sympathetic. In the former, Vicki Woods criticizes Morris for 'harping on' (as women do) about expecting to have 'enjoyed' her job – this is not a sufficient or legitimate reason to resign. It is also insulting to other women: 'most of the world's toilers and labourers go to work because they have to – something that is especially true of women, by the way'. In the second article, Nicola Barry depicts Morris as a simpering, grovelling woman: 'worrying about what others' think ... just doesn't work if you play with the big boys'. Her judgment is pointed: only a woman would have resigned in Morris' fashion. And to reinforce the negative evaluation, Lady Thatcher is exempted from the group: 'I was talking about women, not Maggie'.

Clare Short's resignation: 'Serially dissident'

Gendered adjectives: 'Big, dark and untidy'

In describing the character and personality of Clare Short, journalists employed a much larger number of adjectives than they did for Estelle Morris – more than 200 – and many fewer were used on multiple occasions. There was some, although not very much, positive coverage of Short's abilities and achievements as Secretary of State for International Development. She was recognized as 'committed' to the provision of aid to the developing world, with a 'flair for publicity'; she had been a powerful and efficient presence in her department – had 'excelled in the job she created'; 'punched above her weight in Cabinet' and secured extensive funds for her department from the Chancellor. Others, though, considered her 'un-influential', or more harshly, an 'unmitigated disaster'. Moreover, by the time of her resignation the 'unhappy' Minister's position and reputation had become, for many, 'undermined', 'tarnished' and 'damaged'; she had 'lost' her credibility and was now 'discredited' – a 'devalued currency'.

Short's personality was described using a veritable smorgasbord of adjectives, many of which are highly gendered. For her supporters in the press, she is 'warm', 'convivial' and 'energetic' – a 'strong' minded character with guts, with 'idealist beliefs' which she holds with unshakeable 'moral certainty' and a sense of 'duty'. She is neither 'uppity' nor 'pompous' and always keen 'to speak her mind'. Using more gendered language still, she is 'passionately sincere' and 'impassioned'; she has a 'fine mind' yet speaks 'the language of feeling', has conviction and principles, a sense of justice and the power to 'communicate strong feelings'. In one instance, an example where the evaluation of her was unquestionably positive, Short is regarded as a 'dutiful wife' with regard to the care she had given her late husband who suffered from Alzheimer's.[14]

Other gendered adjectives and evaluations are less sympathetic: Short is 'bossy' and 'mouthy' – all 'heart' and emotion; she 'whinges', 'whines', 'moans', 'wails' and 'bleats'; she is 'scatty', 'daffy' and 'huffy'; a 'moody' and 'brooding woman'. 'Proud' and 'flamboyant' she flounces off and is liable to 'rambling' and 'incoherent' rants. Indeed, her resignation is described in one paper as her having 'spat the dummy'. She is also, although only once, described as a 'feminist' (a negative attribute in their view), while others refer to her as a Kill Joy (a reference to her campaign against topless models in the *Sun* newspaper). Short needs to lighten up, be less of a 'po-faced puritan' and less 'frumpy'. Then there are allusions, implicit and explicit, to her state of mind: is she 'crazy?' one report asks. Others depict her as 'unstable' 'away with the fairies' and short of a 'few marbles'. 'Hot-blooded' and with a 'bleeding heart', Short is a 'woman scorned'. Furthermore, and leaving no little room for misinterpretation, Short is also depicted as a 'petulant princess', a 'spoilt diva' and a 'prima donna'. She is also 'Joan of Arc', Bodaecia and 'Eskimo Nell'.[15] Her resignation constitutes 'career sutee'.

Then there are the negative adjectives that might be regarded as having gendered connotations: vain, ludicrous, ridiculous and preposterous, wayward and erratic, inconsistent, unpredictable and contradictory – someone who 'prevaricates' and 'backtracks', 'breaking her word'; posturing, bombastic and vitriolic. Short is someone who fussed over 'the finer points' rather than seeing the bigger picture; she was 'theatrical' and 'created a fuss'; 'engages her mouth' before her brain – 'shooting her mouth off'; is explosive with a 'volatile' and 'mercurial' temperament – venomous; poisonous; scornful; revengeful; impulsive.

Finally, there are a host of other negative judgments: in interpersonal relations Short was 'spiteful' and 'churlishly ungrateful'. As a member of the government, she was naturally 'rebellious', 'serially dissident', 'consistently off message', 'leaky' and prone to 'disloyal outbursts'. In sum, she was a 'time-bomb ticking', or as one paper put it, 'a millstone around Tony Blair's neck' – 'disruptive', a 'trouble maker' and a 'loose cannon'. As a politician she was 'never exactly smooth', rather 'bungling', with 'faults', prone to making 'gaffes' and 'mistakes' – someone who was 'ignorant' and 'dumb', who was 'unfocused' in her rhetoric and who 'lacked political judgment', 'timing' and 'presentation skills'. At best she was a 'benign irritant' and 'powerless', not to be taken seriously, or a 'disappointment'. More critically, she was considered 'terrifying' and a 'bully', 'arrogant', 'belligerent' and 'truculent': a 'ruthless' if 'reckless' operator, consumed by 'hatred' and 'contempt'. Nonetheless, on two occasions she was considered to have 'chickened out' and 'pulled her punches'. Short is also depicted as 'foolish', 'naïve' and 'gullible'. It gets worse: she is self-interested, self-important, self-centred, self-obsessed, self-righteous, self-pitying (thin-skinned), self-indulgent, self-deceiving (in that she believed in her 'own allure') and 'self-igniting'.

In a number of articles, the representations elaborate a distinction between the **real** and **fake** Clare Short. The **real** Short is the 'egotist' who acts 'like a pop star', who is 'relentlessly ambitious', even though she tries to hide it. She is 'Lady Bountiful' or a 'Dowager', someone who loved the trappings of ministerial office to the extent that she was prepared to make 'compromises' to hold on to it – an 'unprincipled' and 'hypocritical' 'political opportunist' and 'careerist', even as she tries to be depicted as a 'martyr'. In some accounts Short is represented as 'too fond of drawing attention to herself', a 'publicity addict' and 'publicity crazed'. The fake Short, in contrast, is the 'holier-than-thou', 'standard bearer of the left' who dons a 'hairshirt in public', is 'frightfully principled' and acts as a 'political eccentric' – the 'maverick free spirit' whose moral rectitude is 'boldly on display' and whose conscience flaps 'for all to see' – 'purportedly a selfless saint'. The fake Short is also the 'caring mother' reunited with the son she gave up for adoption when she was young – arguably, here, even when Short displays traditional gendered attributes, she is regarded as merely aping traditional gender roles.

One other depiction of Short – just like Morris before her – is that she is **not her own woman**. This has two dimensions: the first claims that she was dependent upon the patronage of Gordon Brown – for one paper his 'catspaw', to another a 'sidewinder';16 the second that she was the acceptable face of rebellion and in that capacity, useful to Blair. Short remained an 'outsider' even whilst nominally at the heart of politics and notwithstanding the fact that she was a 'pints drinking forceful woman'.

Headlines: Come off it ladies – it's time to grow up

Only a minority of the headlines accompanying articles on Short's resignation are positive:

- 'Short's stance is highly admirable';
- 'Foreign aid, Sharp Ms Short will be missed';
- 'Valerie [Amos, the incoming Secretary of State for International Development] will fall Short';
- 'Short pioneered proper path for government aid';
- 'The wisdom of Clare';
- 'Write her off at your peril'.

Others are contradictory, both praising and criticizing her:

- 'Short on friends but long on Commitment; Baroness Amos has a hard act to follow';

- 'Maverick who excelled at job she created: campaign leftie who challenged the Sun's Page 3 Girls, Cannabis ...';
- 'Ms Short's reputation is tarnished, despite the accuracy of her argument'.

Many of the negative headlines emphasize the timing of her resignation:

- 'Ever mistaken, Clare flays Blair five years too late';
- 'Took your time Clare';
- 'About time too, Clare';
- 'Too little too late'.

Then there are those that ridicule her resignation or question the manner of her leaving: 'I quit! tears, tantrums and ta-ras ... how celebs bow out Blair'; 'suicidal blast in Commons: no one hurt'; 'no fiddling around with protocol. She just let rip'; 'she left spitefully, all credibility gone'; 'red alert at Clare'. Other headlines questioned her abilities as a Minister: 'Memo to Lady Amos: ignore Clare Short'; 'Foreign aid can be freed from Short's diktats and prejudice'; 'tiresome, though un-influential, thorn on government's side'; whilst one noted that 'Short's Dept [was] allocated extra aid to the booze cabinet'.

Aside from these negative headlines, others drew upon the contrast between the real and fake Clare Short:

- 'How Clare Short's conscience didn't stop her reckless ways';
- 'Short on principle';
- 'A career destined to end in tears: why the keeper of the party's conscience had to go';
- 'Its hypocrisy';
- 'Wrath of reborn firebrand';
- 'A career of calling a spade a shovel'.
- 'Dowager Short leads mourning for old Labour'.

Others explicitly employ the 'all women' and 'politics as male' gender frames

- 'The Westminster pack has the scent of its favourite prey again. A woman of integrity who falls from grace will be torn to shreds by far ...'
- 'Come off it ladies – its time to grow up';
- 'Clare is selling all women short'.

The allusion to the category of 'mad women' is fore-grounded in one headline for an article written by Mo Mowlam: 'When they question your sanity, it drives you mad' and in those headlines that made reference to Blair's apparently having indicated nonverbally in Cabinet with hand motions that she was 'mad'. The 'not her own woman' thesis is presented in a few headlines: 'Was Brown behind Short's scathing attack on Blair';[17] and 'Don't cry for Clare; As Tony Blair's licensed rebel, Short appeased the powerful and brushed the poor aside'.

There were some clues that he was lying clare: gender frame articles

Table 6. 8 Clare Short articles framed by gender, by sex of author, paper type and partisanship

Sex of author	Male	2
	Female	3
Newspaper[18]	Broadsheet	2
	Midmarket	2
	Tabloid	1
Partisan	Left-wing	2
	Right-wing	3

Three of the gender frames employed in respect of Estelle Morris are shared in the five gender frame articles of Clare Short's resignation: 'politics as male', 'all women' and 'not her own woman'. There was also a fourth frame – the 'love' frame. This refers to articles that frame Short's resignation in terms of her relationship with Blair as analogous to a (doomed) love affair.

Mark Steel's short article in the *Independent* epitomizes the **love** frame. Its headline, 'There were some clues that he was lying Clare', and opening paragraph position Short's resignation as akin to when a 'woman leaves a dreadful bloke'.[19] He goes on:

> 'She's crying "he never listens to me" and everyone else is thinking: "we told you that all along, you idiot". Then, when she blubbers "he promised me he'd involve me in rebuilding Iraq", you almost feel like patting her on the head and saying "we told you he didn't mean it you silly girl"'.

Suzanne Moore's piece in the *Mail on Sunday* employs the same frame:[20] Short is criticized for having 'given in to Tony's charms' and Moore wonders, what 'sweet nothings kept her hooked?' Was it the 'idea that Mr Rumsfeld would be phoning to ask her opinion on the best way to reconstruct Iraq?' she asks, with the implication that Short surely could not have been so naïve. Despite these critical comments, Moore shows how the love frame shares a view of women in public life as 'little more than a bundle of uncontrollable feelings'. To draw out this contrast, she writes of the representation of Robin Cook's resignation as 'all forensic intellect and repressed emotion'. Yet 'women like Short are not allowed intellect instead they are just heart'. Moore also names Mo Mowlam 'bracketed in the emotions department' – 'big powerful, messy women', 'erratic, unstable and moody'. Both are symbolic of all women. This is considered unfair and a double standard: 'did Peter Mandelson [who resigned twice from Blair's cabinet] let down all men, then?' she asks.

The question of Short's mental capacity is another dominant representation, interpreted sometimes as an extension of women's unsuitability for politics more generally. In the *Sunday Telegraph,* Germaine Greer (author of the classic second wave feminist text, *The Female Eunuch)* recounts Blair's behaviour in Cabinet, by which he implied that Short was mad.[21] His actions 'consigned [Short] to the company of batty females', which includes Margaret Thatcher and Mo Mowlam, two women first 'entrusted with high office' only later to be 'reviled as crazy'. This narrative implies not that the actions of 'Tony's cronies', who 'hoodwinked, massaged and knifed' her in the back, was sufficient to 'drive any woman insane' (which she argues they were), but that Short was a 'loose cannon' all along. Neither does the charge against Short appear to have any implications for Blair's reputation. Why is his political judgment not questioned for having had her in his Cabinet for so long, Greer asks? Elsewhere it is suggested that Short had had to be protected and rescued from her own 'rollicking' life by the government machine, although no supporting evidence is provided.

The most extensively employed gender frame is the **not her own woman** frame. Either Short is the client of her 'patron' and 'protector', Gordon Brown, or she is the Cabinet Minister played by the Prime Minister. Illustrations of the former include: 'With Gordon Brown's help (this has been a key) she has raised Britain's game in international development'; 'It was Gordon Brown who argued forcefully for her to stay after her own charge of "reckless" against the PM'. In respect of the latter, Short is the 'licensed jester' and 'acceptable face of rebellion', better to have inside the tent than out and used to 'pacify the Labour left'. She was a Minister 'protected by Blair 'through thick and thin';[22] while he was the man who 'handed her the only Cabinet rank she was qualified to hold'.

The gender frame articles also address the question of women and men's style of politics Women are 'typically hands on' and are reluctant to delegate and to 'admit that management is the art of taking credit for other people's work'. In contrast, successful male career politicians do not make the fundamental mistake of 'actually doing the work' and 'failing to take the credit for it'. In this respect, Greer typifies Estelle Morris's career in the following fashion:

> If Estelle Morris had been a man, bred up to the system of grooming and controlling a squad of subalterns who actually do the footwork and prepare the briefs and draft the settlements and take the blame, she would have avoided letting on the entire world last October that she was not 'up to the job' ... Morris insisted on claiming cock-ups that were in fact none of her making. She never mastered double-speak, and both Short and Mowlam are like her ...

The reaction of women MPs to Short's resignation is described in Quentin Lett's parliamentary sketch in the *Daily Mail*.[23] 'The sisterhood is in a strop' he declares. 'All four MPs directly behind Miss Short were women'. She was 'kissed, hard, by tweedy, sensibly shod Angela Eagle[24] ... another embrace came from Ann Keen' who 'handed Miss Short a postcard. From above I could see it bore the old slogan "Women with Labour for the Children's Sake"'. That Keen is a parliamentary aide to Gordon Brown is also noted. Lett's article concludes by evaluating Short's resignation speech in the Commons: she 'was controlled' and 'straightforward in her fury'; there was no 'boozed-up, emotional, lip-wobbling whine some had expected'.

There is one highly critical gender frame article, by Sue Carroll in the *Mirror*.[25] Short's campaign in the 1980s to ban topless models from the *Sun* newspaper is ridiculed: though Carroll claims she is 'not banging a drum here for topless models', Short is, nonetheless, depicted as a 'po-faced puritanical'. The manner of Short's resignation has, according to Carroll, demeaned her sex 'without [Short] removing so much as her scarf' – putting her actions not on a par with 'Page 3 models', but as *more* damaging to women. By failing to recognize 'her folly' – succumbing to a 'timely bit of ego-stroking from the PM' and retreating with dignity', Short had merely 'confirmed the male perception of the unstable, neurotic PMT woman'. Why, Carroll laments, 'do women strive for a voice only to end up whining and bleating about themselves?'

Notes

1 *Times*, 7 March 2006.
2 *Guardian*, 13 October 2006.
3 Polly Toynbee, *Guardian*, 25 October 2002.

4 To ensure coder reliability a research assistant coded 20 per cent of randomly selected articles – the level of agreement was 84 per cent.

5 This is how Philip Cowley put it.

6 Morris returned to Government as a Minister of State for the Arts in 2003 in the Department of Culture, Media and Sport.

7 March 9 2003. http://news.bbc.co.uk/1/hi/uk_politics/2836925.stm

8 The *Times* and the *Guardian* now take a tabloid and Berliner format, respectively. However, they remain broadsheets in the sense that they are 'high' brow newspapers. I'd like to thank Marian Sawer for this point.

9 This is, of course, not to say that relative to men women politicians receive disproportionate attention in these areas.

10 When these six individual categories of personal information are grouped there are also no statistically significant differences in the coverage by women and men journalists.

11 Positive/negative coding refers to judgements about the Minister's personality, abilities and/or resignation; the neutral category includes headlines that contained both positive and negative comments or describe the Minister's resignation without evaluating it; there was a fourth category for those headlines that did not directly refer to the Minister.

12 *Telegraph*, 29 October 2002.

13 Jackie Ashley, the *Guardian*, 26 October 2002.

14 In two instances she was described as having a 'messy' and 'colourful' private life.

15 This is, to say the least, a crude ballad about two men who go on a sexually violent rampage and are emasculated by a woman – the 'ball-breaking' eponymous Eskimo Nell.

16 Sidewinder: a punch from the side.

17 A few headlines explored the impact of Short's resignation on Gordon Brown's chances of becoming PM after Blair.

18 *Sunday Telegraph, Independent, MOS, Daily Mail* and the *Mirror*.

19 15 May 2003.

20 18 May 2003.

21 18 May 2003.

22 In the *Independent* (13 May 2003) Andrew Grice writes: 'in 1997, he helped her get out of hot water after a late-night incident at Labour's annual conference that could have cost her cabinet job'. There is no further elaboration as to what this refers to.

23 13 May 2003.

24 Arguably, this is a euphemism for Eagle's lesbianism.

25 14 May 2003.

Conclusion

It is sometimes claimed that there is too much attention paid to gender in the study of British politics; that feminist scholars are a 'well-organized' voice in the discipline – and by implication that feminist analysis is no longer a marginalized body of knowledge (Moran 2006). If only that were the case. It is true that gender and politics has emerged as a coherent and burgeoning sub-field in the academic discipline of politics, both in the UK and globally. Feminist political science has some presence in the mainstream: over the last few years three British political science journals have commissioned 'state of the art' gender and politics articles (Mackay 2004a; Childs and Krook 2006a/b; Krook and Squires 2006). Nonetheless, mainstream party scholars often fail to fully engage with feminist analyses. Research monographs, textbooks and conference contributions, routinely ignore or marginalize the gender effects present in British party politics.

Women and British Party Politics seeks to fill in some of the gaps in the extant literature: to provide, in a single volume, discussion of the conceptual frameworks and debates that characterize contemporary gender and politics research, along-side the presentation of empirical research. Moreover, the analysis of the role of women, and particular conceptions of gender at play in British party politics examined in this book, are undertaken in light of a contention that feminization is likely to become a more significant feature of British politics in the future. The book's aims were, in the end, quite limited: to examine the feminization of British party politics in the post-1997 period. Feminization refers to the integration of women in formal political institutions and the integration of women's concerns into political debate and policy (Lovenduski 2005a).

Women and British Party Politics' focus is at the national level, looking at women's mass and elite participation as voters, as members of the three main UK political parties, and as parliamentary representatives at Westminster. Where possible, comparisons are drawn with research on the Scottish Parliament and National Assembly for Wales.

Providing rich description of the characteristics of women's participation in British party politics was one goal of the book, exploring what this meant for ideas about, and the practice of, descriptive, substantive and symbolic representation was the second. The next stage for gender and politics research is, in respect of the former, to develop gendered typologies of parties, understandings of party change and the characteristics of gendered party systems. In respect of the latter, future research should move beyond a fascination with numbers and any simple notion of a direct link between women's presence and symbolic and substantive representation. There is also an urgent need for more comprehensive and systematic empirical research.

Participation and voting. The feminist literature on women's political participation in Britain may not be extensive but it, nonetheless, challenges old assumptions about women's apolitical nature. Women may not participate as much as men in some aspects of traditional and formal party politics, but they are politically interested and active, albeit sometimes differently from men. What remains to be determined is whether women's and men's different forms of political participation in politics have both symbolic and substantive effects. In terms of vote choice, the role of sex and gender is not straightforward; rather than women and men voting differently (a sex difference), other factors combine with sex to determine vote choice (a gender difference). This is most obvious in the gender-generation gap in attitudes and in voting. In this, younger women are more left-leaning, and more likely to vote Labour, than both younger men and older women and men. A motivational gender generation gap is also evident, with women and men's vote choice underpinned by different reasons: younger women are more likely to prioritize education and older women healthcare. Noting these findings, British political parties – who are increasingly competing for women's votes, which are both numerous and seemingly 'up for grabs' – should ensure that they do not target women voters as if they constituted an homogenous bloc.

Feminizing British political parties. British political parties are, as yet, far from fully feminized in respect of either the integration of women or the integration of women's concerns, and may, from feminist perspectives, fall a long way short of integrating feminists and feminist concerns. Nevertheless, a space has opened up for intervention, by both party and civil society gender equality activists, to make demands of British political parties. These challenges, and the parties' responses, can be mapped. Parties' formal policy-making procedures can also be outlined and the form of their women's organizations described. It is not sufficiently clear at this stage, however, how the latter fit in practice, if not on paper, with the former. Women's organizations also look to be under-resourced, with informal rather than formal inputs, and without clear lines of accountability, either downwards to women party members and/or upwards to Party Leaders. Even so, a preliminary framework for distinguishing between party types is outlined; one in which both dimensions of feminization are addressed and in which parties' responses can be categorized as feminist, neutral or anti-feminist.

The process of party change is best illustrated in *Women and British Party Politics* by the discussions of the recent reforms of the Conservative Party's selection procedures – one indicator of feminization. Conservative Party gender equality activists have been mobilized for some time. Previously, they operated largely behind the scenes. Post-2005 they became more vocal, public and strategic in their demands, playing a role in the gendering of the Conservative Party Leadership contest itself. For these reasons, the reforms to the party's selection procedures associated with David Cameron's Leadership – the most visible manifestation of the feminization of the Conservative party at this time – cannot be considered a straightforward, top-down leadership effort. Moreover, the subsequent reforms to candidate selection fall short of measures that *guarantee* the election of substantially greater numbers of Conservative women MPs at the next General Election. If the sex balance of the parliamentary Conservative Party is not significantly altered at that time, it is highly likely that the already mobilized gender equality activists will become more demanding than hitherto. Whether they would be able to successfully contest any counter mobilization is another matter, and would be an empirical question for future research.

Women's legislative recruitment. Feminist political scientists have devoted considerable attention, and over a longer period of time, to women's legislative recruitment. Analytic frameworks in this area are more developed (Norris and Lovenduski 1995) and there is a broad consensus, at least amongst gender and politics scholars, that party demand is the key determinant of women's descriptive representation at Westminster. The asymmetry between the three parties in the House of Commons – Labour women MPs constitute 77 per cent of all women MPs in the 2005 Parliament – reflects the Labour party's use of equality guarantees: AWS in 1997 and 2005.

The choice between different equality strategies is determined, at least in part, by one's understanding of the relative role that various socio-economic, cultural and political factors play in determining women's descriptive representation. If supply-side explanations are perceived to be paramount, equality rhetoric (for example, exhorting women to participate) and promotion measures (for example, training or financial support) should deliver greater numbers of women representatives. If demand is identified as the problem, neither equality rhetoric nor equality promotion is likely to be sufficient: equality rhetoric may encourage greater numbers of women to enter the candidate recruitment pool; equality promotion may ensure that women aspirant candidates are sufficiently better prepared, trained, and resourced; but neither of these can guarantee that party selectorates will select women for seats or positions on electoral lists from which they will get elected, all other things being equal. For this reason, neither the Conservatives nor the Liberal Democrats are *guaranteed* to make significant gains at the next General Election, relying as they are on equality rhetoric and promotion. Thus, if Labour loses seats, it is more than likely that the overall number and percentage of women MPs will decline.

Symbolic Representation. The symbolic effects of women's presence in British party politics are relatively understudied. In *Women and British Party Politics*, symbolic representation is considered in terms of the media representation of women politicians with a single Case Study of the resignations of Estelle Morris and Clare Short from Tony Blair's Cabinet. A multitude of gendered stereotypes and adjectives are used to describe the two women Ministers, and particular gender frames are used. As a single, intra-sex study, the Case Study's findings can only be a modest contribution to the British literature on gender, politics and the media. Furthermore, symbolic representation has other dimensions than media representation (Norris *et al.* 2004): inter alia, gender and politics scholars should investigate how the sex and gender of representatives affects women's feelings about politics; whether their sense of efficacy and political competence is enhanced when institutions have parity of representation, or when women are represented by women (Lawless 2004; High-Pippert and Comer 1998); and whether perceptions of legitimacy are greater when political institutions are descriptively representative.

Substantive representation. For many feminist activists, as well as feminist political scientists, women's political presence matters because of an intuitive sense that women will make a gendered difference when they are present in our political institutions. Indeed, supporters and skeptics, alike, seek answer to the question of what 'difference'. women make in politics. Often the answer is that women will simply 'make a difference'. The nebulousness of this term no doubt goes a long way in explaining why it has seemed so attractive and yet, as argued in Chapter 5, it will no longer do to claim that women will 'make a difference'. *Women and British Party Politics* offers a critical reading of the concept of critical mass, the dominant conceptual framework that has been employed by much of the gender and politics literature to investigate the relationship between women's descriptive and substantive representation. The argument is clear: feminists should walk away from 'critical mass theory', even whilst recognizing that this only partially represents the views of its key authors, Kanter and Dahlerup. Any idea that simply counting the number of women representatives will tell us very much about the likelihood of the substantive representation of women is no longer tenable. Research in the UK, as well as from the wider gender and politics community, has identified several relationships between the proportions of women present in political institutions and the substantive representation of women. Alongside insights from state feminism and comparative literatures, it has become evident that there are multiple actors and multiple sites for women's substantive representation. For these reasons, the focus of gender and politics research should no longer be on '*when* women representatives make a difference' but on '*how* the substantive representation of women occurs'. In this approach, the concept of critical actors is preferred to critical mass theory. Critical actors are those individuals and/or institutions which seek to act for women; they may act on their own or embolden others to participate – they may also stimulate a backlash; crucially, they do not have to be women; what critical actors share is a low threshold for acting for women.

Shifting the overarching research question in this way, and adopting new analytic frames, generates new questions for future research (Celis *et al.* 2007). Addressing these allows us, ultimately, to ask, and then answer, '*what is* the substantive representation of women?' The first question is, '*who* acts for women?' namely, who are the critical actors and with whom do they act? The second question is, '*where* does the substantive representation of women occur?' The third question is, '*why* is the substantive representation of women attempted?' The fourth question is, '*how* is the substantive representation of women expressed?' In sum, the argument here is that the substantive representation of women is likely to take place at many different and interacting levels of government and in a variety of political fora; that over the course of the research the critical actors and the motivations behind 'acting for women' should become identifiable (Celis 2005); and that it is necessary to explore interventions at various points in political processes to identify the claims made in favour of women's substantive representation, the actions taken to promote the substantive representation of women, as well as the outcomes of these attempts.

Studying 'how the substantive representation of women occurs', together with operationalizing the additional questions outlined above, demands a second shift: one in research design and methods. Analysis of the 'micro' rather than the 'macro' level is privileged, namely, the investigation of what specific actors do rather than a focus on what 'women representatives' do? Future research on women's substantive representation should, at least in the first instance, engage in process-tracing and comparison. This approach should facilitate – as in Case Studies 5.5, 5.6 and 5.7 – the identification of critical actors, an appreciation of the contexts within which they act, as well as the wider features of particular policy-making processes. Developing a common research design in this fashion, one that permits comparison across cases, should, in turn, enable gender and politics scholars to identify more precisely how the findings of one research project 'speak' to those of another (Celis *et al.* 2007). As the number of comparisons grows, it will become possible to identify more systematically key variations in conditions consistent with the substantive representation of women across countries and over time.

Underpinning the empirical and conceptual research upon which *Women and British Party Politics* is based is a claim that women's presence in electoral politics is about more than securing justice, honourable and sufficient as that is. Despite continuing debate amongst scholars, feminist conceptions of gender and of representation provide support for a more optimistic reading that women's presence in electoral politics can have both symbolic and substantive effects. Claiming that women's concerns and perspectives will be fully addressed when those who participate in party politics or who sit in our political institutions are overwhelmingly male is highly contested. And of course, there can be no guarantees that the political presence of women will ensure women's representation, either symbolic or substantive. Feminists should be careful not to elide the presence of women in politics with the presence of feminists. Even so, the empirical research presented in *Women and British Party Politics*, provides a pretty good 'snapshot' of the political representation of women in the post-1997 period. Feminization is an ongoing process. Parity of representation remains a long way off at Westminster; and whilst there may well be less substantive representation of women than some feminists hoped for, there is, arguably, a lot more than the skeptics said there would be.

Appendix A Labour Party organization

Local / regional level

Branches (BLP)

Branches are structured around the ward boundaries for the election of councillors. At this level Party members have input in choosing local council candidates.

Constituencies (CLP)

Constituencies are based on the electoral areas for the election of MPs and therefore include several branches. At this level, members of the Party are involved in selecting representation at Conference and parliamentary candidates.

Local and regional policy forums

Local and regional policy forums provide an informal arena for policy discussion and makes submissions to the policy commissions.

Joint Local Government Committee (JLGC)

The JLGC is made up of members from the NEC, Government and Local Government and is responsible for promoting Party representation in local government.

National Level

Annual Conference

Conference is the ultimate authority of the Party, setting down policy frameworks and deciding Party rules. Delegates are elected.

National Policy Forum (NPF)

The NPF is a central institution in the Partnership in Power (PiP) process. It is made up of 183 representatives from all major stakeholder groups in the Party.

The NPF meets several times annually and serves to ensure that the policy is in line with the broad consensus of the Party. The NPF draws together policy consultation documents and monitors the consultation process to ensure all stakeholders participate fully. The NPF submits consultative and final policy documents to Conference in addition to an annual report on the work of the policy commission.

Elections to the NPF – each section of the NPF has its own method of electing NPF representatives. For example, nominations for the CLP section are put forward by CLPs and representatives elected at Conference.

NPF representatives

Constituency LP	55
Regions	22
TU	30
MPs	9
MEPs	6
Peer	2
Govt	8
Socialist Societies	3
Labour Students	1
Cooperative Party	2
Black Socialist Societies	4
Local Govt	9
NEC	32
Total	**183**

National Executive Committee (NEC)

Membership of the NEC is comprised of members of government, MPs, MEPs, councillors, trade unions and CLPs. All key stakeholders are represented. The NEC is the governing body of the Party and is responsible for setting the Party's objectives, the policy making process and overseeing the running of the Party at a national level.

Standing Committees[1]

1. The Women, Race and Equalities Committee
2. Audit Committee and Business Board – responsible for overseeing the business functions of the organisation.
3. Organisation Committee – responsible for party rules and constitution; overall responsibility for membership, investigations, selections, Conferences, electoral law, boundaries strategy and internal elections.

Panels[2]

1. Disputes Panel. This works in a quasi-judicial manner and hears membership appeals, re-admission applications, party disputes and conciliation, minor investigations and local government appeals when these are referred to the NEC.
2. Selections Panel

Policy commissions

There are currently six policy commissions made up of representatives from government, the NPF and the NEC. They are responsible for accepting submissions from branches, CLPs, policy forums and affiliates and preparing policy papers.

Currently the policy commissions (with 16–20 members each) are: Britain in the World; Creating Sustainable Communities; Crime, Justice, Citizenship and Equalities; Education and Skills; Health; Prosperity and Work.

Notes

1 Labour Party, 'Standing Committees', Labour Party Website, http://www.labour. org.uk/neccommittees, accessed 1st June 2006.
2 Ibid.

Appendix B

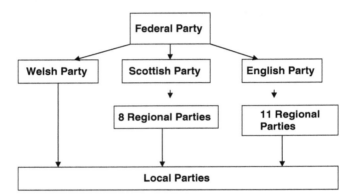

Federal Party

Welsh Party **Scottish Party** **English Party**

8 Regional Parties **11 Regional Parties**

Local Parties

Specified associated organizations
Ethnic Minorities; Youth and Students; Women; Assoc of Lib Dem councillors; DELGA, (Lesbian Gay, Bisexual and Transgender); Parliamentary Candidates Association; Agents and Organizers; ALDTU (trade unionists); ALDES (engineers and scientists).

Other organizations
E.g. Liberal Democrat Peace Group, Liberal Democrat Disability Association.

Figure B.1 Liberal Democrat Party organization

Appendix C Conservative Party policy making bodies

Key policy making institutions in the Conservative Party

- The Party Board is the ultimate decision making body of the Conservative Party. It meets monthly and responsibilities include: fundraising; membership; candidates and works with Conservative Central Office, and elected and voluntary members. Membership is comprised from each section of the Party – the voluntary, political and professional – and there are sixteen members, of whom three are currently women. Members are elected at the National Convention.
- The National Convention is comprised of every association chairman (625) plus approximately 150 representatives from the ten regions and 44 areas. All members of the Party Board and immediate previous National Convention office holders also hold seats, as do a further 100 representatives from recognized organizations. The National Convention meets twice yearly. A two-thirds majority is required for rule changes to be accepted and in some situations this has to be matched by a two-thirds majority vote by MPs. The National Convention provides a focus for views of Party members and acts as a link between the Party Leader and its members.
- Central to the party's 'policy renewal process' is the Conservative Party Forum. Launched in 2002 it provides a means through which party members' views can be sought on current issues and brought to the attention of the party leadership. Membership is open to all members of the Party. Local groups hold regular meetings (inviting visiting speakers/experts etc.) and individual members can contribute their views directly. The views of the CPF are submitted to the Research Department before findings are passed to the relevant Policy Group.
- The Conservative Councillors Association (CCA) represents Conservative councillors in the policy decision making processes of the party. Membership is comprised of elected Conservative councillors, candidates and members of the party who are involved in local government.

Appendix D   Women Ministers 1997–2005

Table D.1   Women MPs by portfolio in Blair's Cabinets 1997–2006[1]

	1997	2001	2005
Ann Taylor	Leader House of Commons; July 1998 Chief Whip	Chief Whip	Stands down at 2005 GE, enters House of Lords
Harriet Harman	Social Security, Women's Minister; July 1998 leaves Cabinet		
Margaret Beckett	Trade & Industry; July 1998, Leader House of Commons	Environment, Food and Rural Affairs	Environment, Food and Rural Affairs; May 2006 Secretary of State for Foreign and Commonwealth Affairs
Clare Short	International development	International development; May 2003, resigns	
Mo Mowlam	Northern Ireland; Oct 1999, Cabinet Office Minister, Chancellor of the Duchy of Lancaster	Stands down at 2001 GE	
Estelle Morris		Education and Skills; Oct 2002 resigns	
Patricia Hewitt		Trade & Industry, Women and Equality	Health
Helen Liddell	Jan 2001, Scotland	Scotland; June 2003, leaves Cabinet	

Table D.1 Women MPs by portfolio in Blair's Cabinets 1997–2006[1]—cont'd

	1997	*2001*	*2005*
Tessa Jowell		Culture, Media and Sport	Culture, Media and Sport, Minister for Olympics
Hilary Armstrong		Chief Whip	Chief Whip; May 2008 Minister for the Cabinet Office and for Social Exclusion (Chancellor of the Duchy of Lancaster)
Ruth Kelly		Dec 2004, Education and Skills	Education and Skills; May 2006, Communities and Local Government and Minister for Women
Jacqui Smith			May 2006, Chief Whip
Hazel Blears			May 2006, Minister without Portfolio and Party Chair

Note

1 This table does not include women members of the House of Lords. In July 1998 Baroness Jay becomes Leader of the House of Lords and Women's Minister and in May 2003 Baroness Amos became Secretary of State for International Development, and later in October 2003, Leader of the House of Lords.

Table D.2 The percentage of women (MPs and members of the House of Lords) in Blair's Cabinets

	Number	*Percentage in Cabinet*	*Percentage in PLP*
1997	5	22.7	24.1
2001	6	26.1	23.1
2005	6	27.2	27.5

Table D.3 Labour's Ministers for women

	Minister for Women in Cabinet	*Parliamentary Under Secretary of State*
1997 GE	Harriet Harman	Joan Ruddock
1998–01	Baroness Jay	Tessa Jowell
2001GE	Patricia Hewitt	Sally Morgan; 2001 Barbara Roche; 2003 Jacqui Smith
2005 GE	Tessa Jowell	Meg Munn
2005–2007	Ruth Kelly	Meg Munn

Appendix E Women's descriptive representation and the devolved institutions, 2007

In both Scotland and Wales, the percentage of women elected in 2007 declined. Women now constitute 33.3 per cent of MSPs and 46.7 per cent of AMs. The reasons are multiple, though the continuing and positive impact of Labour's original equality guarantees – through protecting some incumbent women – is observable. In both countries, women continued to be returned in greater number for constituency seats, although this does differ by party. In Scotland, Labour lost seats overall in 2007, and with them some of its women; though the SNP made overall gains, it fell back from its previous levels of women's representation; the Liberal Democrats failed to make progress; whilst the Conservatives increased the number of their women by two, from three to five. In Wales, Labour women were once again losers, as were women in the Conservative Party.

Table E.1 Members of the Scottish Parliament (MSPs), 2007

Party	Constituency women	Constituency men	Regional women	Regional men	% women
Labour	20	17	3	6	50
SNP	5	16	7	19	25.5
Conservative	0	4	5	8	29.4
L. Democrat	1	10	1	4	12.5
Other	0	0	1	2	33.3
Total	**26**	**47**	**17**	**39**	**33.3**

Table E.2 Members of the National Assembly for Wales (AMs), 2007

Party	Constituency Women	Constituency Men	Regional Women	Regional men	% Women
Labour	15	9	1	1	61.5
Plaid Cymru	2	5	5	3	46.7
L. Democrat	2	1	1	2	50
Conservative	1	4	0	7	8.3
Other	1	0	0	0	100
Total	**21**	**19**	**7**	**13**	**46.7**

Source: Electoral Reform Society Briefing Note 2007

Bibliography

Almond, G. and Verba, S. (1963) *The Civic Culture: Political Attitudes and Democracy in Five Nations* (Princeton: Princeton University Press).

Annesley, C., Gains, F. and Rummery, K. (2007) *Women and New Labour: Engendering Politics* (Bristol: Policy Press).

Atkinson, D. (1988) *Votes for Women* (CUP: Cambridge).

Bacchi, C. (2006) 'Arguing For and Against Quotas', in D. Dahlerup (ed.) *Women, Quotas and Politics* (London: Routledge), 32–51.

Baker, G. (2005) 'Revisiting the Concept of Representation', *Parliamentary Affairs*, 59, 1 1: 155–72.

Barnes, S. and Kaase, M. (1978) *Political Action: Mass Participation in Five Western Democracies* (Beverly Hills, CA: Sage).

Bashevkin, S. (2000) 'From Tough Times to Better Times', *International Political Science Review*, 4: 407–24.

Beckwith, K. (2003) 'Number and Newness', paper given to the author by Beckwith.

Beckwith, K. and Cowell-Myers, K. (2003) 'Sheer Numbers', paper presented at Annual Meeting of the American Political Science Association, Philadelphia.

Benavides, J. C. (2003) 'Women's Political Participation in Bolivia', in *IDEA The Implementation of Quotas: Latin American Experiences* (Stockholm: IDEA).

Bendyna, M. and Lake, C. (1994) 'Gender and Voting in the 92 Presidential Elections', in A. Cook, S. Thomas and C. Wilcox (ed.) *The Year of the Woman: Myths and Realities* (Westview Press: Boulder, San Francisco), 237–54.

Berrington, H. (1973) *Backbench Opinion in the House of Commons 1945–55* (Oxford: Pergamon).

Berrington, H. and Hague, R. (1998) 'Europe, Thatcherism and Traditionalism', in H. Berrington (ed.) *Britain in the 1990s* (London: Frank Cass).

Birch, A. H. (1971) *Representation* (Basingstoke: Macmillan).

Birch, A. H. (1993) *The Concepts and Theories of Modern Democracy* (London: Routledge).

Bird, K. (2005) 'Gendering Parliamentary Questions', *British Journal of Politics and International Relations*, 7, 3: 353–70.

Blackburn, R. and Kennon, A. (2003) *Griffith and Ryle on Parliament, Functions, Practice and Procedures* (London: Sweet and Maxwell).

Bochel, C. and Briggs, J. (2000) 'Do Women Make a Difference', *Politics*, 20, 2: 63–8.

Bourque, S. and Grossholtz, J. (1998) 'Politics, An Unnatural Practice: Political Science Looks at Female Participation', in A. Phillips (ed.), *Feminism and Politics* (Oxford: Oxford University Press), 23–43.

Box-Steffensmeir, J. Deboef, S. and Lin, T-M (1997) *Microideology, Macropartisanship and the Gender Gap* (American Political Science Association).

Bratton, K. A. (2005) 'Critical Mass Theory Revisited: The Behavior and Success of Token Women in State Legislatures', *Politics & Gender*, 1, 1: 97–125.

Bratton, K. A. and Haynie, K. L. (1999) 'Agenda Setting and Legislative Success in State Legislatures: The Effects of Gender and Race', *The Journal of Politics*, 61, 3: 658–79.

Bratton, K. A. and Ray, L. P. (2002) 'Descriptive Representation, Policy Outcomes, and Municipal Day-Care Coverage in Norway', *American Journal of Political Science,* 46, 2: 428–37.

Brazier, A., Flinders, M. and McHugh, D. (2005) *New Politics, New Parliament?* (London: Hansard Society).

Brookes, P. (1967) *Women at Westminster, An Account of Women in the British Parliament 1918–1966* (London: Peter Davies).

Butler, D. and Stokes, D. (1969) *Political Change in Britain: Forces Shaping Electoral Choice* (London: Macmillan).

Butler, D. and Strokes, D. (1974) *Political Change in Britain,* 2nd Edition (London: Macmillan).

Campbell, A., Converse, P., Miller, W. and Stokes, D. (1960) *The American Voter* (New York: John Wiley & Sons).

Campbell, B. (1987) *The Iron Ladies, Why do Women Vote Tory?* (London: Virago).

Campbell, R. (2004) 'Gender, Ideology and Issue Preference: Is There Such a Thing as a Political Women's Interest in Britain?', *British Journal of Politics and International Relations*, 6: 20–46.

Campbell, R (2006). *Gender and the Vote in Britain* (Colchester, Essex: ECPR Press).

Campbell, R. and Lovenduski, J. (2005) 'Winning Women's Votes? The Incremental Track to Equality', *Parliamentary Affairs*, 58, 4: 837–53.

Campbell, R. and Winters, K. (2006a) 'The 2005 British General Election', in R. Campbell, *Gender and The Vote in Britain* (Colchester, Essex: ECPR Press), 115–27.

Campbell, R. and Winters, K. (2006b) 'Gender Differences in Vote Choice: Socialization Not Self-interest?, Paper prepared for the PSA Annual Conference, Reading.

Campbell, R. and Winters, K. (2007) 'Understanding Men and Women's Political Interests: Evidence from a Study of Gendered Political Attitudes?' Paper presented to EPOP Annual Conference, Bristol.

Campbell, R., Childs, S., and Lovenduski, J. (2005) 'Representation in Britain: The Professionalization of politics', Paper presented to Annual Meeting of APSA, Washington, September.

Campbell, R., Childs, S., and Lovenduski, J. (2006) 'Equality Guarantees and the Conservative Party', *Political Quarterly*, 7, 1: 18–27.

Campbell, R., Childs, S. and Lovenduski, J. (2007) 'Descriptive and Substantive Representation: The Difference between Wanting and Needing Women Representatives', paper prepared for ECPR Joint Sessions of Workshops, Helsinki.

Carroll, S. J. (1984) 'Woman Candidates and Support for Feminist Concerns: The Closet Feminist Syndrome', *Western Political Quarterly*, 37: 307–23.

Carroll, S. J. (1988) 'Women's Autonomy and the Gender Gap: 1980 and 1982', in C. Mueller (ed.) *The Politics of the Gender Gap* (California: Sage), 237–56.

Carroll, S. J. (1994) *Women as Candidates in American Politics* (Bloomington and Indianapolis: Indiana University Press).

Carroll, S. J. (1999) 'The Disempowerment of the Gender Gap: Soccer Moms and the 1996 Elections', *PS,* 32, 1: 7–11.

Carroll, S. J. (2001) *The Impact of Women in Public Office* (Bloomington: Indiana University Press).

Carroll, S. J. (2002) 'Representing Women: Congresswomen's Perceptions of Their Representational Roles', in C. Rosenthal (ed.) *Women Transforming Congress* (Norman: University of Oklahoma Press).

Carroll, S. J. (2003) *Women and American Politics* (Oxford: OUP).

Carroll, S. J. and Liebowitz, D. J. (2003) 'New Challenges, New Questions, New Directions', in S. J. Carroll (ed.), *Women and American Politics* (Oxford: OUP), 1–29.

Carroll, S. J. and Schreiber, R. (1997) 'Media Coverage of Women in the 103rd Congress', in P. Norris (ed.), *Women, Media and Politics* (Oxford: OUP), 131–48.

Carver, T. (1996) *Gender is Not a Synonym for Woman* (Boulder: Lynne Reinner).

Celis, K. (2004) 'Substantive and Descriptive Representation: Investigating the Impact of the Voting Right and of Descriptive Representation on the Substantive Representation of Women in the Belgian Lower House (1900–1979)', Paper presented at the Annual Meeting of the American Political Science Association, Chicago, IL.

Celis, K. (2005) 'Reconciling Theory and Empirical Research. Methodological Reflections on Women MP's representing Women('s Interests)', Paper presented at the Annual Meeting of the American Political Science Association, Washington DC.

Celis, K. (2006a) 'Substantive Representation of Women and the Impact of Descriptive Representation. Case: the Belgian Lower House 1900–1979', *Journal of Women, Politics and Policy*, 28, 2.

Celis, K. (2006b) 'Gendering Political Representation. Theory and Empirical Research', Paper presented at the Political Studies Association Annual Conference, Reading.

Celis, K., Childs, S., Kantola, J. and Krook, M. L (2007) 'Rethinking Women's Substantive Representation', Paper prepared for the ECPR Joint Sessions of Workshops, University of Helsinki.

Chaney, P. (2003a) 'The Post-Devolution Equality Agenda', *Policy and Politics*, 32, 1: 63–77.

Chaney, P. (2003b) 'Increased Rights and Representation', in A. Dobrowolsky and V. Hart (ed.), *Women Making Constitutions* (Basingstoke: Palgrave), 173–84.

Chaney, P. (2004a) 'The Post-Devolution Equality Agenda', *Policy and Politics*, 32, 1: 63–77.

Chaney, P. (2004b) 'Women and Constitutional Change in Wales', *Regional and Federal Studies*, 14, 2: 281–303.

Chaney, P. (2006) 'Critical Mass, Deliberation and the Substantive Representation of Women', *Political Studies*, 54, 4: 691–714.

Chaney, P., Mackay, F. and McAllister, L. (2007) *Women, Politics and Constitutional Change* (Cardiff: University of Wales Press).

Childs, S. (2000) 'The New Labour Women MPs in the 1997 British Parliament: Issues of Recruitment and Representation', *Women's History Review*, 9, 1: 55–73.

Childs, S. (2001a) 'In Their Own Words: New Labour Women MPs and the Substantive Representation of Women', *British Journal of Politics and International Relations*, 3, 1: 173–90.

Childs S. (2001b) 'Attitudinally Feminist'? The New Labour Women MPs and the Substantive Representation of Women', *Politics*, 21, 3: 179–86.

Childs, S. (2002) 'Competing Conceptions of Representation and the Passage of the Sex Discrimination (Election Candidates) Bill', *Journal of Legislative Studies*, 8, 3: 90–108.

Childs, S. (2003) 'The Sex Discrimination (Election Candidates) Act and its Implications', *Representation*, 39, 2: 83–92.

Childs, S. (2004) *New Labour's Women MPs: Women Representing Women* (London: Routledge).

Childs, S. (2005) 'Feminizing British Politics: Sex and Gender in the 2005 General Election', in A. Geddes and J. Tonge (ed.), *Britain Decides: The UK General Election 2005* (Basingstoke: Palgrave), 150–67.

Childs, S. (2006) 'Political Parties', in P. Dunleavy et al. (ed.), *Developments in British Politics 8* (Basingstoke: Palgrave), 56–77.

Childs, S. and Krook. M. L. (2006a) 'Gender and Politics: the State of the Art', *Politics,* 26, 1: 18–28.

Childs, S. and Krook, M. L. (2006b) 'Gender, Politics, and Political Science: A Reply to Michael Moran', *Politics,* 26, 3: 203–5.

Childs, S. and Krook, M. L. (2006c) 'Should Feminists Give up on Critical Mass? A Contingent Yes', *Politics and Gender,* 2, 4: 522–30.

Childs, S. and Withey, J. (2004) 'Do Women Sign for Women? Sex and the Signing of Early Day Motions in the 1997 Parliament', *Political Studies,* 52, 4: 552–64.

Childs, S. and Withey, J. (2006) 'The Substantive Representation of Women: Reducing the VAT on Sanitary Products in the UK', *Parliamentary Affairs,* 2006, 59, 1: 10–23.

Childs, S., Lovenduski, J. and Campbell, R. (2005) *Women on Top* (London: Hansard Society).

Chodorow, N. (1978) *The Reproduction of Mothering* (Berkeley, CA: University of California Press).

Clark, J. (1994) 'Getting There: Women in Political Office', in M. Githens, P. Norris and J. Lovenduski (eds), *Different Roles, Different Voices* (New York: Harper Collins), 99–110.

Clark, G. and Kelly, S. (2004) 'Echoes of Butler? The Conservative Research Department and the Making of Conservative Policy', *Political Quarterly,* 75, 4: 378–82.

Clarke, H. D., Sanders, D., Stewart, M. C. and Whitely, P. F. (2004) *Political Choice in Britain* (Oxford: OUP).

Cockburn, C. (1996) 'Strategies for Gender Democracy', *European Journal of Women's Studies,* 3: 7–26.

Considine, M. and Deutchman, I. E (1996) 'Instituting Gender', *Women and Politics,* 16, 4: 1–19.

Conway, M. M. (2001) 'Women and Political Participation', *PS,* 34, 2, June: 231–3.

Cowley, P. (2002) *Revolts and Rebellions: Parliamentary Voting Under Blair* (London: Politico's).

Cowley, P. and Childs, S. (2003) 'Too Spineless Too Rebel', *British Journal of Political Science,* 33, 3: 345–65.

Cowley, P. and Green, J. (2005) 'New Leaders, Same Problems', in A. Geddes and J. Tonge (ed.), *Britain Decides: The UK General Election 2005* (Basingstoke: Palgrave).

Cowell-Meyers, K. (2001) 'Gender, Power, and Peace: A Preliminary Look at Women in the Northern Ireland Assembly', *Women & Politics,* 23, 3: 55–88.

Cowell-Myers, K. (2003). *Women Legislators in Northern Ireland: Gender and Politics in the New Legislative Assembly* (Centre for Advancement of Women in Politics School of Politics, Queens University Belfast, Occasional paper # 3).

Coxall, B., Robins, L. and Leach, R. (2006) *Contemporary British Politics Companion Website* (http://www.palgrave.com/politics/coxall/update3.htm : Palgrave Macmillan).

Crewe, I. (1986) 'On the Death and Resurrection of Class Voting: Some Comments on How Britain Votes'. *Political Studies,* 34, 4: 620–38.

Criddle, B. (1992) 'MPs and Candidates', in D. Butler and D. Kavanagh (eds), *The British General Election of 1992* (Basingstoke: Macmillan), 211–30.

Criddle, B. (1997) 'MPs and Candidates', in D. Butler and D. Kavanagh (eds), *The British General Election of 1997* (Basingstoke: Macmillan), 186–209.

Criddle, B. (2002) 'MPs and Candidates', in D. Butler and D. Kavanagh (ed.), *The British General Election of 2001* (Basingstoke: Palgrave), 182–207.

Criddle, B. (2005) 'MPs and Candidates', in D. Kavanagh and D. Butler (ed.), *The British General Election of 2005* (Basingstoke: Palgrave), 146–67.

Crowley, J. E. (2004) 'When Tokens Matter', *Legislative Studies Quarterly*, 29, 1: 109–36.

Currell, M. (1974) *Political Woman* (London: Croom Helm).

Cutts, D., Childs, S., and Fieldhouse, E. 'This Is What You Get When You Don't Listen', *Party Politics,* forthcoming.

Dahlerup, D. (1984) 'Overcoming the Barriers: An Approach to how Women's Issues are kept from the Political Agenda', in J. H. Stiehm (ed.), *Women's Views of the Political World of Men* (New York: Transnational Publishers), 33–66.

Dahlerup, D. (1988) 'From a Small to a Large Minority: Women in Scandinavian Politics', *Scandinavian Political Studies*, 11: 4, 275–98.

Dahlerup, D. (1998) 'Using Quotas to Increase Women's Political Representation', in A. Kararn, *Women In Parliament Beyond Numbers* (Stockholm: IDEA).

Dahlerup, D. (2002) *Gender Quotas in a Comparative Perspective* (Geneva: ECPR Research Session Report).

Dahlerup, D. (2006) *Women, Quotas and Politics* (Routledge: London).

Dahlerup, D. and Freidenvall, L. (2003) 'Quotas as a Fast Track to Equal Political Representation for Women: Why Scandinavia is No Longer the Model', Paper presented to the 19th International Political Science Association World Congress, Durban, South Africa, June 29 – July 4.

Dahlerup, D. and Freidenvall, L. (2005) 'Quotas as a Fast Track to Equal Political Representation for Women: Why Scandinavia is No Longer the Model', *International Feminist Journal of Politics*, 7, 1: 26–48.

Darcy, R., Welch, S. and Clark, J. (1994) *Women, Elections and Representation* (Lincoln and London: University of Nebraska Press).

Deacon, D., Wring, D. and Golding, P. (2006) 'Same Campaign, Differing Agendas', *British Politics*, 1: 222–56.

Deacon, D., Wring, D. and Golding, P. (2007) 'The 'Take a Break Campaign?': National Print Media Reporting of the Election', in D. Wring, J. Green, R. Mortimore and S. Atkinson (eds), *Political Communication: The General Election Campaign of 2005* (Basingstoke: Palgrave Macmillan).

Deutchman, I. A. and Ellison, A. (1999) 'A star is born: the roller coaster ride of Pauline Hanson in the news', *Media*, Culure & Society, 21, 1: 23–50.

Deutchman, I. A. and Ellison, A. (2004) 'When Feminists Don't Fit: the Case of Pauline Hanson', *International Feminist Journal of Politics* 6, 1: 29–52.

Diamond, I. and Hartsock, N. (1998) 'Beyond Interests in Politics', in A. Phillips (eds), *Feminism and Politics* (Oxford: Oxford University Press), 193–223.

Dobrowolsky, A. and Hart, V. (2003) *Women Making Constitutions* (Basingstoke: Palgrave).

Dods (1997) *The Vacher Dod Guide to the New House of Commons 1997* (London: Vacher Dod Publishing Ltd).

Dod's (2005) *Vacher's Parliamentary Profiles* (London: Dod's Parliamentary Communications).

Dodson, D. (1998) 'Representing Women's Interests in the US House of Representatives', in S. Thomas and C.Wilcox (ed.), *Women and Elective Office* (Oxford: OUP), 130–49.

Dodson, D. L. (2001) 'The Impact of Women in Congress: Re-thinking Ideas about Difference', paper presented to APSA, Women and Politics Special Session, San Francisco, August.

Dodson, D. L. (2006) *The Impact of Women in Congress* (Oxford: OUP).

Dodson, D. and Carroll, S. J. (1991) *Reshaping the Agenda: Women in State Legislatures* (New Brunswick: Center for American Women and Politics).

Dolan, K. (2001) 'Electoral Context, Issues, and Voting for Women in the 1990s', in K. O'Conner (ed.), *Women and Congress: Running, Winning and Ruling* (Binghamton: The Haworth Press), 21–36.

Dolan, K. and Ford, L. E. (1995) 'Women in State Legislatures: Feminist Identity and Legislative Behaviours' *APQ*, 23: 96–108.

Dolan, K. and Ford, L. E. (1998) 'Are All Women State Legislators Alike', in S. Thomas and C. Wilcox (ed.), *Women and Elective Office* (Oxford: OUP), 73–86.

Dovi, S. (2002) 'Preferable Descriptive Representatives: Will Just Any Woman, Black or Latino Do?', *APSR*, 96, 4: 729–43.

Dowding, K. and Kang, W. T. (1998) 'Ministerial Resignations 1945–1997', *Public Administration*, 76, 3: 411–29.

Duerst-Lahti, G. and Verstegen, D. (1995) 'Making Something of Absence. The 'Year of the Woman' and Women's Representation', in G. Duerst-Lahti and R. Mae Kelly (eds), *Gender Power Leadership and Governance* (USA: The University of Michigan Press), 213–38.

Dunleavy, P. and Husbands, C. (1985) *British Democracy at The Crossroads: Voting and Party Competition in the 1980s* (London: Allen and Unwin).

Duverger, M. (1955) *The Political Role of Women* (Paris: UNESCO)

Edwards, J. and McAllister, L. (2002) 'One Step Forward, Two Steps Back? Women in the Two Main Political Parties in Wales', *Parliamentary Affairs*, 55, 1: 154–66.

The Electoral Commission (2002) 'Candidates at a General Election Factsheet' (www.electoralcommission.org.uk).

Elgood, J., Vinter, L. and Williams, R. (2002) *Man Enough for the Job? A Study of Parliamentary Candidates* (Manchester: EOC).

Erickson, L. (1997) 'Might More Women Make a Difference?', *Canadian Journal of Political Science*, 30, 4: 663–88.

Evans, L. (2007) 'Grassroots Influence: Pressure Groups within the Liberal Democrats', *Political Quarterly*, 78, 1: 95–103.

Everitt, J. and Gidengil, E. (2003) 'Tough Talk: Television News Covers Male and Female Leaders of Canadian Political Parties', in M. Tremblay and L. Trimble (ed.), *Women and Electoral Politics in Canada* (Oxford: OUP).

Fairhurst, G. T. and Snavely, B. K. (1983) 'Majority and Token Minority Group Relationships: Power Acquisition and Communication', *Academy of Management Review*, 8, 2: 292–300.

Fine, T. S. (1998) 'Women and Group Consciousness: A Cross Generational Perspective', Paper prepared for delivery at 1998 Annual Meeting of American Political Science Association, Boston, USA.

Finer, S., Berrington, H. and Bartholomew, D. (1961) *Backbench Opinion in the House of Commons 1955–9* (Oxford: Pergamon).

Flammang, J. A. (1985) 'Female Officials in the Feminist Capital', *Western Political Quarterly*, 38: 94–118.

Flynn, P. (1997) Commons Knowledge: Hour to Be a Backbencher (Bridgend: Seren Books).

Fielding, S. (2002) The Labour Party (Basingstoke: Macmillan).

Fountaine, S. and McGregor, J. (2002) 'Reconstructing Gender for the 21st Century: News Media Framing of Political Women in New Zealand', Refereed Conference Paper presented at the Australian New Zealand Communication Association Annual Conference, Greenmount, Brisbane, Australia, 10–12 July 2002.

Franklin, M. (1985) *The Decline in Class Voting in Britain: Changes in the Base of Electoral Choice* (Oxford, Clarendon Press).

Frisch, S. A. and Kelly, S. Q. (2003), 'A Place at the Table: Women's Committee Requests and Women's Committee Assignments in the U.S. House', Paper presented at the Annual Meeting of the American Political Science Association, Philadelphia, PA, August 28–31.

Geddes, A. and Tonge, J. (2005) *Britain Decides: the UK General Election 2005* (Manchester: MUP).

Geisler, G. (2000) 'Parliament is Another Terrain of Struggle': Women, Men and Politics in South Africa', *Journal of Modern African Studies*, 38, 4: 605–30.

Gidengil, E. and Everitt, J. (2003), 'Conventional Coverage/Unconventional Politicians', *Canadian Journal of Political Science*, 36, 3: 559–77.

Gidengil, E. and Everitt, J. (2003), 'Talking Tough: Gender and Reported Speech in Campaign News Coverage', *Political Communication*, 20, 3: 209–32.

Gidengil, E, and Everitt, J. (2003a), 'Conventional Coverage/Unconventional Politicians', Canadian Journal of Political Science, 36, 3: 559–77.

Gidengil, E. and Everitt, J. (2003b), 'Talking Tough: gender and Reported Speech in Compaign News Coverge', *Political Communication,* 20, 3: 209–32.

Gidengil, E., Blais, A., Nadeau, R. and Nevitte, N. (2003) 'Women to the Left', in M. Tremblay, and L. Trimble (ed.), *Women and Electoral Politics in Canada* (Oxford: OUP).

Gilligan, C. (1982) *In a Different Voice: Psychological Theory and Women's Development* (Cambridge, Massachusetts: Harvard University Press).

Goot, M. and Reid, E. (1975) *Women and Voting Studies: Mindless Matrons or Sexist Scientism?* (London: Sage).

Goot, M. and Reid, E. (1984) 'Women: If not Apolitical, Then Conservative', in J. Siltanen and M. Stanworth (eds), *Women and the Public Sphere, A Critique of Sociology and Politics* (London: Hutchinson), 122–36.

Gotell, L. and Brodie, J. (1991) 'Women and Parties: More Than an Issue of Numbers', in H. G. Thorbum (ed.), *Party Politics in Canada* (Scarborough: Prentice Hall), 53–67.

Granovetter, M. (1978) 'Threshold Models and Collective Behavior', *American Journal of Sociology*, 83, 6: 1420–43.

Graves, P. M. (1994) *Labour Women, Women in British Working-Class Politics 1918–1939* (Cambridge: Cambridge University Press).

Greco Larson, S. (2001) 'American Women and Politics in the Media: A Review Essay', *Political Science and Politics*, 34, 2: 227–30.

Greenberg, A. (2001) 'Race, Religiosity and the Women's Vote', *Women and Politics*, 22, 3: 59–82.

Grey, S. (2002) 'Does Size Matter', in K. Ross (ed.), *Women, Politics and Change* (Oxford: OUP).

Guadagnini, M. (2005) 'Gendering the Debate on Political Representation in Italy: A Difficult Challenge', in J. Lovenduski, C. Baudino, P. Meier and D. Sainsbury (ed.), *State Feminism and the Political Representation of Women* (Cambridge: Cambridge University Press).

Gugin, L. C. (1986) 'The Impact of Political Structure on the Political Power of Women: A Comparison of Britain and the United States', *Women and Politics*, 6, 4: 37–56.

Hacker, H. M. (1951) 'Women as a Minority Group', *Social Forces,* 30: 60–90.

Hall, Peter. (1999) 'Social Capital in Britain', *British Journal of Political Science*, 29: 17–61.

Hansard Society (1990) *The Report of The Hansard Society Commission on Women At The Top* (London: The Hansard Society for Parliamentary Government).

Hansard Society (2000) *Women at the Top 2000: Cracking the Public Sector Glass Ceiling* (London: Hansard Society and Fawcett Society).

Harrison, L. (2006a) 'Selecting Women Candidates', Paper presented to the British Liberal Studies Group/Liberal History Group Winter Conference, January 2006, Gregynog, University of Wales.

Harrison, L. (2006b) 'Women's Legislative Representation – Do Political Parties Utilize a Gendered Model of the "Good Candidate" ', unpublished paper given to author.

Hawkesworth, M. (2003) 'Congressional Enactments of Race-Gender: Toward a Theory of Raced-Gendered Institutions', *American Political Science Review*, 97, 4: 529–50.

Hayes, B. (1997) 'Gender, Feminism and Electoral Behaviour in Britain', *Electoral Studies*, 16, 2: 203–16.

Hayes, B. C. and McAllister, I. (1997) 'Gender, Party Leaders, And Election Outcomes in Australia, Britain, and the United States', *Comparative Political Studies,* 30, 1: 3–26.

Heath, A., Jowell, R. and Curtice, J. (1985) *How Britain Votes* (Oxford: Oxford University Press).

Heath, R. M., Schwindt-Bayer, L.A. and Taylor-Robinson, M. M. (2005) 'Women on the Sidelines: Women's Representation on Committees in Latin American Legislatures', *American Journal of Political Science*, 49, 2: 420–36.

Heffernan, R. (2003) 'Political Parties and the Party System', in P. Dunleavy et al. (ed.), *Developments in British Politics 7* (Basingstoke: Macmillan), 119–39.

Heffernan, R. (2001) *New Labour and Thatcherism* (Basingstoke: Macmillan).

Heldman, C., Carroll S. J. and Olson, S. (2000) 'Gender Differences in Print Media Coverage of Presidential Candidates: Elizabeth Dole's Bid for the Republican Nomination', Annual Meeting of the American Political Science Association, 31 August – 3 September, Washington DC.

High-Pippert, A. and Comer, J. (1998) 'Female Empowerment: The Influence of Women Representing Women', *Women and Politics*, 19, 4: 53–66.

House of Commons. *Early Day Motion*, Fact Sheet.

House of Commons. *Parliamentary Questions*, Fact Sheet.

House of Commons. *Procedure Series*, Fact Sheet.

House of Commons. *The Vote Bundle*, Fact Sheet.

House of Commons. *Women in the House of Commons,* Fact Sheet.

Htun, M. and Jones, M. P. (2002), 'Engendering the Right to Participate in Decision Making: Electoral Quotas and Women's Leadership in Latin America', in N. Craske and M. Molyneux (ed.), *Gender and the Politics of Rights and Democracy in Latin America* (New York: Palgrave), 32–56.

Ingle, S. (2004) 'Politics: The Year the War was Spun', *Parliamentary Affairs*, 57, 2: 237–52.

Inglehart, R. and Norris, P. (1998) 'Gender Gaps in Voting Behaviour in Global Perspective', paper presented to the Annual Meeting of APSA, Boston.

Inglehart, R. and Norris, P. (2000) 'The Developmental Theory of the Gender Gap: Women and Men's Voting Behaviour in Global Perspective', *International Political Science Review*, 21, 4: 441–62.

Inglehart, R. and Norris, P. (2003) *Rising Tide: Gender Equality and Cultural Change Around the World* (Cambridge: Cambridge University Press).

Jonasdottir, A. G. (1990) 'On the Concept of Interest, Women's Interests, and the Limitations of Interest Theory', in K. B. Jones and A. G. Jonasdottir (eds), *The Political Interests of Gender, Developing Theory and Research with a Feminist Face* (London: Sage), 33–65.

Judge, D. (1999) *Representation* (London: Routledge).

Kahn, K. F. (1994) 'The Distorted Mirror: Press Coverage of Women Candidates for Statewide Office', *Journal of Politics*, 56, 1: 154–73.

Kahn, K. F. (2003) 'Assessing the Media's Impact on the Political Fortunes of Women', in S. J. Carroll (ed.), *Women and American Politics: New Questions, New Directions* (Oxford: OUP), 173–83.

Kanter, R. M. (1977a) 'Some Effects of Proportions on Group Life', *American Journal of Sociology*, 82, 5: 965–90.

Kanter, R. M. (1977b) *Men and Women of the Corporation* (New York: Basic Books).

Karvonen, L., Djupsund, G. and Carlson, T. (1995) 'Political Language', in L. Karvonen and P. Selle (eds), *Women in Nordic Politics* (Aldershot: Dartmouth), 343–79.

Kathlene, L. (1994), 'Power and Influence in State Legislative Policy Making' *APSR*, 88, 3: 560–76.

Kathlene, L. (1995), 'Position Power Versus Gender Power: Who Holds the Floor?', in G. Duerst-Lahti and R. M. Kelly (ed.), in *Gender Power, Leadership, and Governance* (Ann Arbor: University of Michigan Press), 167–94.

Kathlene, L. (1998) 'In a Different Voice, Women and the Policy Process', in S. Thomas and C. Wilcox (ed.), *Women and Elective Office* (Oxford: OUP), 188–202.

Kathlene, L. (2001) 'Words that Matter', in S. J. Carroll (eds), *The Impact of Women in Public Office* (Bloomington: Indiana University Press), 22–48.

Katz, R. and Mair, P. (1995) 'Changing Models of Party Organization and Party Democracy', *Party Politics*, 1, 1: 5–28.

Kelly, R. (2004) 'The Extra-Parliamentary Tory Party: McKenzie Revisited', Political Quarterly, *75, 4: 398–404.*

Kenney, S. (1996) 'New Research on Gendered Political Institutions', *Political Research Quarterly*, 49: 445–66.

Kingdon, J. W. (1984) *Agendas, Alternatives, and Public Policies* (Boston: Little, Brown).

Kittilson, M. C. (2005) 'In Support of Gender Quotas', *Politics and Gender*, 1, 4: 638–45.

Kittilson, M. C. (2006) *Challenging Parties, Changing Parliaments* (Columbus: Ohio State Univ. Press).

Krook, M. L. (2003), 'Gender Quotas: A Framework for Analysis.' Paper presented to the General Conference of the European Consortium for Political Research. Marburg, Germany, September 18–21.

Krook, M. L. (2005) *Politicizing Representation: Campaigns for Candidate Gender Quotas Worldwide,* Ph.D. Diss., Columbia University.

Krook, M. L. (2006) 'Reforming Representation: The Diffusion of Candidate Gender Quotas Worldwide', 2, 3: 303–27.

Krook, M. L. and Squires, J. (2006) 'Gender Quotas in British Politics', *British Politics*, 1, 1: 44–66.

Krook, M. L., Lovenduski, J. and Squires, J. (2006) 'Western Europe, North America, Australia and New Zealand', in D. Dahlerup (ed.), *Women Quotas and Politics* (London: Routledge), 194–221.

Kropf, M. and Boiney, J. (2001) 'The Electoral Glass Ceiling? Gender, Viability, and the News in the US Senate Campaigns', in K. O'Conner (ed.), *Women and Congress: Running, Winning and Ruling* (Binghamton: The Haworth Press).

Labour Party (2005) Patnership in Power (London: The Labour Party)

Lawless, J. L. (2004) 'Politics of Presence? Congresswomen and Symbolic Representation', *Political Research Quarterly*, 57, 1: 81–99.

Lee, F. L. F. (2004) 'Constructing the Perfect Women: The Portrayal of Female Officials in Hong Kong Newspapers', *Media, Culture and Society*, 26, 2: 207–25.

Lovenduski, J. (1990) 'Feminism and West European Politics: An Overview', in D. W. Urwin and W. E. Paterson (eds), *Politics in Western Europe Today* (London: Longman), 137–61.

Lovenduski, J. (1993) 'Introduction: The Dynamics of Gender and Party', in J. Lovenduski and P. Norris (eds), *Gender and Party Politics* (London: Sage), 1–15.

Lovenduski, J. (1994) 'Will Quotas Make Women More Women-Friendly?', *Renewal*, 2, 1: 9–18.

Lovenduski, J. (1996) 'Sex, Gender and British Politics', in J. Lovenduski and P. Norris (ed.), *Women in Politics* (Oxford: Oxford University Press), 3–18.

Lovenduski, J. (1997) 'Gender Politics: A Breakthrough for Women?', *Parliamentary Affairs*, 50, 4: 708–19.

Lovenduski, J. (1998) Gendering Research in Political Science', *Annual Review of Political Science*, 1: 333–56.

Lovenduski, J. (2001), 'Women and Politics: Minority Representation or Critical Mass', in P. Norris (ed.), *Britain Votes 2001* (Oxford: Oxford University Press).

Lovenduski, J. (2005a) *Feminizing Politics* (Cambridge: Polity).

Lovenduski, J. (2005b) *State Feminism and the Political Representation of Women* (Cambridge: Cambridge University Press).

Lovenduski, J. and Norris, P. (1989) 'Selecting Women Candidates: Obstacles to the Feminisation of the House of Commons', *European Journal of Political Research*, 17, 533–62.

Lovenduski, J. and Norris, P. (1991) 'Party Rules and Women's Representation: Reforming the British Labour Party', in I. Crewe et al. (ed.), *British Elections and Parties Yearbook* (Hemel Hempstead: Harvester Wheatsheaf), 189–206.

Lovenduski, J. and Norris, P. (1993) *Gender and Party Politics* (London: Sage).

Lovenduski, J. and Norris, P. (1994a) 'The Recruitment of Parliamentary Candidates', in L. Robins, H. Blackmore and R. Pyper (eds), *Britain's Changing Party System* (London: Leicester University Press), 125–46.

Lovenduski, J. and Norris, P. (1994b) 'Labour and the Unions: After the Brighton Conference', *Government and Opposition*, 29, 2: 201–17.

Lovenduski, J. and Norris, P. (1996) *Women in Politics* (Oxford: Oxford University Press).

Lovenduski, J. and Norris, P. (2003) 'Westminster Women: The Politics of Presence', *Political Studies*, 51: 84–102.

Lovenduski, J. and Randall, V. (1993) *Contemporary Feminist Politics* (Oxford: Oxford University Press).

Lovenduski, J., Norris, P. and Burness, C. (1994) 'The Party and Women', in A. Seldon and S. Ball (eds), *Conservative Century, The Conservative Party Since 1900* (Oxford: Oxford University Press), 611–35.

Lowndes, V. (2000) 'Women and Social Capital: A Comment on Hall's 'Social Capital in Britain', *British Journal of Political Science*, 30: 533–40.

Lowndes, V. (2006) 'It's Not What You've Got But What You Do With It', in B. O'Neill and E. Gidengil (ed.), *Gender and Social Capital* (New York: Routledge).

Mackay, F. (2001a) *Love and Politics* (London: Continuum).

Mackay, F. (2001b) 'The Case of Zero Tolerance: Women's Politics in Action?' in E. Breitenbach and F. Mackay (eds), *Women and Contemporary Scottish Politics* (Edinburgh: Polygon).

Mackay, F. (2003) 'Women and the 2003 Elections', *Scottish Affairs*, 44: 74–90.

Mackay, F. (2004a) 'Gender and Political Representation in the UK: the State of the 'Discipline', *British Journal of Politics and International Relations*, 6, 1: 99–120.

Mackay, F. (2004b) 'Women and Devolution in Scotland', Briefing note prepared for the Scottish Parliament Cross-Party Group on Women and the EOC.

Mackay, F. (2004c) 'Women's Representation in Wales and Scotland', *Contemporary Wales*, 17: 140–61.

Mackay, F. (2005) 'The Impact of Devolution on Women's Citizenship in Scotland', summary of paper presented to International Women's Policy Research Conference, Washington DC, June.

Mackay, F. and Kenny, M. (2005) *Access, Voice ... and Influence?' A Report for Engender.* Given to the author.

Mackay, F., Meehan, E., Donaghy, T. and Chaney, P. (undated) 'Gender and Constitutional Change in Scotland, Northern Ireland and Wales', Unpublished Report.

Mackay, F., Myers, F. and Brown, A. (2003), 'Towards a New Politics', in A. Dobrowolsky and V. Hart (ed.), *Women Making Constitutions* (Basingstoke: Palgrave).

Mactaggart, F. (2000) 'Women in Parliament: Their Contribution to Labour's First 1000 Days', Research Paper prepared for the Fabian Society (London: Fabian Society).

Maguire, G. E. (1998) *Conservative Woman* (Oxford: Macmillan and St Anthony's).

Mansbridge, J. (1999) 'Should Blacks Represent Blacks and Women Represent Women? A Contingent 'Yes'', *The Journal of Politics*, 61, 3: 628–57.

Mansbridge, J. (2003) 'Rethinking Representation', *American Political Science Review*, 97, 4: 515–28.

Mansbridge, J. (2005) 'Quota Problems: Combating the Dangers of Essentialism', *Politics and Gender* 1, 4: 622–38.

Marwell, G. and Oliver, P. (1993) *The Critical Mass in Collective Action: A Micro-Social Theory* (New York: Cambridge University Press).

Mateo Diaz, M. (2005) *Representing Women: Female Legislators in West European Parliaments* (Essex: ECPR).

Matland, R. E. (2006) 'Electoral Quotas', in D. Dahlerup (ed.), *Women, Quotas and Politics* (Routledge: London), 275–92.

Matland, R. E. and Studlar, D. T. (1996) 'The Contagion Effect of Women Candidates in Single-Member District and Proportional Representation Electoral Systems: Canada and Norway', *The Journal of Politics*, 58: 3, 707–33.

Mazur, A. G. (2002) *Theorising Feminist Policy* (Oxford: Oxford University Press).

McLean, I. (1991) 'Forms of Representation and Systems of Voting', in D. Held (ed.), *Political Theory Today* (Cambridge: Polity), 172–196.

Meier, P. (2005) 'The Belgian Paradox: Inclusion and Exclusion of Gender Issues', in J. Lovenduski, C. Baudino, P. Meier, and D. Sainsbury (eds), *State Feminism and the Political Representation of Women* (Cambridge: Cambridge University Press).

Merriam, C. (1924) *Non-voting Causes and Methods of Control* (Chicago: The University of Chicago Press).

Meyer, B. (2003), 'Much Ado about Nothing? Political Representation Policies and the Influence of Women Parliamentarians in Germany', *Review of Policy Research*, 20, 3: 401–21.

Moran, M. (2006) 'Gender, Identify and the Teaching of British Politics: A comment', *Politics* 26, 3: 200–2.

Mortimore, R. (2005) 'Opinion Polls Since 2001', in S. Henig and L. Bason (eds) *Politieos guide to the General Election* (London: Politics).

Mueller, C. M. (1988a) *The Politics of the Gender Gap: the Social Construction of Political Influence* (London: Sage).

Murray, R. (2005) 'The Power of Sex and Incumbency', Paper presented at the 2005 PSA Annual Conference.

Norris, P. (1985a) 'The Gender Gap in Britain and America', *Parliamentary Affairs*, 38, 2: 192–201.

Norris, P. (1985b) 'Women's Legislative Participation in Western Europe', *West European Politics*, 8, 4: 90–101.

Norris, P. (1986) 'Conservative Attitudes In Recent British Elections: an Emerging Gender Gap?', *Political Studies*, 34: 120–8.

Norris, P. (1991) 'Gender Differences in Political Participation in Britain: Traditional, Radical and Revisionist Models', *Government and Opposition*, Winter: 56–74.

Norris, P. (1993) 'Conclusions: Comparing Legislative Recruitment', in J. Lovenduski and P. Norris (eds.), *Gender and Party Politics* (London: Sage), 309–30.

Norris, P. (1994a) 'Labour Party Factionalism and Extremism', in A. Heath, R., Jowell and J. Curtice (eds), *Labour's Last Chance? The 1992 Election and Beyond* (Aldershot: Dartmouth), 173–90.

Norris, P. (1994b) 'The Impact of the Electoral System on Election of Women to National Legislatures', in M. Githens, P. Norris and J. Lovenduski (eds), *Different Roles, Different Voices* (New York: Harper Collins), 114–21.

Norris, P. (1994c) 'Political Participation', in M. Githens, P. Norris and J. Lovenduski (eds), *Different Roles, Different Voices* (New York: Harper Collins), 25–6.

Norris, P. (1994d) 'Elections and Political Attitudes', in M. Githens, P. Norris and J. Lovenduski (eds), *Different Roles, Different Voices* (New York: Harper Collins), 47–50.

Norris, P. (1994e) 'Political Recruitment' in M. Githens, P. Norris and J. Lovenduski (eds), *Different Roles, Different Voices* (New York: Harper Collins), 85–88.

Norris, P. (1995) 'Labour Party Quotas for Women', in D. Broughton, D. M. Farrell, D. Denver and C. Rallings (eds), *British Elections and Parties Yearbook 1994* (London: Frank Cass), 167–80.

Norris, P. (1996) 'Women Politicians: Transforming Westminster?', in J. Lovenduski and P. Norris (eds), *Women in Politics* (Oxford: Oxford University Press), 91–104.

Norris, P. (1997a) *Passages to Power* (Cambridge: Cambridge University Press).

Norris, P. (1997b) *Women, Media, and Politics* (Oxford: Oxford University Press).

Norris, P. (1997c) 'The Puzzle of Constituency Service', *Journal of Legislative Studies*, 3, 2: 29–49.

Norris, P. (1998) 'A Gender-Generation Gap' http://www.ksg.harvard.edu/people/pnorris/Gendergap.htm

Norris, P. (1999a) 'New Politicians? Changes in Party Competition at Westminster', in P. Norris and G. Evans (ed.), *Critical Elections* (London: Sage), 22–43.

Norris, P. (1999b) 'Gender: A Gender-Generation Gap?' in P. Norris and G. Evans (eds), *Critical Elections* (London: Sage), 148–163.

Norris, P. (2000a) 'Gender and Cotemporary British Politics' in C. Hay (ed.), *British Politics Today* (Cambridge: Polity).

Norris, P. (2000b) 'Women's representation and Electoral Systems' in R. Rose (ed.), *Encyclopaedia of Electoral Systems* (Washington DC: CQ Press).

Norris, P. (2001). 'The Gender Gap: Old Challenges, New Approaches', in S. J. Carroll (ed.), *Women and American Politics: Agenda Setting for the 21st Century* (Oxford: Oxford University Press).

Norris, P. (2004) *Electoral Engineering* (Cambridge: Cambridge University Press).

Norris, P. and Inglehart, R. (2000) 'Cultural barriers to Women's Leadership: A Worldwide Comparison', Paper for special session IPSA World Congress, Quebec City.

Norris, P. and Lovenduski, J. (1989) 'Women Candidates for Parliament: Transforming the Agenda?', *British Journal of Political Science*, 19, 1: 106–15.

Norris, P. and Lovenduski, J. (1993a) 'Gender and Party Politics in Britain', in J. Lovenduski and P. Norris (eds), *Gender and Party Politics* (London: Sage), 35–59.

Norris, P. and Lovenduski, J. (1993b) 'If Only More Candidates Came Forward: Supply-side Explanations of Candidate Selection in Britain', *British Journal of Political Science*, 23: 373–408.

Norris, P. and Lovenduski, J. (1995) *Political Recruitment* (Cambridge: Cambridge University Press).

Norris, P., Lovenduski, J. and Campbell, R. (2004) *Gender and Political Participation* (London: Electoral Commission).

Norton, N. (1999) 'Uncovering the Dimensionality of Gender', *Legislative Studies Quarterly*, 24, 1: 65–86.

Norton, N. (1995) 'Women, It's Not Enough to Be Elected: Committee Position Makes a Difference', in G. Duerst-Lahti and R. M. Kelly (eds), *Gender Power, Leadership, and Governance* (Georgia Ann Arbor: University of Michigan Press), 115–40.

Norton, N. (1997) 'Analysing Roll-Call Voting Tools for Content: Are Women's Issues Excluded from Legislative Research', *Women and Politics*, 17, 4: 47–69.

Nunn, H. (2002) *Thatcher, Fantasy and Politics* (London: Lawrence and Wishart).

Oliver, P. and Marwell, G. (1988) 'A Theory of Critical Mass. Interdependence, Group Heterogeneity, and the Production of Collective Action', *American Journal of Sociology* 91, 3: 522–56.

Olson, M. (1965) *The Logic of Collective Action* (Cambridge: Harvard University Press).

Parry, G., Moyser, G. and Day, N. (1992) *Political Participation and Democracy in Britain* (Cambridge: Cambridge University Press).

Peake, L. (1997) 'Women in the Campaign and in the Commons', in A. Geddes and J. Tonge (eds), *Labour's Landslide, the British General Election 1997* (Manchester: Manchester University Press), 165–77.

Pennock R. J. (1968) 'Political Representation: an Overview', in R. J. Pennock and J. W. Chapman (eds), *Representation* (New York: Atherton Press), 3–27.

Pennock, R. J. and Chapman, J. W. (1968) *Representation* (New York: Atherton Press).

Perrigo, S. (1999) 'Women, Gender and New Labour', in G. R. Taylor (ed.), *The Impact of New Labour* (Basingstoke: Macmillan).

Perrigo, S. (1986) 'Socialist-Feminism and the Labour Party: Some Experiences from Leeds', *Feminist Review*, 23: 101–8.

Perrigo, S. (1995) 'Gender Struggles in the British Labour Party from 1979 to 1995', *Party Politics*, 1, 3: 407–17.

Perrigo, S. (1996) 'Women and Change in the Labour Party 1979–1995', in J. Lovenduski and P. Norris (ed.), *Women in Politics* (Oxford: Oxford University Press), 118–31.

Phillips, A. (1991) *Engendering Democracy* (Cambridge: Polity).

Phillips, A. (1993) *Democracy and Difference* (Cambridge: Polity).

Phillips, A. (1995) *The Politics Of Presence* (Oxford: Clarendon Press).

Phillips, A. (1996) 'Why Does Local Democracy Matter', in L. Pratchett and D. Wilson (eds), *Local Democracy and Local Government* (Basingstoke: Macmillan), 20–37.

Phillips, A. (1998a) *Feminism and Politics* (Oxford: OUP).

Phillips, A. (1998b) 'Democracy and Representation: Or, Why Should it Matter Who Our Representatives Are?, in A. Phillips (ed.), *Feminism and Politics* (Oxford: Oxford University Press), 224–40.

Phillips, A. (1999) *Which Equalities Matter?* (Cambridge: Polity).

Pitkin, H. F. (1967) *The Concept of Representation* (Berkeley, Los Angeles: University of California Press).

Pitkin, H. F. (1969) *Representation* (New York: Atherton Press).

Poggione, S. (2004) 'Legislative Organization and the Policymaking Process: The Impact of Women State Legislators on Welfare Policy', Paper presented at the Annual Meeting of the Southern Political Science Association, New Orleans, LA.

Putnam, R. (1995) 'America's Declining Social Capital', *Journal of Democracy*, 6, 1: 65–78.

Putnam, R. (2000) *Bowling Alone: The Collapse and Revival of American Community* (New York: Simon and Schuster).

Putnam, R., Leonardi, R. and Nanetti, R. (1993) *Making Democracy Work: Civic Traditions in Modern Italy* (Princeton: Princeton University Press).

Puwar, N. (2004) *Space Invaders* (Oxford: Berg).

Quaile Hill, K. and Hurley, P. A. (1999) 'Dyadic Representation Reappraised', *American Journal of Political Science*, 43, 1: 109–37.

Raaum, N. C. (1995) 'The Political Representation of Women: A Bird's Eye View', in L. Karvonen and P. Selle (eds), *Women in Nordic Politics* (Aldershot: Dartmouth), 25–55.

Randall, V. (1987) *Women and Politics, An International Perspective* (Basingstoke: Macmillan).

Rao, N. (1998) 'Representation in Local Politics: A Reconsideration and some New Evidence', *Political Studies*, 46: 19–35.

Reingold, B. (1992) 'Concepts of Representation Among Female and Male State Legislators', *Legislative Studies Quarterly*, 17: 509–37.

Reingold, B. (2000) *Representing Women* (Chapel Hill: University of North Carolina Press).

Rhode, D. (2003) *The Difference 'Difference' Makes'* (California: Stanford Law and Politics).

Rose, R. and McAllister, A. (1986) *Voters begin to Choose* (London: Sage).

Rosenthal, C. S. (1998) *When Women Lead* (New York: Oxford University Press).

Ross, K. (1995) 'Gender and Party Politics: How the Press Reported the Labour Leadership Campaign, 1994', *Media, Culture and Society*, 17: 499–509.

Ross, K. (2000) *Women at the Top 2000: Cracking the Public Sector Glass Ceiling* (London: Hansard Society and Fawcett Society).

Ross, K. (2002) *Women, Politics, Media* (NJ: Hampton Press).

Ross, K. (2003) *Women Politicians and Malestream Media* (Belfast: CAWP Occasional Paper).

Ross, K. and Sreberny-Mohammadi, A. (1997) 'Playing House – Gender, Politics and the News Media in Britain', *Media, Culture and Society*, 19: 101–9.

Ross, K. and Sreberny-Mohammadi, A. (2000) 'Women in the House', in A. Sreberny and L. van Zoonen (eds), *Gender Politics and Communication* (Cresskill, NJ: Hampton Press).

Russell, A. (2005) 'The Party System in 2004', *Parliamentary Affairs*, 58, 2: 351–65.

Russell, A. and Fieldhouse, E. (2005) *Neither Left nor Right? The Liberal Democrats and the Electorate* (Manchester: Manchester University Press).

Russell, M. (2000) *Women's Representation in UK Politics* (London: The Constitution Unit).

Russell, M. (2001) *The Women's Representation Bill* (London: The Constitution Unit).

Russell, M. (2003) 'Women in Elected Office in the UK, 1992–2002', in A. Dobrowolsky and V. Hart (eds), *Women Making Constitutions* (Basingstoke: Palgrave).

Russell, M. (2005) *Building New Labour* (Basingstoke: Palgrave).

Russell, M., Mackay, F. and McAllister, L. (2002) 'Women's Representation in the Scottish Parliament and National Assembly for Wales', *Journal of Legislative Studies*, 8, 2: 49–76.

Saint-German, M. (1989) 'Does their Difference Make a Difference?', *Social Science Quarterly*, 70, 4: 956–68.

Sampert, S. and Trimble, L. (2003) 'Wham Bam, No Thank You Ma'am: Gender and the Game Frame in National Newspaper Coverage of Election 2000', in M. Tremblay, and L. Trimble (eds), *Women and Electoral Politics in Canada* (Oxford: Oxford University Press), 211–26.

Sapiro, V. (1998) 'When are Interests Interesting', in A. Phillips (ed.), *Feminism and Politics* (Oxford: Oxford University Press), 161–92.

Saward, M. (2006) 'The Representative Claim', *Contemporary Political Theory*, 5: 297–318.

Sawer, M. (2000) 'Parliamentary Representation of Women', *IPSR*, 21, 4: 361–80.

Sawer, M. (2002) 'The Representation of Women in Australia', *Parliamentary Affairs*, 55, 1: 5–18.

Sawer, M. (2004) 'When Women Support Women...', Paper presented to 'Women and Westminster Compared' Conference, Ottawa.

Sawer, M., Tremblay, M. and Trimble, L. (2006) *Representing Women in Parliament: A Comparative Study* (New York: Routledge).

Schelling, T. C. (1978) *Micromotives and Macrobehavior* (New York: W. W. Norton & Company).

Schwindt-Bayer, L. (2004) 'Women's Representation in Latin American Legislatures: Policy Attitudes and Bill Initiation Behavior', Paper presented at the Annual Meeting of the Midwest Political Science Association, Chicago, IL, April 15–18.

Schwindt-Bayer, L. A. (2006), 'Still Supermadres? Gender and the Policy Priorities of Latin American Legislators', *American Journal of Political Science* 50, 3: 570–85.

Seltzer, R. Newman, J. and Leighton, M. (1997) *Sex as a Political Variable: Women as Candidates and Voters in U.S. Elections* (Boulder: Lynne Rienner).

Seyd, P. (1999) 'New Parties/New Politics', *Party Politics*, 5, 3: 383–406.

Seyd, P. and Whiteley, P. (1992) *Labour's Grass Roots* (Oxford: Clarendon Press).

Shaw, S. (2000) 'Language, Gender and Floor Apportionment in Political Debates', *Discourse and Society*, 11, 3: 401–18.

Shepherd-Robinson, L. and Lovenduski, J. (2002) *Women and Candidate Selection* (London: Fawcett Society).

Short, C. (1996) 'Women and the Labour Party', in J. Lovenduski and P. Norris (eds), *Women in Politics* (Oxford: Oxford University Press), 19–27.

Siltanen, J. and Stanworth, M. (1984a) *Women and the Public Sphere, A Critique of Sociology and Politics* (London: Hutchinson).

Skard, T. and Haavio-Mannila, E. (1985) 'Women in Parliament', in E. Haavio-Mannila (ed.), *Unfinished Democracy: Women in Nordic Politics* (New York: Pergamon), 51–80.

Skjeie, H. (1991) 'The Rhetoric of Difference: On Women's Inclusion into Political Elites', *Politics and Society*, 19, 2: 233–63.

Skjeie, H. (2001) 'Quotas, Parity, and the Discursive Dangers of Difference', in J. Klausen and C. S. Maier (eds), *Has Liberalism Failed Women* (New York: Palgrave), 165–76.

Smith, K. (1997) 'When All's Fair', *Political Communication*, 14:71–82.

Sones, B., Moran, M. and Lovenduski, J. (2005) *Women in Parliament, The New Suffragettes* (London: Politico's).

Squires, J. (1995) 'Rethinking Representation', Paper presented to the Political Studies Association Annual Conference, York University.

Squires, J. (1996) 'Quotas for Women: Fair Representation?', in J. Lovenduski and P. Norris (eds), *Women in Politics* (Oxford: Oxford University Press), 73–90.

Squires, J. (1999) *Gender in Political Theory* (London: Polity).

Squires, J. (2003) 'Reviewing the UK Equality Agenda in the Context of Constitutional Change', in A. Dobrowolsky and V. Hart (eds), *Women Making Constitutions* (Basingstoke: Palgrave), 200–15.

Squires, J (2005) 'Is Mainstreaming Transformative?' *Social Politics*, 3: 366–88.

Squires, J. (2007) *The New Politics of Gender Equality* (Basingstoke: Palgrave).

Squires, J. and Wickham-Jones, M. (2001) *Women in Parliament: a Comparative Analysis* (Manchester: EOC).

Squires, J. and Wickham-Jones, M. (2002) 'Mainstreaming in Westminster and Whitehall', *Parliamentary Affairs*, 55, 1: 57–70.

Squires, J. and Wickham–Jones, M. (2004) 'New Labour, Gender Mainstreaming and the Women and Equality Unit', *British Journal of Politics and International Relations*, 6, 1: 81–98.

Sreberny-Mohammadi, A. and Ross, K. (1996) 'Women MPs and the Media: Representing the Body Politic', in J. Lovenduski and P. Norris (eds), *Women in Politics* (Oxford: Oxford University Press), 105–17.

Steel, G. (2003) 'Class and Gender in British General Elections', Paper prepared for the Midwest Political Science Association Annual Meeting, Chicago.

Stephenson, M. (1997) *The Best Man for the Job, The Selection of Women Parliamentary Candidates* (London: The Fawcett Society).

Stephenson, M. (1998) *The Glass Trapdoor* (London: The Fawcett Society).

Stephenson, M. (undated) *Fawcett Society Survey of Women MPs* (London: The Fawcett Society).

Stokes, W. (2005) *Women in Contemporary Politics* (Cambridge: Polity).

Studlar, D. T. and McAllister, I. (2002) 'Does a Critical Mass Exist?', *European Journal of Political Research*, 41, 2: 233–53.

Swers, M. L. (1998) 'Are Women More Likely to Vote for Women's Issue Bills Than Their Male Colleagues?', *Legislative Studies Quarterly* 23, 3: 435–48.

Swers, M. L. (2001a) 'Understanding the Policy Impact of Electing Women: Evidence from Research on Congress and State Legislatures', *PS*, 34, 2: 217–19.

Swers, M. L. (2001b) 'Research on Women in Legislatures: What we have Learned, Where are We Going?', in K. O'Conner (ed.), *Women and Congress: Running, Winning and Ruling* (Binghamton: The Haworth Press), 167–85.

Swers, M. L. (2002) *The Difference Women Make: The Policy Impact of Women in Congress* (Chicago: University of Chicago Press).

Swers, M. L. (2004) 'Legislative Entrepreneurship and Women's Issues: An Analysis of Members' Bill Sponsorship and Cosponsorship Agendas', Paper presented at the Annual Meeting of the Midwest Political Science Association, Chicago, IL, April 15–18.

Tamerius, K. L. (1995) 'Sex, Gender, and Leadership in the Representation of Women', in G. Duerst-Lahti and R. Mae Kelly (eds), *Gender Power Leadership and Governance* (USA: The University of Michigan Press), 93–112.

Tinker, I. (2004) 'Quotas for Women in Elected Legislatures', *Womens's Studies International Forum* 27: 531–46.

Thomas, S. (1991) 'The Impact of Women on State Legislative Policies', *Journal of Politics*, 53, 4: 958–76.

Thomas, S. (1994) *How Women Legislate* (Oxford: Oxford University Press).

Thomas, S. (1998) 'Women and Elective Office', in S. Thomas and C.Wilcox (eds), *Women and Elective Office* (Oxford: Oxford University Press), 1–14.

Thomas, S. (2003) 'The Impact of Women in Political Leadership Positions', in S.J. Carroll (ed.), *Women and American Politics* (Oxford: Oxford University Press), 89–110.

Thomas, S. and Welch, S. (1991) 'The Impact of Gender on Activities and Priorities of State Legislators', *Western Political Quarterly:* 445–55.

Tingsten, H. (1937) *Political Behaviour* (Totowa, NJ: Bedminster).

Tolleson Rinehart, S. (1992) *Gender Consciousness and Politics* (London: Routledge).

Towns, A. (2003) 'Understanding the Effects of Larger Ratios of Women in National Legislatures: Proportions and Gender Differentiation in Sweden and Norway', *Women & Politics*, 25, 1–2: 1–29.

Toynbee, P. and Walker, D. (2001) *Did Things Get Better?* (London: Penguin).

Toynbee, P. and Walker, D. (2005) *Better or Worse? Has Labour Delivered?* (Bloomsbury: London).

Tremblay, M. (1998) 'Do Female MPs substantively Represent Women?', *Canadian Journal of Political Science*, 31, 3: 435–65.

Tremblay, M. (2003) 'Women's Representational Role in Australia and Canada: The Impact of Political Context', *Australian Journal of Political Science*, 38, 2: 215–38.

Tremblay, M. and Pelletier, R. (2000) 'More Feminists or More Women', *International Political Science Review*, 21, 4: 381–405.

Tremblay, M. and Steele, J. (2004) 'Gender Parity Lost? The Nunavut Experience', Paper presented to 'Women and Westminster Compared' Conference, Ottawa.

Tremblay, M. and Trimble, L. (2003) *Women and Electoral Politics in Canada* (Ontario: OUP).

Trimble, L. (2004) 'When do Women Count?', Paper presented to 'Women and Westminster Compared' Conference, Ottawa.

Trimble, L. (2006) 'Gender, Political Leadership and the Press', paper given to author.

Trimble, L. and Arscott, J. (2003) *Still Counting: Women in Politics Across Canada* (Canada: Broadview).

Trimble, L. and Sampert, S. (2004) 'Who's in the Game? Framing of the Canadian Election 2000 by the Globe and Mail and the National Post', *Canadian Journal of Political Science*, 37, 1: 37–58.

Trimble, L. and Tremblay, M. (2003) 'Women Politicians in Canada's Parliament and Legislatures, 1917-2000', in M. Tremblay and L. Trimble (eds), *Women and Electoral Politics in Canada* (Oxford: Oxford University Press), 37–58.

Vallance, E. (1979) *Women in the House* (London: The Anthlone Press)

Van Acker, E. (2003) 'Media Representations of Women Politicians in Australia and New Zealand: High Expectations, Hostility or Stardom', *Policy and Society*, 22, 1: 116–36.

Vega, A. and Juanita, M. F. (1995) 'The Effects of Gender on Congressional Behavior and the Substantive Representation of Women', *Legislative Studies Quarterly*, 20, 2: 213–22.

Veitch, J. (2005) 'Looking at Gender Mainstreaming in the UK Government', *International Feminist Journal of Politics*, 3, 1: 600–6.

Verba, S., Norman N. and Kim, J. (1978) *Participation and Political Equality: A Seven Nation Comparison* (New York, Cambridge University Press).

Vickers, J. (1997) 'Toward a Feminist Understanding of Representation', in J. Arscott and L. Trimble (eds), *In the Presence of Women* (Toronto: Harcourt Brace), 20–46.

Voet, R. (1992) 'Political Representation and Quotas: Hannah Pitkin's Concept(s) of Representation in the Context of Feminist Politics', *Acta Politica*, 27, 4: 389–403.

Voet, R. (1994) 'Women as Citizens', *Australian Feminist Studies,* 19, Autumn: 61–77.

Wangnerud, L. (2000) 'Testing the Politics of Presence', *Scandinavian Political Studies*, 23: 67–91.

Ware, A. (2003) 'Book Reviews', *Party Politics*, 9, 4: 523–5.

Watts Powell, L., Brown, C. W. and Hedges, R. B. (1981) 'Male and Female Differences in Elite Political Participation: An Examination of the Effects of Socio-economic and Familial Variables', *Western Political Quarterly*: 31–45.

Waylen, G. (2004), 'Gender and Representation in New Democracies: the Case of South Africa', Paper presented to PSA Annual Conference.

Webb, P. (2000) *The Modern British Party System* (London: Sage).

Welch, S. (1977) 'Women as Political Animals? A Test of Some Explanations for Male-Female Political Participation Differences', *American Journal of Political Science*, 21, 4: 711–29.

Weldon, S. L. (2002) 'Beyond Bodies: Institutional Sources of Representation for Women in Democratic Policymaking', *The Journal of Politics,* 64, 4: 1153–74.

Weldon, S. L. (2004) 'The Dimensions and Policy Impact of Feminist Civil Society', *International Feminist Journal of Politics*, 6, 1: 1–28.

Whip, R. (1991) 'Representing Women: Australian Female Parliamentarians on the Horms of a Dilemma', *Women and Politics*, 11: 1–22.

Williams, M. (1998) *Voice, Trust, and Memory* (Princeton: Princeton University Press).

Winters, K. and Campbell, R. (2007) 'Hearts or Minds? Men, Women and Candidate Evaluations in the 2005', in D. Wring, J. Green and R. Mortimore (eds), *Political Communications: The General Election Campaign of 2005* (Basingstoke: Palgrave Macmillan).

Woodhouse, D. (1993) 'Ministerial Responsibility in the 1990s: When Do Ministers Resign?', *Parliamentary Affairs*, 46, 3: 277–92.

Yoder, J. (1991) 'Rethinking Tokenism: Looking Beyond Numbers', *Gender and Society*, 5: 178–92.

Young, I. M. (1990) *Justice and the Politics of Difference* (Princeton, New Jersey: Princeton University Press).

Young, I. M. (2002) *Inclusion and Democracy* (Oxford: Oxford University Press).

Young, L. (2000) *Feminists and Party Politics* (Ann Arbor: University of Michigan Press).

Young, L. (2003) 'Can Feminists Transform Party Politics', in M. Tremblay, and L. Trimble (eds), *Women and Electoral Politics in Canada* (Oxford: Oxford University Press), 76–90.

Young, L. (2004), 'Women's Representation in the Canadian House of Commons', Paper presented to 'Women and Westminster Compared' Conference, Ottawa.

Epilogue

The view from the 'Feminist' of the House:
The Rt Hon Harriet Harman QC MP, and Deputy
Leader of the Labour Party*

If she could wave a magic wand Harriet Harman would transform the House of Commons into a Parliament with equal numbers of women and men forthwith. When she first arrived, over twenty years ago, and seven months pregnant, women comprised fewer than 3 per cent of the House. The young MP for Camberwell and Peckham never believed that it would take so many elections to see significant increases – relatively speaking – in the number of women MPs. Yet Harman is mindful that in the 2005 Parliament women remain a minority of representatives at Westminster, at fewer than 20 per cent; moreover, in the absence of sex parity, and when so many women MPs owe their election to Labour's policy of All Women Shortlists, she maintains that women's presence in the UK Parliament cannot be taken for granted.

Getting women elected is not, for Harman, an end in itself. If, in the past, women politicians had to claim that they could do politics as well as men, so that they would be allowed in; today's women politicians, make a different claim: 'we are bringing something extra, we are bringing our understanding of women's lives', our 'difference' to politics; the fact that 'we are women is not an excuse, or a problem, **it's our cause**'. In Harman's view, the new generation of women politicians are politicians **because** they are women. The consequence of a parliament comprised of 50 per cent women? One that is 'sighted on women's concerns'; women representatives understand the 'daily struggles' women face.

Being able to act on women's concerns in Parliament is, according to Harman, about numbers (although her subsequent comments make it clear that it is not just about numbers). Having a certain rarity value as a woman MP is 'worthless if you cannot do anything'. Being in the party of government with 100 or so women means that progress for women can be made – 'efforts', she argues 'that depend

* Interview with Harriet Harman.

upon state intervention' – on after-school clubs, childcare, domestic violence, and on maternity pay and leave. Hitherto marginal to the mainstream parliamentary agenda, there are now 'always women in meetings pushing these issues forward'. Sure, she acknowledges, women work with good, cooperative men in the party and government, but if women's presence is not big enough, men will not act.

Such self-consciously feminist beliefs underpinned Harman's successful bid for the Deputy Leadership of the Labour Party in 2007. She believes that voters expect to see women and men 'working together'. She also contends that all male leadership teams are 'less representative and less complete'. In contrast, mixed leadership teams are more likely to have the 'right approach' and to have a 'wider reach'. If standing for Deputy Leader of the Labour Party **as a woman** risked gendered criticism from her opponents – and it did – so be it. Harman saw this as throwing down a gauntlet for a wider debate around gender and politics. Discussion thereafter would, she believed, centre on the precise ways in which the sex and gender of our politicians matter.

Index

Figures, Tables and Boxes in **BOLD**
Case studies in *italics*

Lightning Source UK Ltd.
Milton Keynes UK
UKHW02f2323220818
327669UK00010B/236/P